INTO THE FIRE

INTO THE FIRE

PLOESTI

THE MOST FATEFUL MISSION
OF WORLD WAR II

DUANE SCHULTZ

WESTHOLME
Yardley

Frontispiece: *The Sandman*, a B-24D of the 98th Bombardment Group "Pyramiders" piloted by Lt. Robert W. Sternfels, emerges from the smoke and fires of the bombed Astra-Romana refinery. Taken as a mirror image by an automatic camera in a nearby bomber, it is an iconic photograph of World War II. (*National Archives*)

First Westholme Paperback: September 2008

Copyright © 2007 Duane Schultz

Westholme Publishing, LLC

Eight Harvey Avenue

Yardley, Pennsylvania 19067

Visit our Web site at www.westholmepublishing.com

10 9 8 7 6 5 4 3 2 1

ISBN: 978-1-59416-077-6

ISBN 10: 1-59416-077-5

Printed in United States of America

"It was the worst catastrophe in the history of the Army Air Corps. It wasn't a raid, it was a full-scale battle."
—Col. John R. Kane

If you do your job right, it is worth it, even if you lose every plane.
—Maj. Gen. Lewis Brereton

We knew it was a disaster and knew that in the flames shooting up from those refineries we might be burned to death. But we went right in.
—Lt. Norman Whalen

We were dragged through the mouth of hell.
—from a Ploesti Mission debriefing report

Contents

PART VI. AFTERMATH

PROLOGUE: FROZEN IN TIME

"**H**E LOOKED LIKE CLARK GABLE, could talk his way into or out of virtually anything, and loved to wear his cowboy boots and pearl-handled revolvers into battle." That was how a Wichita, Kansas, newspaper described 1st Lt. Gilbert B. Hadley when he was buried in 1997, 54 years after he died in the cockpit of his airplane. His boots and pearl-handled revolvers were found in the plane with him, ghostly remnants of another time and place, another world.

Hadley was a member of the "Greatest Generation," though probably he would not have thought of himself that way. He was too much of a hell-raiser to have such grand thoughts, certainly not on the day he died in 1943. A flamboyant, rowdy 22-year-old pilot of B-24s from Arkansas City, Kansas, Gib liked to have a good time and to fly his lumbering four-engine bomber like it was a fighter plane.

He joined the army a month before the attack on Pearl Harbor, after completing two years at the local junior college. The family could not afford to send him away to college for a four-year degree, so he did what so many other boys did in his circumstances. He joined the army and was intelligent enough to be accepted for pilot training. The Army Air Corps sent him to flying schools in the area and he took delight in flying low over his house and the homes of friends, seeming to barely miss the rooftops. He attempted the maneuver in single-engine trainers and, later, in B-24s, frightening everybody but himself.

Gib named his plane *Hadley's Harem*, because he liked to think he had a way with the ladies, and he was also popular with the men who flew with him. He wanted to be one of the guys, not standoffish with the enlisted members of his crew the way some officers were. "He chewed us out for saluting him," remembered Staff Sgt. Leroy Newton from Monrovia, California, a 19-year-old at the time of the raid. "He let us fly the plane when it was in the air and nothing was happening. He was a budding legend happening right under our feet. There wasn't a thing we wouldn't have done for him."

Sergeant Newton was one of the lucky members of *Hadley's Harem*. He survived the crash that August evening that took Gib Hadley's life and that of his co-pilot, 22-year-old 2nd Lt. James Lindsay, from Gilmer, Texas. Newton survived the war, and tried not to think much about *Hadley's Harem* and Gib and the horrors of that terrible day in 1943. He put them out of his mind for 50 years until 1993, when he learned there would be a reunion of the men who flew with him on the famous mission to the Ploesti oil fields of Romania.

Newton went to the 50th reunion, the first such gathering he attended. He was amazed to see a photograph of himself and the six other survivors of *Hadley's Harem* on a beach in Turkey surrounded by more than a dozen armed men. The picture brought back a flood of memories. He decided to go back, to stand on that beach again and try to find whatever might be left of the plane. "The seven of us really owed our lives to him,"

Newton said of Gib Hadley. "It's miraculous he could fly the thing that far. [He and co-pilot Lindsay] gave me a good 50 years on my life, and I feel this was a good payback."

Newton went to Turkey in 1994 and walked the beaches for miles, looking for anything familiar to identify the spot where they came ashore. He knew there was no chance of finding the plane until he found the right beach, but he did not recognize anything. On the last day of his trip a local newspaper reporter interviewed him and published a story about the airplane that had crashed off the coast five decades before and the wounded Americans who had straggled ashore. By the time the article appeared, Newton had returned home, disappointed that his search had been fruitless.

A short time later he received a letter from a Turkish diver who had read about him. The diver wrote that he had discovered the aircraft back in 1972 while filming underwater for a documentary about turtles. Newton was skeptical but decided to go back one more time. The diver took him directly to *Hadley's Harem*, lying 750 feet offshore in 90 feet of water, broken in three pieces.

The remains of the pilots were in the cockpit, along with a pair of cowboy boots and two pearl-handled revolvers. The bodies were retrieved, positively identified through DNA analyses, and returned to the United States for burial with full military honors.

The B-24's forward section, including the cockpit, was raised, cleaned, and put on display in the Rahmi M. Koc Museum in Istanbul, where it remains as the only survivor of the 177 planes that took off from Benghazi in Northern Africa early on the morning of August 1, 1943.

The other bombers live only in memories, photographs, and the imagination of those of us who look back with wonder, admiration, and gratitude for what those men endured and the terrible price they paid. "I tell you," wrote Lt. John McCormick, pilot of *Vagabond King*, after the mission was over, "there wasn't a man among us who will ever be the same."

The battle over Ploesti's skies on August 1, 1943, lasted 27 minutes from the time the first bomb was dropped until the last one fell and the surviving planes turned south to head home. Of the 177 Liberators assigned to the mission, 54 had been lost by day's end. Only 93 returned to base, and 60 of those were so badly damaged they never flew again. Of the others, 19 landed at Allied airfields such as Cyprus, 7 in Turkey, and 3, including *Hadley's Harem*, crashed into the sea. The remainder crashed in and around Ploesti.

One of the bombardment group commanders described the mission as the "worst catastrophe in the history of the Army Air Corps." A 1999 research report prepared for the Air War College at Maxwell Air Force Base in Alabama concluded that the mission to Ploesti was "one of the bloodiest and most heroic missions of all time." One of the crewmen who was shot down referred to it as "the greatest ground-air battle ever fought."

The casualties were staggering. Of the 1,726 airmen on the mission, 532 were killed, captured, interned, or listed as missing in action. In addition, 440 of those who returned to Benghazi were wounded, some so severely they never returned to active service.

More decorations and awards for bravery under fire were bestowed on the men who attacked Ploesti than for any other mission in the history of American aerial combat. All received the Distinguished Flying Cross. Five Medals of Honor were awarded to the Ploesti airmen, more than for any other mission; three of the medals were given posthumously.

A U.S. Marine Corps combat pilot wrote in 1993 that the raid was "a watershed event in the history of aerial warfare," carried out against one of the most heavily defended targets in the world. It was also the first and last large-scale bombing raid carried out at such a low altitude. The planes flew at tree-top level, making it impossible for the crews of ships damaged over the target area to bail out. Most of those men burned to death before their planes crashed, and many planes were flaming coffins by the time they plowed into the ground.

The sacrifice was horrendous, the battle a nightmare of exploding fuel tanks, shrapnel shearing off limbs, and unparalleled bravery as pilots flew through sheets of flames caused by bombs dropped by earlier waves of B-24s. But the planners, cursed by the survivors, believed that no cost was too great to destroy the Ploesti refineries.

Without oil, the officials reasoned, German planes and tanks would grind to a halt. Destroying the refineries would end the war. It was that simple, the planners said, and had it succeeded, the cost in lives and planes would have seemed more bearable in light of the far greater number of lives saved by shortening the war.

Sadly, that was not to be. Intelligence about the Ploesti defenses was misleading at best, woefully inadequate, and downright wrong. The bomb groups became separated as some took a wrong turn before they reached the target, so three refineries were not hit at all. Most of those that were bombed were repaired quickly. Other refineries, which had not been in operation, were easily activated. Within weeks, "Ploesti was producing at a higher rate than before the raid."

Leroy Newton returned to Ploesti in 1997 and found lingering reminders of the bombing.

> It was strange to me to have flown over it and now, fifty-four years later, to be standing on it. The debris is all pushed aside with some shelled-out buildings still in place. Many of the blast walls surrounding the huge storage tanks have large blown-out holes with rubble still lying where it fell. Left standing are all the tall poured concrete AA towers, minus the guns. Ploesti is strangely frozen in time but still pumping oil through leaky and patched-up piping.

What else remains of the heroism and sacrifice—a few towers that once held guns? The nose section and cockpit of *Hadley's Harem* in a museum? No, that's not all. There are also the men. Those who survived the mission to Ploesti moved on with their lives, but singular sights and sounds, images and feelings remained with them until they died, memories that highlighted and focused their recollection of the historic mission.

It is by collecting and assembling those memories and images that what we call history is compiled and written, out of the past, from images frozen in time. We cannot allow these memories to disappear; they continue to haunt us many decades later. Images and scenes such as these.

"Look, there's another one," a waist gunner wrote. "The flak got him bad. Burning near the bomb bay doors. Trying to climb. Look at him climb. Burning and climbing. There goes a chute. Look at the guy's face. He can't believe it. Two more chutes. No, they can't make it . . . all those planes, all those guys burning to death."

One bomber, its wings sheared off, skidded down a Ploesti street and plowed into a women's prison, where it exploded and set the building on fire. Still another mortally hit B-24 lurched into a climb while two crewmen bailed out. Suddenly the ship fell to the ground in a slow motion, blinding explosion. The two crewmen, suspended underneath their parachutes, fell flailing into the flames.

A stricken Liberator scraped along the ground with the fuselage buckling under the pressure while the crew braced themselves as best they could and hung on. "Two pieces of metal began to squeeze my head in a vice-tight grip," the navigator wrote. "Tighter and tighter they pressed as I slipped into darkness. For one brief moment, a mental picture of my father flashed before me. I felt no pain, just a numb feeling of weightlessness making me giddy. 'This isn't such a bad way to die,' I thought."

"When we got there it was just like an inferno, it was hot as hell. Over the target, when I saw all those planes go down, I just got a don't-give-a-shit attitude and didn't care if we went down or not. Be out of the war and all its misery."

"Near the refinery a house was on fire, burning in the upper story. A man with shirtsleeves rolled up to the elbow, carrying a small child in one arm and sheltering a woman with the other, ran towards the burning building. The child had long brown hair; the woman an attractive figure. I have always hoped that they survived."

The ship was called *Sad Sack II*, and it lived up to its name. Even before it reached the target it was damaged by flak that killed the rear gunner, knocked out one engine and riddled the plane with holes. Then both waist gunners were seriously wounded. *Sad Sack II* flew straight on through a raging column of fire and was attacked by a German fighter. The tail of the ship was hit, making it hard to control. The fighter spun around and attacked head on, shooting the pilot in the face and wounding the copilot. Flak exploded in the nose, killing the navigator.

Sad Sack II was burning, torn apart by continuing gunfire. The pilot lay crumpled over the controls with flames consuming his legs. The copilot's legs were broken. The plane was no more than a pile of twisted metal that tore across a cornfield and shuddered to a halt.

Another aircrew waved at the men in the neighboring plane as they passed over the target just as flak exploded in its bomb bay. Gasoline poured out of the ruptured bomb-bay tank, setting the length of the plane on fire. "It was a horrible sight," one of the onlookers in the first plane recalled, "watching the burning plane and knowing that the men in there were fighting for their lives and there was nothing we could do to help." No one bailed out.

A copilot, who had survived many missions, went crazy from the terror and had to be manhandled out of his seat. The navigator dragged him aft and sat on him to keep him from running amok. An airman jumped from another plane that was enveloped in flames. His parachute opened and he drifted so close to another ship that the crew clearly saw his charred legs. They could only imagine his pain.

In another plane a crewman bailed out when the pilot managed to pull their burning ship up to an altitude of 300 feet. He was the only crew member to escape. His parachute opened, but he was so low when he jumped that he was badly injured when he hit the ground. "I don't know how I made it," he said. "I wish I had ridden her to the ground and died with the five men who didn't have the guts to jump."

An 88-mm German shell exploded directly in the nose of a B-24, killing the bombardier and the navigator. The explosion wrecked one engine, set fire to two others, and caused the plane to turn almost upside down. The pilot fought to get it back under control but had trouble with the rudder pedal. "I was not getting much pressure on the right pedal. I reached down. My right leg below the knee was hanging from a shred of flesh."

A 20-mm shell from a German fighter plane tore off the American pilot's head. The bombardier pulled the body away from the controls while the copilot struggled to keep the ship level. One engine was dead, five other crew members were wounded, and gas was leaking from the bomb bay tank. The bombardier stuffed his flight jacket into the gas tank's gap and tried to cover the pilot as best he could.

Another B-24 took a hit in the bomb bay, opening a large hole in the gas tank. Fuel streamed out through the open bomb bay doors, soaking the plane's underbelly. The gas was so thick that men in an adjacent plane could no longer see the waist gunner. One spark would have been enough to set the plane ablaze.

The ship ahead dropped its bombs on one of the refinery's boilers, which exploded upward, sending a huge column of flame directly in the path of the plane with the gas leak. The pilot faced a quick choice: stay on course and bomb his assigned target, which meant that his plane would certainly catch on fire, or take evasive action to avoid the flames and drop his bombs elsewhere.

The navigator of a nearby plane watched; he knew his friend Pete was the pilot. "My stomach turned over. Poor Pete! Fine, conscientious boy, with a young wife waiting for him at home. He was holding formation to bomb, flying into a solid room of fire, with gasoline gushing from his ship. Why do men do such things?"

Pete made his choice and hit the target, but the plane was a flying torch, on fire from nose to tail. He headed for a dry creek bed and managed to maintain control, but a wingtip struck the bank of the creek. The ship cartwheeled end over end, leaving a spiraling, flaming trail of debris.

Many of those who managed to bail out of their crippled planes were horribly wounded.

In one case, Romanian peasants reportedly killed an American pilot to put him out of his misery after his parachute failed to open and he was still alive after he hit the ground. Triage points were established around the refineries and the city. A school in Ploesti was a collection point for thirty American flyers who lay "burned and broken, naked and dying." A flak battery barracks was used as another aid station where several other Americans were laid out, unconscious. All were beyond medical help and were being administered morphine to ease their deaths.

The last of the planes to return to the base in North Africa landed in the evening. The survivors "tumbled out of their ships, furious at their leaders for what had happened. Others were in tears. The wounded were stoic, exhausted, or unconscious. The dead could show no emotion as they were pulled out of the bombers, sometimes in pieces."

Chaplain James Patterson, nicknamed "Chappie," met each plane in his group as it landed. He knelt over a wounded man who had just been removed from his plane through the waist gunner's open hatch.

"I made it back from Ploesti, Chappie," the man said. "See you later." A moment after that he was dead. Patterson covered his face with a blanket while one of the gunners watched. The man lit a cigarette, held up the match up, and watched the flame flicker and die.

"Is life like that, Chappie?"

"Yes, Sergeant," Patterson said, "life is like that."

Captain Robert Adlen did not go on the Ploesti mission but his plane did, along with all the men in his squadron. They had become like brothers. Adlen had completed his tour of duty but volunteered for the mission anyway. He was grounded a few days before with a bad case of dysentery. He waited for the planes to return and recorded his thoughts in his diary.

"Our squadron is no more.

"I hope the price was worth it.

"It's so dead and silent, and the club is like it never was before. [It's] empty.

"Now I'm the only one living in the tent."

PART I

THE PLAN

B-24s practice low-level flying in North Africa. (*U.S. Air Force*)

1

OPERATION SOAPSUDS

WINSTON CHURCHILL'S MATTE-BLACK converted B-24 Liberator bomber, which he had named *Commando*, took off from a base in England on the evening of January 12, 1943. The prime minister was on his way to Casablanca, in North Africa, for a secret meeting with Franklin D. Roosevelt to discuss their plans for the war against Germany.

Roosevelt had given Churchill the airplane to use as his personal transport six months earlier. It had been flown to England by a young American, Capt. William J. "Bill" Vanderkloot, who stayed on as Churchill's personal pilot.

The accommodations were spartan, hardly suitable for Great Britain's prime minister, but it was the only long-range aircraft that could be spared in the summer of 1942, only seven months after the Japanese attack on Pearl Harbor. There was no heating system, and at high altitudes the temperature was below freezing and wind roared through the ship. Dealing with these conditions brought Churchill close to dying. In an attempt to keep passengers warm, someone had installed a small gasoline-powered engine with metal vents that blew hot air to various portions of the plane's interior.

"I was woken up at two in the morning," Churchill wrote, "when we were over the Atlantic five hundred miles from anywhere, by one of these heating points burning my toes, and it looked to me as if it might soon get red-hot and light the blankets."

He woke Sir Charles Portal, his chief of air staff, and alerted him to the problem. The two men searched throughout the plane and found two additional heating vents that seemed risky. "From every point of view I thought this was most dangerous," Churchill wrote. "The hot points might start a conflagration, and the atmosphere of petrol would make an explosion imminent." Portal took the same view. "I decided that it was better to freeze than to burn, and I ordered all heating to be turned off and we went back to rest shivering in the ice-cold air about eight thousand feet up. I am bound to say this struck me as rather an unpleasant moment."

Churchill had another unpleasant moment a few hours later when he woke up nearly frozen. Lord Moran, his personal physician, found him on hands and knees trying to stuff a blanket into a crevice in the wall to keep out the chilling wind. "The P.M. is at a disadvantage in this kind of travel," Moran wrote, "since he never wears anything at night but a silk vest [T-shirt]. On his hands and knees, he cut a quaint figure with his big, bare, white bottom."

Churchill was on his way to Casablanca to discuss, among other issues, the bombing of the oil refineries at Ploesti, which he considered the "taproot of German might." He was determined that they be destroyed as soon as possible. American planners agreed.

In the months before the U.S. and British leaders met at Casablanca, a high-level group of American military officers had focused on the need to shut down the refineries. The group, the Joint Strategic Survey Committee (JSSC), had been formed in November 1942, to provide advice to the Joint Chiefs of Staff on long-range strategic planning. As part of their plans for the defeat of Germany, the JSSC listed several crucial targets whose destruction would seriously hamper the Nazi war effort. At the top of the list was Ploesti. Shutting down the oil refineries was paramount, the JSSC concluded, if the Allies were to win the war.

The choice of Ploesti as a prime target was an obvious one both for Churchill and the members of the JSSC. Germany, with the most highly mechanized military machine in the early days of the war, with the possible exception of Japan, could supply less than one percent of its own crude-oil needs.

That left Romania, a reluctant ally of Germany since 1941, whose huge oil fields and refineries, once they were brought under Nazi control, supplied the majority of the fuel needed to keep Hitler's planes and tanks in operation. Without Romania's resources, Germany would be unable to continue a large-scale war. Hitler admitted as much when he wrote that if the refineries at Ploesti were put out of commission, the results for the Third Reich would be disastrous.

Yet even with all of Romania's oil production, the German military was experiencing shortages by 1943, confining the massive German battleship fleet to port and forcing the Luftwaffe to shorten training times for new pilots. The army was in even greater difficulty.

So reduced were inventories that not even calling off the Eastern offensive could have restored the balance. The Germans were now burning up half again the amount of oil they were taking in. In 1943 the figures showed twenty-two million tons consumed, fourteen million tons received, and almost nothing in reserve.

No wonder Hitler was concerned about the continued safety of Ploesti by the time Churchill and Roosevelt met in Casablanca in January 1943. This small town in Romania that few Americans had heard of was increasingly the focus of Allied military planning.

The Casablanca conference lasted ten days, January 14–24, gathering top American and British military leaders with their staffs, as well as the president and prime minister and their advisors. They were quartered in lavishly appointed villas and hotels overlooking the sea, in an area surrounded by double lines of barbed wire and guarded by General Patton's troops. When Roosevelt was shown into the opulent bedroom of his villa, he whistled and exclaimed, "Now all we need is the Madame of the house!"

Despite the holiday atmosphere, serious meetings and spirited discussions were held throughout the days and nights, resulting in decisions that would determine the course of the war, at least through 1943. Agreement was reached on plans to retake Burma from the Japanese, to invade Sicily, to increase troop numbers in England for an eventual invasion of Europe, to mount a joint British-American strategic bombing offensive against Germany, and to launch an aerial assault against Ploesti by the U.S. Army Air Force.

American leaders, particularly Army Chief of Staff George C. Marshall, and Air Force Chief Henry H. "Hap" Arnold, were highly enthusiastic about the mission to bomb Ploesti. They were also optimistic about the outcome of the raid. Preliminary estimates by their staffs predicted that American bombers would destroy at least 30 percent of Ploesti's production capacity and shorten the war against Germany by at least six months.

As usual with such forecasts, there was a large element of faith and an overly hopeful belief in the supremacy of air power. But few people recognized that at the time, or if they did, they were reluctant to voice any doubts in the face of the plan's unanimous endorsement by Marshall, Arnold, and other military leaders. The mission to Ploesti was on.

American planes had already attacked Ploesti some six months before the Casablanca conference. The Russians had bombed the refineries nearly a year before that, in July 1941. It was not much of a raid, only six planes, but the Russians claimed to have destroyed storage tanks and railway tank cars and set huge fires. German fighters shot down four of the six Russian planes. Although the Russians later attacked other oil-related targets, they never tried to bomb Ploesti again.

The first American attack on the refineries in Romania took place on June 12, 1942, led by Col. Harry A. Halverson, a pioneer in the development of air power. "Short and square-set, a tough old pro," Halverson had come up through the ranks of the Army Air Corps during the years between the wars, along with Carl Spaatz, Ira Eaker, and Pete Quesada, all destined to play major roles in the war.

"Hurry-Up Halverson" was given a tough assignment in January 1942, a month after Pearl Harbor. He was ordered to bomb Tokyo in a follow-up raid to the one being led by Col. Jimmy Doolittle. Given 23 B-24s, fresh from the factory, the men in Halverson Project Number 63 (known as HALPRO) were to take off from a base in Florida and fly 13,000 miles to Chekiang, on the east coast of China. From there they would launch their bombing mission on Tokyo.

The crews flew south from Florida to Natal, Brazil, in late April 1942 and from there across the South Atlantic Ocean to Africa's west coast. Then it was north and east to Khartoum in Sudan, just south of Egypt, covering a distance of 8,000 miles from their base in Florida.

By then, however, mid-May, the Japanese had captured the China airfield that was to have been their base of operations. There was no other facility in China within the range of the B-24 aircraft from which to reach Japan, so the mission was cancelled. But one question remained. What to do with the B-24s, now stuck in North Africa? Halverson kept his men and planes fit by putting them through training missions, but had no idea what he was training them for. All he could do was keep busy and wait for new orders.

On June 5, 1942, the United States declared war on Hungary, Bulgaria, and Romania, the last of which provided a highly valuable target for Halverson's men: Ploesti. Orders were sent to Khartoum to move the outfit to an RAF base at Fayid, Egypt, to reduce the distance to their new target. Still, the men would have to fly 1,300 miles to Ploesti. The U.S. government requested permission from Moscow to land the planes behind Russian lines, to reduce the return trip distance, but no reply was received.

The crews were briefed prior to the mission by an RAF officer, whose prohibitions made it clear that no one was likely to return. The crews were told to take off at night, cross the Mediterranean Sea, and circle Turkey to avoid it because it was a neutral country. "You are not, and I repeat not, to enter neutral Turkish territory."

They would fly over German-occupied Greece to Romania, but the detour around Turkey meant the planes would not have sufficient range to reach the refueling site in Iraq once the raid was completed. They were also ordered to drop their bombs from an altitude of 30,000 feet.

The plan as specified by the RAF was impossible. Halverson's B-24s could not reach 30,000 feet with the added weight of the extra fuel tank installed in the bomb bay, together with the 3,000 pounds of bombs they had been ordered to carry. Further, they could not reach Ploesti and go on to Iraq even if they installed two extra gas tanks and carried no bombs at all! "To us," one pilot said, "the briefing was straight out of 'The Wonderful Wizard of Oz.'"

Following the briefing, the lead navigator summoned the other navigators to a secret meeting in his room where he unfolded a *National Geographic* map of the Middle East and pinned it to the wall. He traced a line with his finger to how far off a straight course for Ploesti they would need to fly to avoid Turkey. He believed it was nothing short of a suicide mission. But what choice did they have? If they violated orders and flew over Turkey and bombed from a lower altitude, they would be court-martialed—that is, if anyone survived.

The door to the navigator's room burst open and Colonel Halverson strode in. He looked at the map on the wall and pointed to a crease where it had been folded. The crease ran from Egypt straight through Turkey to the Black Sea bordering Romania. "Can we help it," Halverson said, "if the *National Geographic* put their line through Turkey?"

The navigators smiled in relief, but Halverson was not finished. "Furthermore, I suggest that we bomb at fourteen thousand feet."

At 10:30 that night, June 11, 1942, 13 bombers took off from the base in Egypt, all that were still in flyable condition of the original 23-plane force from Florida. The 8,000-mile journey over ocean and desert without adequate maintenance and replacement parts had taken a toll.

One plane returned to Fayid when an engine cut out, but the other 12 reached the target and dropped their bombs on what the crews thought was a refinery. The clouds were so thick, however, that it was difficult to tell. Six planes flew safely to the refueling base in Iraq and two landed in Syria. The other four were forced to land in Turkey; the crews were interned for more than six months and their airplanes were confiscated.

Nine days after the raid, HALPRO's planes and crews were renamed the First Provisional Bombardment Group of the Middle East Air Force. Four months later, on October 31, 1942, they became part of the newly organized 376th Heavy Bombardment Group. Unofficially they called themselves the "Liberandos," a wordplay on the name of their plane, the Liberator. In August 1943, some would return to Ploesti as part of a larger force that would do more damage and be far more costly than the first time they made the long flight to Romania.

That first raid on Ploesti did little damage and received almost no publicity. Three days after the attack the *New York Times* published a brief article: U.S. Bombers Strike Black Sea Area—Base Is Mystery. Nothing more was revealed about the target, not even its name.

Official Army Air Force reports expressed cautious optimism about the raid's results, but in truth the refineries had hardly been touched. Two days after the mission the RAF issued a more realistic assessment. "The general impression is that the majority of aircraft jettisoned their bombs from above the clouds or on breaking cloud. It is highly improbable that any damage has been done."

Despite the lack of tangible success, the HALPRO mission was important for the morale of Air Force leaders. It had demonstrated the type of air operation that could be mounted in the future. Prior to that time, the only offensive missions American air power had participated in had been conducted in conjunction with the RAF. The flight to Ploesti was the first time American bombers flew on their own over enemy territory in Europe.

It was the largest American heavy bomber mission of the war to date, proving that a heavy bomb load could be carried a distance of 1,300 miles to a target deep inside enemy territory. The mission also validated the usefulness of the B-24 for what its designers claimed it to be, the longest range plane in the U.S. arsenal.

There was another effect of this first mission to Ploesti, which was unexpected and unwelcome, but by the time it became known, it was too late to do anything about it.

The raid alerted the Germans that Ploesti was vulnerable to destruction by air, a realization that induced them to strengthen their defenses. They were certain the Americans would return, and with a greater air force next time.

And so Ploesti became the most heavily defended target in Europe, but the Allies would not realize the extent of these defenses until the mission on August 1, 1943. Those aircrews would pay a terrible price, the unintended legacy of Operation HALPRO.

After that first raid in 1942, Gen. Alfred Gerstenberg, who was responsible for Ploesti's defense, clearly saw what it portended. "This is the beginning," he wrote.

When the Casablanca conference ended, Hap Arnold, Army Air Force chief of staff, ordered Col. Jacob E. Smart to plan the new mission against Ploesti. Jake Smart was a highly intelligent, 35-year-old bomber pilot who served as a member of Arnold's advisory council. Arnold had enough confidence in Smart to give him complete authority and responsibility for all the details of the raid. The result, as one air force historian put it, was that "no mission before or after was put together with such care, forethought and training."

Although Smart would later characterize his Ploesti plan somewhat flippantly as "a bad idea I dreamed up," it seemed brilliant at the time. Most of his superiors gave unqualified approval to his unorthodox approach.

The first thing Smart did was assemble a knowledgeable staff. In London he procured an American Air Force intelligence officer, who was also an artist and architect, to prepare detailed models and maps of the target area. He also tapped a combat-tested B-24 pilot and one of the best air force navigators, who had already completed a tour of combat duty in Europe.

From the RAF he brought in a group captain experienced in desert operations, because Smart knew that the only air bases in Allied hands from which planes could reach Ploesti were in the desert of North Africa. He also selected an RAF wing commander experienced in flying low-level attack missions, and a British army officer who for eight years had been an engineer at one of the Ploesti refineries. The man had intimate knowledge of the target areas.

With his highly competent staff assembled, Smart pored over previous studies and surveys, which had concluded that close to 1,400 bombers would be needed to do significant damage to the refineries if they flew at high altitude, the way the air force had been training for years. High-altitude bombing was considered the only acceptable means to conducting successful raids.

The route planned for Operation Tidal Wave, the low-level bombing attack on the oil refineries at Ploesti, Romania. The island of Corfu was used as a navigational landmark. After the raid, surviving planes ended up in Romania, Turkey, Cyprus, and North Africa, while others were forced to ditch in the Mediterranean.

Smart knew he would have nowhere near that number of B-24s available to carry out those scenarios. There probably were not 1,400 Liberators in all theaters of operation in 1943. Even if there were that many planes, they would not all be at his disposal in North Africa. He could count on no more than 200 aircraft.

Further, the refineries were not conveniently located in a central cluster or adjacent to one another. They had been built in a 6-mile ring around the town. Smart had to decide how he could drop the bombs from a high altitude and strike only the perimeter without hitting the city center and killing the civilian population. In addition, there were two major refineries outside the circle around Ploesti, one 18 miles north and the other 5 miles south.

Smart saw only one solution. If the planes could not accurately hit the targets from a high altitude, then they would have to go in at treetop level. That way they could be sure of inflicting the greatest possible damage to the refineries with the least possible harm to civilians.

Flying low also increased the chance of having the advantage of surprise because the planes would be approaching the target undetected by radar. Thus the enemy would be less prepared for an attack. The Germans were aware of the American doctrine favoring high-level bombing missions and would be unlikely to imagine the appearance of U.S. aircraft just above the tree tops.

On the other hand, Colonel Smart recognized a major drawback to a low-level bombing raid and that was the type of aircraft. Smart admitted that "of all aircraft, there is probably none less suited to low-level work than the B-24." The plane looked like a flying boxcar, and at a low altitude would be vulnerable to machine gun and small arms fire.

Smart knew his plan would be unpopular with the crews who would have to fly the mission. "Nobody with any sense," he wrote, "wanted to fly a B-24 in low, but we had no choice. It was the only way we could do it." He believed that the pilots could be trained to keep tight formations while avoiding obstacles on the ground, and that flying low would give the ships' gunners the chance to kill anyone who was firing small arms at them.

Another decision Colonel Smart made was to prohibit all reconnaissance flights over Ploesti in the months before the

An intelligence photograph of two of the oil refineries at Ploesti, Romania. Astra-Romana would be the target for the 98th Bombardment Group, while Standard would be the target for the 93rd. Key: 1. stabilization plant; 2. distillation plant; 3. boiler house; 4. pumping station. (*National Archives*)

mission. The reason was sound: He did not want to alert the Germans that an attack was being planned. Nevertheless, General Gerstenberg was already convinced that Ploesti was a major target because of the previous HALPRO raid, and he had persuaded his superiors to provide superior antiaircraft defenses.

"Had photographs been taken," wrote a U.S. Air Force historian later, "they would have revealed a very heavily defended target with more flak guns than those protecting Berlin and a fighter strength of nearly two hundred fifty first-line aircraft. Unknown to the planners also, the German early warning net was far-flung and efficient." The Germans were ready for the American mission to Ploesti, no matter how thoroughly Colonel Smart and his staff had considered every detail of the operation.

Hap Arnold approved Smart's plan in early May 1943. The next step was to present it to Roosevelt, Churchill, and other top leaders meeting in Washington, D.C., May 13-24, for the so-called Trident Conference. The final plan, as presented at that meeting, called for an attacking force composed of five bombardment groups.

Two of the groups were already in North Africa as part of the Ninth Air Force, but two others were in England as part of the Eighth Air Force. The fifth unit had just arrived in England and was scheduled to become part of the Eighth. The plan called for the groups based in England to be dispatched temporarily to North Africa for the Ploesti attack, after which they would return to England.

At the Trident Conference, Sir Charles Portal, Churchill's Chief of Air Staff, objected to that temporary reassignment on the grounds that it would weaken the effectiveness of the bombing offensive against Germany at a time when the Eighth Air Force was far from maximum strength. In addition, Portal expressed concern that if the assault on Ploesti failed to destroy the refineries, the Germans would strengthen their defenses further, making future raids on the refineries that much more difficult.

Gen. George C. Marshall, U.S. Army Chief of Staff, countered that any damage the bombers could inflict on the refineries would hamper the German war effort to some degree and therefore was worth the effort and potential cost. Marshall's argument prevailed, perhaps in great part because the focus of the meeting was the upcoming invasion of Sicily, so relatively little time was spent on what was perceived, in contrast, to be a small operation.

The Trident Conference endorsed Jake Smart's plan and sent

him off to North Africa to present it to the American commander there, Lt. Gen. Dwight "Ike" Eisenhower, and his deputies, Air Chief Marshall Sir Arthur Tedder and U.S. Army Air Force Lt. Gen. Carl "Tooey" Spaatz.

They reviewed the plan on May 24 and were not enthusiastic. In fact, they were quite critical. One of Spaatz's staff officers, Gen. Gordon Saville, called the operation "ridiculous and suicidal." General Eisenhower wrote, after the war, that he had doubted the wisdom of the mission. All three questioned how effective a single strike could be. They had already seen too many instances of manufacturing facilities reported destroyed that were fully operational again in a matter of days.

Tedder estimated that the attacking force would lose 40 percent of its planes and that the odds of destroying as much as half the refineries' capacity were no greater than one in ten. Still, even in the face of this grim assessment, in the end Tedder gave his support, arguing that if somehow it turned out to be more effective than he predicted, the results would have a significant effect on Germany's war machine.

Eisenhower agreed, and he granted his approval to Colonel Smart's plan. It would have been awkward for him at that stage in his career (he was not yet Supreme Commander of all Allied Forces) to oppose an operation that had earned the endorsement of the president, the prime minister, General Marshall, and other British and American leaders at the Trident Conference.

Even with Eisenhower's approval, Smart's plan was not ready to become operational. Following the Trident Conference in Washington, the major participants, except Roosevelt, headed for a conference in Algiers, June 1-3.

Churchill was no longer flying in *Commando*, the spartan B-24 given him by the Americans. The RAF, perhaps thinking it unseemly for their prime minister to be transported in a U.S. airplane, and an uncomfortable one at that, provided Churchill with a luxuriously converted Lancaster bomber. "Very comfortable," approved Field Marshall Sir Alan Brooke, "with a special cabin for PM, dining rooms, berths for four besides PM, and lavatory."

The primary focus of the Algiers conference was the coming invasion of Sicily and the final stages of the war against the German forces in North Africa. Consequently, little time was devoted to the Ploesti raid. The general feeling was that since it had already been approved by all major parties, there was nothing left to discuss. General Eisenhower gave formal approval to the mission at the meeting but was reluctant to commit himself to either a low-altitude or high-altitude approach.

Colonel Smart, perhaps surprised that this issue was still open for discussion, arranged a private meeting with Churchill and made his case for a low-level attack.

The imaginative Churchill, a lifelong lover of surprise raids, responded enthusiastically. He offered four crack Royal Air Force Lancaster crews to lead the Americans to the target.

Smart replied that the Lancaster bomber and the Liberator had differing characteristics of range, load, altitude, and speed, and that it would be impossible for the two types to maintain close formation on the long journey to Romania. Churchill yielded. Smart did not have to bring up the additional consideration that American airmen would resent the implication that they could not find the target themselves.

Colonel Smart was not yet finished giving high-level briefings on his plan to destroy the Ploesti refineries. He still had to mollify Maj. Gen. Ira Eaker, commander of the Eighth Air Force in England, who was not pleased that two of his veteran B-24 groups would be taken away from him, along with a third group newly arrived from the States. Although assured that the transfer would be temporary, he knew that all too often temporary turns out to be permanent.

Smart briefed Eaker on the mission and assured him that he would have his three groups back after the raid, assuming any of them survived. Eaker knew he could not refuse to cooperate, not when his superiors, up to the president of the United States, had already approved.

And so General Eaker did what he could to facilitate the transfer. Colonel Smart wrote, "General Eaker has given me everything I have asked for and more." Eaker provided a total of 128 B-24 Liberators and crews, to be available for as long as needed to achieve a successful bombing raid. Many would never return to England.

By the middle of June 1943, when it appeared that every detail had been considered, agreed upon, and arranged, Churchill raised another matter. He was not happy with the code name the Americans had assigned to the mission. It did not have a sufficiently heroic ring to be entered for all time in the war histories yet to be written. He also protested that it would hardly bolster the morale of the aircrews and so he proposed a new name to Roosevelt.

During the early years of World War II, code names for U.S. operations were selected in several ways, in an effort to simplify the process. At first, colors were used, for example, Operation Red, but the list of colors quickly ran out. Then a list of 10,000 common English-language adjectives and nouns was compiled. Operations planners would select one at random as the code-name for their mission. And that was how some unknown person, possibly a member of Colonel Smart's staff, chose Operation Soapsuds as the code name for the mission to bomb Ploesti's oil refineries. It could just as easily, and inappropriately, have been called Operation Cornflakes.

No one in the U.S. military hierarchy had objected to "Soapsuds," and that would have remained the mission's designation had not Churchill urged something grander. Roosevelt agreed. On June 26, 1943, Churchill sent a telegram to President Roosevelt marked "Personal and Most Secret."

> On reflection, I thought "Soapsuds" was inappropriate for an operation in which so many brave Americans would risk or lose their lives. I do not think it is good for morale to affix disparaging labels to daring feats of arms. I am very glad that the United States Chiefs of the Staff have agreed with ours to substitute "Tidal Wave" for "Soapsuds." I wish all our problems were as simply settled.

Operation Tidal Wave was ready to begin.

Maj. Gen. Lewis H. Brereton addressing the 376th Heavy Bombardment Group, the Liberandos, on June 30, 1943. (*U.S. Air Force*)

2

SOME IDIOTIC ARMCHAIR
WARRIOR IN WASHINGTON

THE BRITISH CALLED HIM "Hot-Foot Louie" because when
he walked, he strode rapidly and with purpose. "He always
seemed to be in a hurry," the *New York Times* wrote in 1943, "even
when seated."

Others described him as "chronically querulous," "blunt,
assertive, and pugnacious," possessing a "reckless, restless vigor"
and "a fierce temper." He was also known as a "cocky, aggressive,
intelligent, experienced, pretty damn able commander." People
found it hard to be neutral; some thought he was difficult to get
along with, others genuinely liked him and thought he was an
outstanding officer.

At the age of 53, Maj. Gen. Lewis Hyde Brereton was fighting his second worldwide war and was no doubt the only Air
Force general to have graduated from the U.S. Naval Academy.
Further, he had experienced a period of such intense anxiety
and fear of flying at one point in his career that he was grounded, clearly not a good career move for a pilot wishing to advance
in the service.

Worse, he then sought psychoanalytic therapy, quite openly,
with the best known American psychoanalyst—a personal

friend of Sigmund Freud—at a time when a strong stigma was attached to treatment for emotional problems, especially in the military. Nevertheless, Brereton not only stayed in the service but rose to the rank of general by the time World War II began.

Born in Pittsburgh, Pennsylvania, the young Brereton grew up wanting to go to West Point but was unable to secure an appointment. Instead, he followed his brother to the Naval Academy where he received the nickname "Louie." He displayed a blatant disregard of rules and regulations. He once told *Life* magazine journalist Clare Boothe Luce that his performance at Annapolis was "distinguished by the amount of time he spent in confinement."

He graduated in 1911 and resigned his naval commission to join the army, the service he had wanted originally. He learned to fly but two years later, after two crashes, he asked to be relieved from flying duty. He served in other branches of the army, but by 1917 was a pilot once again with the rank of major. During World War I he served under the legendary pilot Billy Mitchell, flew many dangerous missions, compiled a record for bravery, and earned an impressive number of medals including the Distinguished Service Cross.

Brereton's postwar career was less illustrious. It began promisingly enough with a plum assignment as air attaché in Paris, a post he received on Mitchell's recommendation. His superior officer there rated Brereton above average in intelligence but also inattentive to duty, indolent, in need of constant supervision, and careless with money.

He did not do well as a flight instructor when he returned to the United States, his performance being rated only average. An air force historian suggested that his less than outstanding record during the 1920s may have reflected the "postwar problems faced by someone successful in war who continued to have trouble adjusting to peacetime activities." Brereton was also dealing with personal problems, including the death of his parents and marital and financial difficulties, and he had a tendency to drink heavily.

His fitness reports showed no improvement by 1927. He was described as an average officer "who does not apply himself with wholehearted interest to the extent expected by an officer of his rank and experience."

It was during that obviously troubled year that he was granted two months' sick leave because of his fear of flying, perhaps triggered by a near mid-air collision and a crash that forced him to bail out. He consulted Dr. A. A. Brill, a distinguished psychoanalyst.

Nevertheless, he was selected to attend the army's Command and General Staff School, whose graduates are typically earmarked for promotion to higher rank and greater responsibility. Even so, his performance was below average. The staff declined to recommend him for additional military studies.

Yet over the next decade Brereton was given responsible commands and his performance ratings showed some change for the better. By 1935 he was promoted to lieutenant colonel and impressed younger officers with his overall conduct as a commander and his attention to detail. One of those officers was a young pilot named Jake Smart.

Brereton's reputation as a commander improved so much that eventually he was appointed an instructor at the Command and General Staff School at which he had performed so poorly several years before. This time he earned outstanding efficiency reports and the recommendation for higher command. He seemed to have turned his life around. In 1936 he was promoted to colonel and four years later to brigadier general. A year after that he was rated ninth in excellence out of a field of 80 brigadiers.

When Japanese air forces attacked Pearl Harbor, Hawaii, on December 7, 1941, Louie Brereton was a highly regarded major general chosen by Douglas MacArthur to command his air force in the Philippines. More than half of Brereton's aircraft were destroyed on the ground the first day of the war. The controversy over blame for the fiasco—whether MacArthur's fault or Brereton's—remains unresolved, but neither man was formally reprimanded.

Brereton took his command to Java, Dutch East Indies, and served as deputy commander for air of the grandly titled but meagerly equipped ABDACOM, the American-British-Dutch-Australian Command. When the Japanese took the islands he was ordered to India to command the newly formed 10th Air Force, operating under Vinegar Joe Stilwell.

He developed the habit of wearing British military uniforms, having lost his own in the Philippines. He kept an Oriental rug on the floor of his personal airplane, which irritated Stilwell, and carried a riding crop. Stilwell complained that Brereton had gone "too British."

On April 2, 1942, Brereton led two B-17s and one LB-30 (the British export version of the B-24) on a night raid to the Japanese-occupied Andaman Islands off the coast of India in the Bay of Bengal. All three planes returned safely and Brereton was awarded the Distinguished Flying Cross. Clare Boothe Luce reported him as saying, "Boys, bombing Japs makes me feel dammed fine."

After receiving the medal he wrote to a friend: "About the only fun a professional soldier looks forward to outside of

killing people is to pin a ribbon on his belly." There was probably a bit of hype in both statements, designed to raise public
morale back home at a time when the U.S. was still reeling from
the string of defeats at the hands of the Japanese.

By early June 1942 the British 8th Army was in full retreat
across the desert to Egypt. Even Cairo seemed doomed to fall.
On June 23 George C. Marshall ordered Brereton to take every
plane that could fly to Egypt to help the British. Three days
later he left India with a force comprising one LB-30, four B-
24s, and four B-17s, an all too tragic indication of the army air
force's shortage of aircraft.

The situation improved over the summer. Brereton got more
planes, enough to form the Ninth Air Force, which he commanded, and the British won a major victory over the Germans
at El Alamein. With Brereton's air support, the British pushed
Rommel and his combined German-Italian forces farther to the
west.

Historians consider this the beginning of the road to ultimate victory against the Nazis; Brereton would play an important role. But first he would have to deal with the raid on
Ploesti. It was his responsibility, as commander of the Ninth
Air Force, to see that it succeeded.

Brereton believed there was only one thing wrong with the
plan for Operation Tidal Wave developed by Colonel Smart
and approved at Casablanca, Washington, and Algiers: he was
not sure it would work. Regardless of the high-level endorse-
ments, the final tactical decision on how best to carry out the
raid was his to make as commander of the units that would fly
the mission.

He realized that if he criticized the approved plan, he would
be challenging the authority and judgment of Hap Arnold,

George C. Marshall, and President Roosevelt. Such an open protest could have only one result. He would be relieved of command and replaced by someone who would do as he was told.

The operation would get under way as Colonel Smart envisioned it whether or not Brereton remained in command. If it succeeded, Brereton would win praise and glory, and if it failed, he would be the likely scapegoat for the inevitable blame.

He pored over the target folders for two weeks before concluding that he had no choice but to execute the raid as planned. He also resolved to initiate a thorough training program to ensure the maximum rate of survival. He wanted to bring back as many men and planes as possible because he was going to be with them, personally leading the mission.

On July 6, 1943, Brereton confided his thoughts to his dairy.

> I knew that the Liberator was definitely not suited for a low-level attack, but I felt that the surprise element would weigh heavily in our favor. It was necessary to assure the heaviest possible damage in the first attack. I invited no discussion whatsoever among the commanders [about a low-level attack]. While I do not believe there was a single commander who would have not preferred a high-altitude attack, the decision was accepted by all. I stressed the necessity for absolute ruthlessness in the immediate relief of any commander who at any time during the training period showed a lack of leadership, of aggressiveness, or of complete confidence.

Louie Brereton was right about one thing. All of his commanders were opposed to a low-level attack, but they realized that they, too, had no choice. Unless they agreed to take their men in at treetop level, they would be sacked immediately. The matter was no longer open for discussion. However, some were determined to protest anyway.

The first to object was 43-year-old Brig. Gen. Uzal G. Ent, chief of the Ninth Air Force's bomber command. Ent would be more closely involved with training the aircrews because his headquarters were in Benghazi where the bombers were based, while Brereton was headquartered in Cairo. A West Point graduate and career army man, Ent was an ordained Lutheran minister, a balloon pilot, and husband of a former Ziegfeld Follies showgirl, which made him the envy of those who had seen her picture.

General Ent was nicknamed "P.D.," short for Pennsylvania Dutch, and he was popular with superiors and subordinates alike. But he did have one problem as a combat leader: he was considered a mediocre pilot. This did not stop him from volunteering for a number of combat missions and it was not about to stop him from going on the Ploesti raid.

No one questioned Ent's bravery, not since the day in 1938 when he and another officer were in the National Balloon Race over Pennsylvania, his home state. Lightning set the balloon on fire, killing Ent's partner. Ent had a quick decision to make: bail out of the burning balloon and save his life, in which case the balloon would go down over a town, possibly injuring innocent people, or stay with it and try to steer away from the populated area at the risk of burning to death. He chose to stay with the balloon and brought it down outside of town, without injury to himself or anyone else. For his bravery he was awarded the Distinguished Flying Cross, a decoration rarely given in peacetime.

Now, in 1943, Ent chose another brave act that could have cost him his career. He openly and adamantly criticized

Brereton's decision to take a low-level approach to Ploesti's oil fields. He put his protest in writing, in the form of a petition for the subordinate commanders of the five bombardment groups to sign.

"We estimate," Ent wrote to Brereton, "that seventy-five aircraft will be lost at low level. Fifty percent destruction [of the refineries] is the best we can hope for. You have guessed our recommendation, [that is] to attack at high level until the target is destroyed or effectively neutralized."

Ent soon realized, however, that nothing would alter Brereton's stand. Brereton returned Ent's petition marked "disapproved."

The concern about the outcome did not lessen as more men learned the magnitude of the distance to the target and the altitude at which they would have to make their attack. Ent put away his petition and ceased his formal protests. If he could not change or stop the operation, at least he could train the men properly so they had the best chance of coming back alive.

The plan to hit the target at treetop level was not the only issue to draw criticism. Some of the flyers saw other points of weakness. They were concerned about the lack of recent aerial reconnaissance photos of the target, leaving group commanders with no current information about the defenses in and around Ploesti. All that was available to them were intelligence estimates of the defenses based on outdated information of dubious quality.

Other crewmen argued that they would not take the Germans by surprise, no matter how low they flew. A formation of nearly 200 sizable airplanes would surely be spotted at some point along the 700-mile route. And it was not farfetched to suppose that the Germans had spies among the Arab population living near the airbases. There would be no hiding the take-off of so many planes. A spy with a radio transmitter could inform the enemy of their departure before all the ships were even in the air. The Germans would not have to know where they were headed. They would raise their alert levels at all possible targets, including Ploesti.

The surprise element would indeed be difficult to achieve. General Gerstenberg had set up a wide-ranging series of radar detection stations as well as a radio tracking unit to intercept and decode radio transmissions from the Ninth Air Force. That gave the Germans the ability to track the movements of all Allied aircraft in the area.

Another source of serious concern to the Liberator crewmen was the barrage balloons rumored to be in place over the refineries, each linked to the ground by a thick cable. Were those cables thick enough to shear off an airplane's wing? Might they snag on a wing and bring the cable down until the wing's leading edge struck the explosive device at the top of the cable?

"What about the balloons?" one pilot asked. "Who takes them out? And the people who had [planned] the missions said, 'We think you'll break the cables.' Well, that wasn't very much satisfaction to the people who were involved: 'think you'll break the cables!' It's all right to think it, but it's pretty important to know it if you're going to be one of the participants."

There were so many unknowns about the mission, including the capability of the planes for covering so great a distance with the weight of the additional fuel and bombs they would need to carry. What kinds of defenses awaited them over the target? And at what altitude would they ultimately have to fly? Could they hold the huge bombers in tight formations if they were so low a lucky rifle shot could bring them down? Surely not, some said. There must be some mistake, others added. But what if it's true?

On January 14, 1943, the opening day of the Casablanca conference, a navigator with the 98th Bombardment Group, called the "Pyramiders" after the pyramids of Egypt where they were stationed, wrote in his diary: "I wish I could believe myself that I expect to come back alive in one piece."

On the next day, while the Ploesti mission was being decided in Casablanca, some 2,300 miles to the west the navigator, Capt. Robert Adlen, wrote about how war-weary he and his buddies were from five months of almost daily combat.

> It's strange, and then again, perhaps not strange, but most of the boys here seem more "shot" than less. Each night you can see them gather in the club room drinking, smoking, playing poker, singing at the top of their voices and raising hell in general.
>
> Nothing wrong in that, but they have to do it to keep themselves from cracking. Most of them have from 200 to 300 combat hours and their nerves are pretty well shot. Johnny Burger walks around punchdrunk half the time. Young Neal, who never drank or smoked, isn't that way anymore. Holloway sweats out these tough missions, he says. Benish was permanently grounded. The Killer [Colonel Kane] wanted him to fly and Benish couldn't even land the ship. He made two attempts and then let his co-pilot do it [and] Benish used to be the hot test pilot for the group. Kandaras was wounded; still on flying status and gets himself tight every other few nights. You can't even get Ohlson to go on a mission anymore. I wonder how long I'll last. I remember at home you couldn't even get me on a roller coaster a second time.

The Pyramiders of the 98th had been flying constantly since their arrival in Palestine in July 1942. They had been on alert to evacuate if Rommel took Egypt and reached the Suez Canal, which at the time seemed likely. Then the British began to push Rommel back, and the 98th moved westward from one primitive airfield to other, following the successive victories of the British Army and the landing of American troops in the Casablanca area in November. By the summer of 1943, the Pyramiders were still flying missions almost every day.

The commander of the Pyramiders was 36-year-old Col. John Riley Kane, known as "Killer." With that nickname and a colorful personality, he quickly became the war correspondents' favorite. They knew they could always get a good story out of Killer Kane. Or at least make one up.

As a result he became by far the best known of the five bombardment group commanders slated to lead their men to Ploesti. More magazine and newspaper articles were written about him than about all the others combined. Many people back home came to believe that Kane was the leader of the raid.

One popular magazine, *Coronet*, wrote a highly flattering article in 1944 describing him as the "hero" of the raid. In 2002, nearly 60 years after the mission, an aviation magazine published an article entitled "Killer Kane's Raid!" It was not his raid, of course, but then, as now, publicity can shape reality—that version of reality in the news reports out of North Africa in 1943.

Coronet wrote of Kane as a man who "can fly a fully loaded Liberator bomber with one hand and he can chew tobacco with his oxygen mask on. He sounds like an enraged bull when he speaks into a field telephone at his desk, and his wrath with men who snafu a raid is terrible to behold. Some men hate Kane, and they spread the story that he is called the Killer because he has no regard for the lives of his pilots. Others gossip that he isn't as brave as the uncontrovertible [*sic*] evidence of his record shows. The Killer, being a man of action, scarcely realizes this."

One of the stories told about Kane is the day he silenced the Luftwaffe. The Pyramiders were bombing Rommel's Afrika Corps when an attack by German fighter planes caused Kane to miss the run to the target. He banked the plane to make another run and gave orders for his pilots to follow him in. German pilots zeroed in on his radio frequency and tried to drown out his orders with taunts and jokes. Kane shouted, "Get the hell off the air, you bastards!" As the story goes, the Germans obeyed his orders to be quiet.

The nickname "Killer" seemed appropriate for Kane's aggressive, even belligerent, personality and reflected his tough, domineering manner, but it actually came from a comic strip character. One of Kane's friends was a pilot named Rogers who, inevitably, was called Buck, after the fictional space traveler. In that popular comic strip, Rogers had a sidekick named Killer Kane. And John Riley Kane certainly lived up to it.

Most people either respected Kane or hated him; few were neutral. Capt. Robert Adlen was initially impressed with Kane when he took command, praising him for his interest in the welfare of his men. But that changed once they started flying combat missions. Adlen recorded his evaluation in his diary.

> Since Kane took the outfit over three months ago, it has lost twice as many ships as it did in the previous six months. The name of Killer sure fits him. Instead of killing the enemy, he's killing the men in his own groups with his ideas.

I hate the bastard. I don't want to wish him any bad luck, nothing more than a piece of ack-ack in his head. We all wish he gets out of this outfit soon, but that doesn't seem likely because the 9th Bomber Command won't have him. Can't blame them.

Kane's navigator, Lt. Norman Whalen, who knew him better than most because he flew with him nearly every day, was far less critical. "He was a controversial figure," Whalen wrote, "and he told the higher-ups what he thought. Colonel Kane was very direct and outspoken. He expressed himself without holding back on what he felt." And in a 2002 interview Whalen said, "I'd go back up with him tomorrow if he was still around and asked me."

Col. Jake Smart, who devised the plan for the Ploesti operation that Kane had termed "idiotic," described Kane some years after the war as follows:

> [A] courageous, able bomber pilot; a stern, intense, and unforgiving commander; a firm believer in the righteousness of his own values and his judgment and highly skeptical of those of others. Kane felt a deep responsibility for the care and well being of the young men in his group. He regarded them as lambs that would be led to the slaughter. He steeled himself to lead them to Hell and back home—if he could.

The son of a Baptist preacher, Kane was born in 1907 in Eagle Springs, Texas, and grew up in Louisiana and Missouri as his father moved from one church to another. As with many ministers' sons, the church was not the place for young John Riley. He was too brash, outspoken, and boisterous for life as a small-town preacher. He decided to become a doctor and in 1924 enrolled at Baylor University in Waco, Texas, majoring in zoology and German, part of the standard pre-med training. He become a teaching assistant, joined the Baylor Chamber of Commerce, and played football for two years. He acknowledged that he was not a good player and joked that he was a "punching bag" for the other players. He was better at basketball, but on a trip to an out-of-town game, the team bus was rammed by a train. Ten players were killed; Kane was one of 12 to survive.

When he graduated from Baylor in 1928, he enrolled at the medical school of Washington University in St. Louis, Missouri, but stayed two years before deciding that medicine was not right for him. "I found out I couldn't stand all that medical smell, chloroform and ether and all. It actually made me sick."

He returned to his grandfather's farm in Eagle Springs, Texas, where he worked for a year, then decided he wanted to be a pilot. He went to Brooks Field in San Antonio and earned his wings and a commission as a second lieutenant but still did not have a job. The Depression was under way and the military, like most other employers, was laying off people.

Kane was discharged from active duty and placed in the reserves. There were few jobs to be had anywhere. "I sponged off my dad for a long time," he wrote, "and then went back to the farm." A year later the army called him back to active duty, and he spent the next few years training pilots for the rapidly expanding Army Air Corps.

At the time of the Japanese attack on Pearl Harbor in 1941, Kane had reached the rank of captain. A year later he was a major, sent to North Africa to join the 98th Bombardment Group. The following year he was a colonel and commander of the group. He had completed his first tour of combat duty, 30 missions, and had flown 13 more in his second tour. And he was well known as Killer Kane.

When he was informed of the plan for a low-altitude bombing raid on Ploesti, he immediately pronounced it stupid and suicidal, and said that it had obviously been dreamed up by "some idiotic armchair warrior in Washington." But, as always, after he had made his objections known in his characteristic way and was told that the mission would be carried out as planned whether he remained in command or not, he stopped

Commander of the 98th Bombardment Group, 36-year-old Col. John Riley "Killer" Kane. (*John Andrew Prime*)

criticizing it publicly and proceeded to do his duty. "We're going to knock out Ploesti," he told his men, "or die trying." A historian commented that Kane probably "figured it would be both."

The other outfit already flying combat out of North Africa in 1943 was the 376th Heavy Bombardment Group, the Liberandos. The men from the HALPRO mission had originally formed this group, but by 1943, most of them had been killed or transferred out and replaced by fresh crews from the U.S. The Liberandos had been flying almost daily missions for as long as Killer Kane's men had.

Together they had more combat time than any outfit in the Eighth Air Force in England, including the three groups that would join them for the Ploesti raid. The Liberandos' commander was Col. Keith Compton, a highly competent pilot who despised Killer Kane. The feeling was mutual.

The 93rd Bombardment Group in England was known as "Ted's Traveling Circus," after its first commander, Col. Edward "Ted" Timberlake. The group had flown to England in September 1942, in the first nonstop flight of American bombers across the North Atlantic. They conducted short-run bombing raids to France and carried out anti-submarine patrols over the Bay of Biscay in conjunction with RAF Coastal Command.

Parts of the 93rd were sent to Libya for temporary duty to help with the bombing campaign against Rommel's Afrika Corps, and, later, in raids against Italy. They returned to England in the winter of 1943. That spring, Colonel Smart chose Timberlake to join his planning staff as operations officer.

Timberlake selected Lt. Col. Addison Baker, one of his squadron commanders, to take over the 93rd. The 35-year-old Baker had been an auto mechanic in Akron, Ohio, when he joined the army in 1929. He had completed flight training as a second lieutenant in 1931 but was forced to leave active duty a year later because of military budget cuts. He went to Detroit and opened a service station, continuing to fly as a member of the National Guard. In 1940 he was recalled to active duty.

The other B-24 group that had been flying combat missions from England for nearly a year was the 44th Bombardment Group, known as the "Flying Eight Balls." Some said they chose the name for the obvious mathematical reason that four plus four equals eight. Another version is that they got the name because they had a reputation as a hard-luck outfit because they had suffered a high number of losses. Unofficially they had another nickname—the "Flying Screwballs"—bestowed by their rivals in Ted's Traveling Circus.

The 44th was commanded by Col. Leon Johnson who, at 39, was one of the oldest men in the outfit. Born in Kansas, he decided to go to West Point after a friend came home on leave in his fancy dress cadet uniform. Johnson graduated in 1926 and spent three years in the infantry before attending flight school to become a bomber pilot. He had been flying combat missions since his arrival in England in June 1942 and had won more medals for bravery than had Killer Kane.

Corp. Andy Rooney, a 24-year-old reporter for the U.S. Army's daily newspaper, *The Stars and Stripes*, described Johnson as "a good commander, good pilot, and all-round regular guy." Corporal Rooney also admired Johnson's car, a seven-passenger Packard touring car. "[Johnson] often went down to London in it and he'd amaze the enlisted men hitchhiking along the road by stopping to pick them up until he had a full load."

The last of the three Liberator groups in England that would be transferred to North Africa for the Ploesti operation was the 389th Bombardment Group, the "Sky Scorpions." Led by Col. Jack Wood, they flew new B-24s, fresh from the factory, and did not arrive until June 11, 1943. Thus, they had not been in England long enough to gain any combat experience. That would soon change.

In late May 1943, a few weeks before the Sky Scorpions arrived, the veteran crews of the Flying Eight Balls and Ted's Traveling Circus were flying low-level practice runs along the English coast. Having experience with only high-altitude combat missions, and still unaware of the plan for the Ploesti raid, they reacted to this unorthodox type of training with surprise, some anxiety, and considerable opposition.

In addition, the Norden bombsights, designed specifically for high-altitude bombing, had been removed from the airplanes, replaced by a simple device that could be effective only at low altitudes. Clearly the crews realized they were being trained and equipped for an unusual mission that would have them bombing from no higher than a few hundred feet, and perhaps even lower.

Rumors were rife about what kind of target would require a low-level attack and where it might be. Some did speculate about the refineries at Ploesti. To counteract that notion, the planners planted their own rumor that the likely target was the German battleship *Tirpitz*, which lay at anchor in a fjord on Norway's coast beyond the range of the RAF.

To add credence to the rumor, the planners arranged for a visit from a few Norwegian naval officers, whom they instructed to "walk around the B-24 bases and go in and out of operations rooms. The Norwegians had no idea why, but they enjoyed their post-exchange privileges."

Colonel Johnson of the Flying Eight Balls protested against the idea of a low-level bombing raid. The Eight Balls had recently lost 7 of 18 planes on a raid against German submarine pens. A few days before, twin-engine B-26 medium bombers had attempted an attack on a target in Holland by roaring in at a very low altitude. All were shot down.

Johnson was told firmly that he would obey his orders or be relieved. He then told his men that there was no point in protesting to him any further about the idea of a low-level raid. "Colonel Johnson told us in a calm, positive voice that if it was the desire of the Air Force to fly low-level missions, we would fly those missions and he would lead us. There was complete silence in the room. If he was leading, we were going to follow."

Still, many airmen remained concerned, unwilling to accept that the air force brass would send them over any target, whatever and wherever it was, so close to the ground in their B-24s. One pilot noted: "We did practice at low levels, but no one really believed that they would send us in that low."

Jersey Bounce and three other planes of the 93rd Bombardment Group on their way to Ploesti. (*National Archives*)

3

A Bird's-Eye View of
Impending Death

GERMAN FIGHTER PILOTS called the American Liberator bombers "furniture vans," because they looked so clumsy and made such tempting targets. They were also known as "flying coffins." RAF pilots made jokes about the ungainly big-bellied planes. "Great cargo ship," one said; "never do as a bomber." A Romanian fighter pilot who saw them over Ploesti said they looked like big, fat birds.

Men who flew B-17s called the Liberators "pregnant cows." And even those who flew the B-24s had dubbed it the "flying box car," "an aluminum cigar," "a banana boat." Several historians have noted that few, if any, of the pilots coming out of flight school were eager to fly that bomber. One author preparing a book about the Liberator wrote: "When the book was started, I thought that the B-24 was an unattractive aircraft. When the book was finished, I thought the B-24 was a *supremely* unattractive aircraft!"

A World War II waist gunner assigned to B-24s recalled the plane as "a hollow tube with aluminum ribs holding it sacrosanct. Take a thin tube and drop a floor into it, hammer on a couple of wings, put a tail on its rear; and that was a B-24. A flying eggshell, that's all it was. We were all together in a flying eggshell."

The B-24 was quite unlike its sleeker, more graceful and glamorous cousin, the B-17 Flying Fortress. The author of the book about the Liberator acknowledged that the B-17 was "the bomber that caught and held the American public's imagination." The B-24 was a more modern aircraft—it carried a greater payload than the B-17. The Liberator had a greater range than the fortress. The B-24 was also faster than the B-17, but none of this mattered. The B-17 was the quintessential bomber in America's eyes. Numerous wartime and postwar movies were based around B-17s, but none were based on B-24s.

The B-24 waist gunner agreed, reminiscing about the war 60 years later.

> Those [B-17s] were beautiful in the air. With great swooping wings, they looked like huge gliders. I especially liked to watch them take off. They would hit the end of the runway and start a slow rolling climb. It looked like those babies could fly themselves; they appeared so effortless in lift off and flight.
>
> Those B-17s could take a hell of a beating and keep flying. They could return to base on one engine and with both wings shot off. Maybe they could do it with no propellers, too? We [in our B-24s] were faster but we couldn't take a hit to save our rear.

The journalist Andy Rooney agreed. In 1995 he wrote: "The B-24 was never the bomber the B-17 was. If you have to go to Berlin or Schweinfurt, take a B-17 and your chances of getting home were vastly improved. The B-17 could take a punch like no other aircraft ever built."

During the war, the maker of the B-24, Consolidated Aircraft Corporation, hired the advertising firm of Young & Rubicam to conduct a survey to find out which of the two bombers had the higher recognition value. The results, after interviewing 2,421 civilian men, showed that the Flying Fortress was better known than the Liberator; 70 percent of those interviewed had heard of the B-24, and 90 percent had heard of the B-17.

Surveys of 3,000 flight personnel in the Eighth Air Force in England in 1944 compared the morale of the aircrews assigned to these planes. The majority of the men flying each type of plane thought theirs was better. However, only 76 percent of B-24 crews believed their plane was the better of the two compared to 92 percent of Flying Fortress crews.

Regardless of the B-24's reputation, there were certainly a lot of them. More than 19,000 Liberators were built during the war. At the peak of production in 1944, a Liberator rolled off the assembly line every hour and forty minutes.

The B-17 had been designed by Boeing and was in production at its Seattle, Washington, plant in 1938 when the Army Air Corps sought out another aviation company to complement Boeing's single production line. Army staffers visited Consolidated Aircraft in San Diego, California, builder of the Navy's popular PBY seaplane, the "Catalina." The Army's need came at a good time for Consolidated because their PBY contract was ending. The company had already started to lay off some of its work force.

Building a plane for the Army was seen as a golden opportunity for Consolidated, but the management was more ambitious. They did not merely want to produce someone else's airplane, even though it would have been highly profitable to do so. They wanted to design and build their own, a new plane that would fly a greater distance at a higher altitude and speed, and carry a larger bomb load than the B-17. And they were determined to complete that task in no more time than it would have taken to retool their production line to turn out B-17s.

Their plan for the new bomber was radical. The designers gave the plane a nose wheel, a tricycle landing gear that no other heavy bomber had. It would allow for faster takeoffs and landings. The B-17 had a tail wheel on which it rested; the fuselage sloped up from tail to nose when the ship was on the ground.

The B-24 had a new type of wing, the so-called Davis wing. At first glance it appeared too narrow and thin to keep a heavy bomber in the air. The wing was not much bigger than the wings on twin-engine bombers but its unique airflow design provided greater lift and enhanced performance at high altitudes. The new wing was attached high on the fuselage, which provided more cargo space for bombs.

The wing's narrowness, however, while providing an advantage at high altitudes, was also the major point of vulnerability in combat. It was later observed that "battle damage to any major structural component of the Davis wing almost always resulted in the wing folding back along the side of the fuselage and the loss of the aircraft and its crew." The wider wing of the B-17, in contrast, was able to sustain considerable damage and remain structurally sound to bring the plane and its crew home safely.

The fuselage of the new bomber was large and slab-sided, taller than the B-17, contributing to its ungainly appearance. The advantage of the design was that it provided additional space for the bomb load.

The company assembled a full-size wooden mock-up to present to army officials. They inspected it on February 1, 1939, and in only three weeks' time accepted Consolidated Aircraft's proposal, offering a contract to build the new plane. The prototype, designated XB-24USAAC s/n 39-556, was ready to fly on December 29, 1939.

The initial flight test lasted 17 minutes and was pronounced a success. The unorthodox design elements seemed to work the way they were supposed to. The company declared that a major new weapon of war was ready for production. The employees chose its name, considered appropriate for its mission in the coming war: the Liberator.

But the Liberator proved a difficult airplane to fly. Andy Rooney wrote that "the B-24 handled like a car with mushy steering." It took a great deal of physical strength to pull and push on the control wheel to keep the plane in tight formation; several hours of that maneuvering on a mission took a demanding physical toll on the pilots. The Young & Rubicam survey of B-17 and B-24 crews found that Liberator pilots made many more negative comments about how hard it was to fly in formation and how stiff the controls were to operate.

One Liberator pilot wrote: "Men who are picked to fly B-24s should be picked for their physical abilities; there should be no pilots under 160 pounds because the physical strain of formation flying is too much." During the Ploesti raid, some pilots would spend as long as 16 hours at the controls.

The Liberator was also an uncomfortable plane for the crew, although no worse than the B-17 or more other military aircraft. Space was limited and human comfort and convenience were secondary, if they were considered at all.

On board the B-24, moving from one part of the plane to another could be dangerous. Passage from the cockpit to the rear required crewmen to cross a narrow catwalk in the middle of the bomb bay. One waist gunner wrote: "It was so tight in there that you couldn't walk through without brushing into the bombs on either side. One misstep and you would put your weight upon the bomb bay doors. These could not support extra mass and it would be a free ride to the ground."

The bomb bay doors opened by sliding up and down like an old-fashioned rolltop desk. If during a bombing run the doors would not open, the bombs could be released anyway because the doors were designed to give way under the weight of the bombs. Or the weight of a man.

Before a bomb run commenced, the bombardier had to enter the bomb bay, stand on the catwalk, and pull a pin from the nose of each bomb. "The only way to do this was by hanging onto the bomb racks and on the bombs themselves. All this amid the noise, the gusts of wind, and the vibration."

The radio compartment was located one step down from the cockpit toward the nose. The radioman had a difficult job. He "sat for hours on end, static crackling in his ears, giving position reports every 30 minutes, assisting the navigator in taking fixes, and informing headquarters of targets attacked and [the] results. [Also,] the radio operator was responsible for first-aid equipment he fervently hoped would stay unused."

Forward of the radio compartment was a crawl space, a narrow tunnel that led to the nose. It snaked past the retracted front wheel where the catwalk was less than a foot wide. The wheel well was covered by a thin sheet of aluminum that was not designed to support a man's weight. Occasionally, a navigator or bombardier stretched out on the wheel doors to take a break from cramped quarters in the nose, or simply to rest on the return trip from a mission. And more than once the doors broke under their weight, dropping them to their death; they wore no parachutes because the quarters were too tight to permit them in flight.

The Liberator's Plexiglas nose offered the best view, and the most frightening. Some crewmen described it as being perched on the end of a girder atop a skyscraper under construction, except that in the B-24's "greenhouse," which got uncomfortably hot in the sun, there was nothing below them but emptiness, a "bird's eye view of impending death." The nose had no armor plate or even aluminum skin to give the illusion of protection. When newly trained navigators and bombardiers arrived in England, they were surprised to find they were in great demand. They soon learned why; they had the highest casualty rates of any crewmen.

Pilots, copilots, bombardiers, and navigators were officers. The other six members of the usual ten-man crew, including the engineer, radioman and gunners, were sergeants, even those fresh out of training school. There were no privates or corporals in bomber crews, for a reason relating to Hermann Goering, head of the Luftwaffe, who had been a fighter pilot in World War I.

Whatever his faults and excesses, and there were many, Goering had great respect for airmen. As a result, he personally saw to it that captured British and American airmen were held in prisoner-of-war camps administered by the Luftwaffe, rather than those run by the German Army or the Gestapo. And he insisted that his camps provide better food and facilities than the camps for captured ground troops.

In addition, the Luftwaffe provided differential treatment of its prisoners by rank. Officers fared better than enlisted men; sergeants better than privates or corporals. Consequently, the U.S. Army Air Force decided that all enlisted men flying combat missions would be made sergeants. If captured, they would still be subject to harsh discipline and the rigors of confinement, but would be treated better than captured infantrymen who were privates.

The least envied enlisted men aboard the B-24 (and this was true for the B-17 as well) was the ball turret gunner. He hung in a Plexiglas, aluminum-ribbed sphere underneath the plane. The turret was positioned too low on the Liberator to be down during takeoff and landing, so the gunner did not get into position until the aircraft was near enemy territory.

The gunner entered the turret through a metal door at the rear. He had to curl almost in a fetal position to fit, usually lying on his back between the twin .50-caliber machine guns with his feet in stirrups on either side of a 13-inch window. He had to remain in this awkward position, with his knees drawn close to his ears, sometimes for several hours.

The turret was too cramped to allow the gunner to wear a parachute. If the plane was hit, the turret had to be brought back up inside the fuselage. But if the raising mechanism had been damaged by flak, the gunner would be trapped. The ball turret gave the gunner an excellent view; he could clearly see the flak rising up toward the plane, and the enemy fighters firing machine guns and cannon, which appeared to be coming directly at them.

Few ball turret gunners survived a direct hit. If the plane managed to return to base, there was little left of the body to bury. A popular poem at bomber bases throughout England was Randall Jarrell's "The Death of the Ball Turret Gunner," which closed with these grim words: "When I died they washed me out of the turret with a hose."

None of the B-24 gunners had an easy time, though none was as physically uncomfortable in their firing positions as the ball turret gunner. The air force trained more than 227,000 gunners during World War II. At the high point, seven training schools in the United States were turning out some 3,200 every week. The rumor was that a gunner's average life span in combat was 17 seconds. Despite the obvious risks, the majority of men who became gunners were volunteers.

The tail gunner was isolated at the extreme end of the fuselage. It, too, was a lonely spot. Like the ball turret gunner, the tail gunner could not stay at his post during takeoffs and landings because of the high acceleration, or G-forces, that built up at the tail end of the aircraft.

Getting into the tail turret once airborne was difficult and dangerous because the fuselage was so narrow. Gunners had to make sure that a valve inside the turret was shut off before they entered. If the valve happened to be open, gunners could be trapped when they grabbed at a gun handle to haul themselves forward. That action would set the turret in motion, pinning them in the narrow opening.

The top turret gunners, who also served as flight engineers, fired their guns from a bubble atop the fuselage behind the cockpit. To get into position, they had to hoist themselves up into the turret, then pull down and latch a hinged drop seat. To get out, they put their weight on a foot rest, which allowed them to move the seat back into its upright position, then dropped themselves back inside the airplane.

Like the ball turret gunners, top turret crewmen had an excellent view but were essentially out in the open, without even fragile aluminum skin for protection. One turret gunner wrote: "Once inside it seemed as though there was nowhere to run, nowhere to hide. You could look down and see the whole sweep of the top side of the bomber. Your head was stuck up and ready to be chopped off. What a view. What a place to be when the Messerschmitts came."

There were two waist gunners standing back to back in the belly of the fuselage, firing single .50-caliber machine guns mounted on steel tube arms. When firing, the men stood in front of 5-foot-wide open windows with the barrels of their weapons protruding outside the plane in the 200-mile-per-hour slipstream. Considerable physical strength was needed to keep the guns aimed properly, and even more when the men had to angle the guns toward the nose in the face of such strong winds.

One of the most persistent and aggravating problems of flying the B-24 was managing the flow of gasoline from the fuel tanks to the engines. One military writer noted that the plane's fuel system was "complicated beyond reason and confounded easy operation."

There were 18 fuel cells, or tanks, located in the wings with a capacity of 2,793 gallons. For extremely long-range missions, like Ploesti, two additional fuel cells were placed in the bomb bay, adding another 790 gallons. It was the job of the flight engineer, when he was not operating the top turret, to monitor the amount of fuel in each cell to keep the weight of fuel in each wing equal. This was necessary so that the plane would stay in balance. It was a constant juggling operation, making sure that as the fuel tanks going to an engine were emptying, new ones were switched to take their place. If the engineer did not react in time, the engine would stop running.

It was even more complicated for the added tanks in the bomb bay. The gasoline from those cells had to be transferred to a wing tank before it went dry, and the transfer of fuel was done by hand. If the aircraft came under attack at the same time, the task was obviously more dangerous.

The fuel system was also vulnerable to accidents as well as enemy fire. The fuel gauges, one for each tank, consisted of single glass tubes connected directly to each tank; the amount of fuel in each tube indicated the level of fuel in the tank. These tubes broke easily, particularly when bullets and shells passed through the plane, and the gas would leak out, often bursting into flame inside the flight deck.

The fuel lines between tanks, and between tanks and engines, often leaked, leaving puddles of highly flammable gas. One spark, and a fire would erupt or the plane would explode, disappearing in a ball of flame and smoke.

There were other problems flying B-24s, whether on routine training flights or combat missions. The cockpit had no windshield wipers. When landing in the rain, pilots had to stick their head out the side window to look for critical landmarks such as lights and runways.

There were no toilets, only small tubes in which the men could urinate. At high altitudes, urine froze in the tubes before they could empty out. Waxed paper bags were provided for defecation.

Cold temperatures were not a problem during the Ploesti mission, but they had created hazards on other high-altitude raids. Oxygen masks, necessary above 10,000 feet, could freeze to a man's face. Saliva could freeze in the mask and block the flow of oxygen, causing a loss of consciousness. The man could die unless another crew member noticed and took corrective action. It was dangerous to touch any metal surface, such as the guns or the skin of the fuselage, with bare hands. They would freeze and stick to the metal.

One ball turret gunner described a flight at 30,000 feet.

Oxygen masks had built-in microphones that seemed to cause the ice to form around your face, causing frostbite. Goggles were necessary, even in the sheltered part of the ship, to keep our eyelids from freezing shut. Guns were hardly able to fire due to the frost. We had to fire them at short intervals to make sure they would fire when needed.

Even without the cold, flying in the B-24 was stressful. A waist gunner recorded his impressions:

The noise was more than deafening, and speech would be a shout unless the intercom was used. This was a flying metallic can. The sheet metal groaned, cracked, vibrated, and shook. It was like flying in a sieve. The wind would blow though the open slots, gaps, and hatches in great unabated gales. When it rained the entire aircraft was flooded and we splashed among the puddles. This was never meant to be a comfort cruise, not for us and not for those on the receiving end of our intentions.

Finding those on the receiving end of their intentions was a major headache for the Ploesti planners. They needed highly detailed maps and photographs of the refineries. Because they would not be bombing from 30,000 feet and wanted to hit only the circle of refineries—not the town in the center of that circle—the planners wanted to provide the crews with sufficient detail to know what their designated target looked like as they approached it at low altitude.

A 46-year-old architect, who had been an infantryman in World War I, provided the solution. Gerald K. Geerlings's idea was to provide the crews of each plane with highly detailed photographs, maps, and drawings of exactly what they would see as they flew over the countryside on their way to the target—as well as the specifics of the refinery area itself.

Instead of preparing the usual "top down" overview of what would be visible from high altitudes, Geerlings proposed making oblique maps and drawings showing the ground and the target at an angle of 25 to 40 degrees, approximating what the landscape would look like as the aircraft approached the target at a low level. It was a simple but revolutionary idea that had never been used in planning a bombing raid. That type of oblique drawing would have been of no use for high-altitude missions when pilots and navigators were looking down at a target from such a height that it would be difficult to recognize specific objects such as buildings.

Geerlings's solution was deemed an excellent idea, but there was one major problem. Neither Colonel Smart's planning staff, nor apparently anyone else in the Air Force, had such pictures or drawings to use.

There were some in Britain, however. Some time prior to this, the British government had issued an appeal to its citizens to donate postcards or photographs they had saved from trips abroad, throughout Europe. The public responded with enthusiasm and sent thousands of pre-war scenes from all over the Continent. The images had been stored at a university library.

Geerlings examined their picture files from Ploesti and nine other European locations, so as to allay any suspicion of undue interest in Ploesti alone. He photographed all ten sets of material and returned to London with scenes for his oblique maps.

But he required more information. He knew that the Admiralty Library in London also contained material that could be useful. To maintain the security of the operation, however, he could not simply ask to see the relevant materials. One historian wrote:

> Here a bit of cloak and dagger activity came into play. Geerlings was able to get a job as a fire watcher at night. With his new job, he was able to search through the files without being suspected or interrupted. He worked 14 nights, then resigned his position for a better one. He walked away from his night job with almost all the information he needed for the mission. The spying worked; none of the library staff suspected a thing.

With his file of postcards and photographs, Geerlings brought his skill as an architect to the task. He drew an 11-page accordion folder showing in detail the route to be flown to the target. The result was more like a chart than a map, with 11 checkpoints to show navigators when they had successfully reached each of a series of locations along the way. Geerlings prepared another set of even more detailed charts—drawings of actual sites—showing how each refinery would look when approached from an altitude of 400 feet. There was more.

The idea was taken one step further by making drawings of individual targets such as boiler houses, cracking plants, and distillation plants so that the pilots and bombardiers would know exactly what to look for as they bore down on the target.

Each plane was to be assigned a highly specific target, for example, the southeast corner of a certain wall or a particular building. Each pilot and bombardier would have his own drawing of how that target would appear as it was approached at 200 miles per hour. This was the forerunner of the precision bombardment the Air Force had been touting, but rarely achieving, at high altitudes.

The next step for Geerlings was to build detailed models out of cardboard and paper showing the route and the target, displaying not only the refineries but also the town of Ploesti. Five models were constructed, the largest measuring 8 by 14 feet, and they were so accurate that a member of Colonel Smart's staff who had once lived in Ploesti was able to identify his old neighborhood and even the house in which he had lived.

These unprecedented detailed and accurate charts, drawings, and models still did not complete the planning stage of the mission. The next step of this extraordinary operation involved two unusual men, a child's tricycle, and a picture of a naked woman.

The men—one American, one British—were flamboyant, eccentric, colorful personalities of the type for which the phrase "larger than life" is no exaggeration. The American, 33-year-old John Reagan McCrary, known as "Tex," was a sometime journalist and publicist who by 1943 was a public relations officer for the Eighth Air Force.

Born in Texas, McCrary attended the elite Phillips Exeter Academy and Yale University, where he became editor of the newspaper and a member of the exclusive Skull and Bones secret society. During the war, Tex McCrary achieved greater visibility when he married the model and actress Jinx Falkenburg, a beauty who had been the first Miss Rheingold.

The British member of the pair was Wing Commander Arthur Patrick Hastings, Viscount Forbes, an aristocrat and would-be soldier-of-fortune. Some Americans who served with him on Col. Jake Smart's planning staff called him "silly pants," according to McCrary, "until they got to know him."

Forbes owned an airplane in the years before the war, at a time when few people could afford even automobiles. He flew over most of Europe, stopping here and there to describe the sights for a London newspaper. He was in the Balkans in 1939 when the war began and volunteered to fly as a diplomatic courier between Belgrade, Warsaw, and Bucharest.

Shortly after he was made a wing commander in the RAF and appointed air attaché in Bucharest, the capital of Romania. Unofficially, he helped several Polish pilots escape to England through Romania. When Romania became allied with Hitler, Forbes returned to England by way of Cairo. In 1942 he joined Colonel Smart's staff because of his intimate knowledge of the Romanian countryside.

Forbes and McCrary were assigned to make a top-secret training film for the Ploesti raid, probably the first time a film was devised to train crews for a designated mission. It took three weeks of intensive effort to produce a 45-minute film, as well as a series of brief silent films, each depicting a specific target, showing how it would appear to a bomber crew approaching at low level and high speed.

They made the film using a child's tricycle as a dolly to hold the camera. One of the men (which one was not recorded) mounted the tricycle and pedaled toward and around a model of the entire refinery complex. To hold the viewers' attention, McCrary and Forbes opened the movie with a shot of a comely naked woman and the voiceover announcement that Ploesti was a "virgin target," never bombed before.

At first, McCrary and Forbes disagreed on whether to emphasize, or even mention, the mission's difficulties and dangers. Forbes argued that if the film were being made for RAF crews, "I would say that we should come right out with it and tell them that half of them might not get back [but] with your boys, well, I don't know."

McCrary was insulted by the implication that Americans could not accept the truth about danger the way the British could, but in the end he agreed with Forbes that the primary emphasis in the commentary should be on the raid's importance for the overall war effort. McCrary said later:

> And so at the end of the film, we had a "conclusion" which was like a locker-room fight talk. We flashed on screen pictures of Doolittle's bombers taking off for Tokyo [in April, 1942] and pictures of the first Flying Fortress raid on Europe. The commentary said,
>
> *These jobs were big jobs—but the job that you men have been selected to do, this job is the biggest job of the war.*
>
> Then we put a picture of President Roosevelt on the screen, saying "The Nazis and the Fascists have asked for it, and they are going to get it."

The voiceover downplayed the threat posed by the reinforced defenses at Ploesti. McCrary and Forbes almost scoffed at them, ridiculing the German preparations as essentially worthless, certainly nothing to worry about. Andy Rooney screened the film before the raid and described Tex's "soothing voice" making light of the defensive forces the bomber crews would be facing. McCrary told the crewmen:

> The defenses are nothing like as strong here as they are on the Western Front. The fighter defenses at Ploesti are not strong and anyway, the majority of fighter planes will be flown by Romanian pilots who are thoroughly bored by the war. The heavy antiaircraft [fire] should not bother you at low altitude. All the antiaircraft guns are manned by Romanians so there's a pretty good chance there may be incidents like there were in Italy at the beginning of the

war when civilians could not get into the [bomb] shelters because they were filled with antiaircraft gunners. The defenses at Ploesti may look formidable on paper but remember they are manned by Romanians.

It was propaganda, of course, wishful thinking and totally wrong. McCrary and Forbes knew it, and some of the men slated for the mission knew it as well. Andy Rooney added: "No one headed for Ploesti on a B-24 slept any better because of having seen that film."

PART II

THE PREPARATIONS

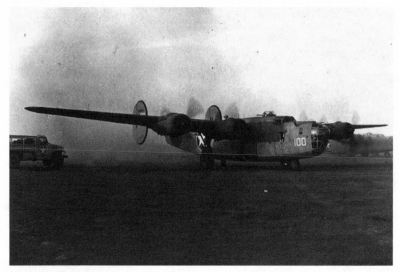

Teggie Ann, the lead plane for the Ploesti mission, commanded by Col. Keith Compton, just before takeoff on the morning of August 1, 1943. (*Pete Aspesi*)

4

WHEN ARE YOU GOING
TO BOMB PLOESTI?

B Y THE SUMMER OF 1943, Ploesti had become a death trap
for anyone who dared attack it. The Germans made it a
fortress, and that was not an exaggeration, or wartime propaganda, or wishful thinking. American airmen who had seen Tex
McCrary's training film and believed his comments about the
inadequate defenses around the oil refineries were dead wrong.

The defenses had been carefully designed by 48-year-old
Gen. Alfred Gerstenberg, who had been a fighter pilot in World
War I in Jagdstaffel Number 11, one of the superb squadrons
commanded by Manfred Von Richtofen, the "Red Baron." A fellow pilot and close friend of Gerstenberg was the young, dashing, and then quite slender Hermann Goering.

Gerstenberg was one of the few German airmen who had
been able to sustain a military flying career in the years after
World War I, when the Versailles Treaty had left Germany with
no air force. Officially, the Luftwaffe had been disbanded and its
planes destroyed or given to the victorious allies. However,
Germany was able to maintain a secret air force with the help of
the Soviet Union, which provided the Luftwaffe with a base at
Lipetsk, some 230 miles southeast of Moscow, at which to train

a new generation of pilots. Gerstenberg was one of those chosen to join the Soviet Army and train pilots from 1926 until 1933.

When Hitler came to power in 1933, the Russians abruptly ended their hospitality. Gerstenberg returned to Germany to join a reconstituted Luftwaffe. A patriot, Gerstenberg was ready to give his life for his country, but he refused to join the Nazi Party or to wear a swastika as part of his uniform. Such behavior prevented many Germans, both civilian and military, from advancing (or even remaining) in their chosen professions. Gerstenberg, however, enjoyed the patronage of Goering, who was then chief of the Luftwaffe.

In 1938 Gerstenberg was appointed military attaché at the German Embassy in Bucharest, Romania, a post he held until June 15, 1942, when that nation became an ally of Hitler. Gerstenberg, promoted to the rank of general, was given command of Luftwaffe operations there. He was an urbane, sophisticated, and cultured man, a welcome guest in the homes of Romania's political, social, and cultural elite. One of his staff officers recalled: "[Gerstenberg] was a dedicated man. To better fulfill his duties he learned to speak Polish, Russian, and Romanian. He worked 16 hours a day with one goal in mind: to make Ploesti too costly for the enemy to attack."

Hermann Goering provided all the manpower, weapons, and supplies Gerstenberg needed to protect the refineries, but geography was also an important factor. Ploesti sat in a valley formed by two sloping ridges. Aircraft approaching the refineries at low altitude had to fly below the ridge tops. And it was there, on both sides of the valley, that Gerstenberg placed his deadliest weapons, the 88- and 105-mm antiaircraft guns.

A staggering 237 of them lined the ridges, and fully 80 percent were manned by trained German troops, not by

Romanians, as Tex McCrary had touted in his training film. Gerstenberg had also mounted hundreds of smaller caliber weapons and machine guns from one end of the valley to the other. These were placed atop specially constructed concrete towers (some of which Leroy Newton of *Hadley's Harem* had found in place as late as 1997). Guns were also mounted on bridges, water towers, and church steeples. A number were hidden in dummy haystacks; these opened like the petals of a flower so the gunners could fire.

Railroad tracks ran down the center of the valley, and there Gerstenberg placed a specially built flak train with antiaircraft guns in every car. The train was capable of racing at high speed below any enemy pilots foolish enough to fly low. More than 100 barrage balloons hung over the refineries, each tethered to the ground by a thick steel cable. In addition, each had a bomb dangling beneath it to blow up any plane that became ensnared.

General Gerstenberg had a formidable number of fighter planes. Only 20 miles east of the refineries was a base housing 52 top-of-the-line Messerschmitt 109s. A few miles beyond was an airfield with 17 ME-110s, twin-engine fighters that could outfly any bomber in the air.

About half of the fighter aircraft were flown by Romanian pilots, most of whom had trained in Germany. Their style may have been more flamboyant and less disciplined than German pilots, but they were every bit as daring and aggressive, if not more so. Gerstenberg also had access to some 20 Romanian-built fighter planes stationed about 30 miles from Ploesti, near Bucharest.

By any standard, Romania's oil refineries in 1943 were the most heavily defended territory in all of German-occupied Europe or in Germany itself. No one involved with Operation

Tidal Wave had the slightest idea of what they were about to confront.

In the final days of June the three bombardment groups in England—the 93rd, Ted's Traveling Circus; the 44th, the Flying Eight Balls; and the 389th, the Sky Scorpions—received orders to prepare to move to a secret destination identified only as "DS Secret."

Many of the men believed the rumor that they were preparing to attack a German battleship based in Norway, so they packed cold-weather gear. They were more than a little surprised to find themselves in the North African desert, living under primitive and demanding conditions, far removed from the relative comfort of barracks life in England.

The newly arrived aircraft were easy to distinguish from those of the Liberando and the Pyramider outfits, which had been in the desert for more than a year. The ships from England were painted in traditional U.S. Army olive drab; the desert planes were pink, painted to blend in with the desert floor if spotted by German pilots flying overhead.

To the newcomers, life in the desert was grim, bleak, and unpleasant. What they remembered most about the airfields around Benghazi in the summer of 1943 was the sand. There was no escape from it. The sand was like a fine-grained red dust and it found its way into everything. The tents soon turned from green to red. Even faces turned red from the sand. Margaret Cotter, a Red Cross worker, wrote: "The days were hot as blazes, with dead, still air, except for the cutting sandstorms, which often blew sharp in our faces, penetrating our tents and our clothing and dusting us with the same red tint we'd noticed on the soldiers when we'd arrived."

Col. Leon Johnson, commander of the Flying Eight Balls, recalled years later how "the dust moved every day. The sand was in everything. Several years after the mission, I found red sand in the seams of my underwear."

"Daily, for hours and hours on end, the desert sandstorms blew with high velocity winds," wrote Maj. Robert Sternfels of the 98th. "Micro-sized particles of sand penetrated every crack or joint in the tents, cooking utensils and mess halls, invading the prepared food and somehow even into covered jars of jam. It seemed like one could never wash out the grit between one's teeth."

The blowing sand was even more destructive of the planes. It made its way inside aircraft engines, fouling sparkplugs and damaging the cylinders. Under normal conditions, the engines were expected to last some 300 hours before overhauling. In the desert, they had to be rebuilt every 50 to 60 hours.

Tracks in the gun turrets became so fouled with sand that they would no longer rotate. The sand scoured Plexiglas so severely that it was no longer possible to see through windows and turrets. Ground crew had to clean sand off each .50-caliber shell before the ammunition could be placed in the belts that fed the bullets into the guns. The blowing sand could render the exposed planes as useless as if they had been damaged by enemy fire.

And then there was the stultifying, unrelenting heat; summertime temperatures routinely reached 125 degrees in the shade—but there was no shade. "The sun beat down on mortals with unbridled ferocity. Tents became uninhabitable moments after sunrise. Anything metallic was hot to the touch. Aircraft literally became ovens. Legend has it that several loaves of bread were baked in a B-24." Ice was the stuff of dreams, refrigeration a rarity, and air conditioning nonexistent.

There were only two ways to escape the heat, and both were temporary. One was to take a swim in the Mediterranean Sea. Another was to take a plane up to a deliciously cool high altitude. The men suddenly discovered that a lot of their ships needed "test flights," and there was no shortage of volunteers to take them up. Often the cargo for the test flights included bottles of beer. That was the only way to get the beer cold enough to drink once the men were back on the ground.

Mealtimes provided a break because of the chance to socialize, not for the food. "Chow in camp was mostly canned rations, consisting of powdered eggs and potatoes, dried beef, hash and Spam. Then there was what was charitably referred to as 'desert butter,' a yellow concoction that wouldn't melt no matter how hot the day."

The water was not so palatable, either, and there was not much of it. Water had to be trucked to the airfields from wells in the area. It was stored in so-called "lister bags," made of a rubberized fabric. The bags were hung from a metal tripod out in the merciless sun. In a few short hours the water would be hot enough to shave comfortably with.

Chlorine was added to the water to prevent dysentery and that made the taste bitter. Most of the men preferred what the army called "lemonade," a mix of lemon powder and water, in an attempt to mask the chlorine taste. Each man was allowed a ration of one canteen a day. There was no water to waste for washing clothes. Garments were soaked in gasoline and left to dry in the heat. The clothing smelled bad, but then so did the men.

To conserve as much water as possible, the six men housed in each tent put in an equal amount of water each day to fill one helmet. Then they drew straws to see who would wash his face first. The last man that day got "leftover soapsuds and dirty water." The opportunity for a shower was rare.

"Take a shower?" recalled a man from the 389th. "Sure! Walk about two miles each way and by the time you get back, you're dirty." One could take a swim in the Mediterranean, but that required hitching a ride to get there. And by bedtime, the salt from the sea tightened the skin so much that a man would itch as if he'd been bitten by a swarm of fleas.

To add to the misery, if these conditions were not awful enough, there were the bugs, rats, locusts, scorpions, and other assorted animals and vermin. One pilot recalled, "There were grasshoppers all over. They were in the clothes, beds, and mess kits. We were issued netting to keep them out of our beds. No matter how tight you tucked it in at night, come morning there would be at least several crawling on the inside of the netting."

Kangaroo rats roamed at night, burrowing into small spaces such as boxes, bags, piles of clothing, and food. They could grow as long as 15 inches from nose to tail, with big heads out of proportion to their bodies. Some men thought they were cute, with their huge eyes and bulging food storage pouches in their cheeks. They had short front legs and long rear legs, which caused them to jump like kangaroos. A few of the men captured some rats and built a track for them to run, complete with a bookie to take bets on the races. When men in the desert are that bored, kangaroo rat races can be a much-needed source of excitement.

Less exciting were the plagues of locusts, insects with wingspans up to eight inches. The swarms were large enough to block out the sun, and they settled on everything—planes, tents, bodies. The men were constantly brushing them away. "To make things more exciting for the diners," wrote a crewman in the Sky Scorpions, "some GI, as he was leaving the mess tent, would kick a tent stake, which resulted in hundreds of locusts, clinging to the underside of the tent, becoming dislodged and falling into the mess kits."

Another recalled an old story:

> You can tell a rookie from an old-timer by the way he acts when confronted with locusts in the mess kit. The rookie will stop eating, get up, and leave the mess tent. A short-timer will remove the locusts and continue eating. An old-timer cannot eat until he has a few in his mess kit, and will, on occasion throw a few in his food so he feels at home.

Of course, the men inevitably found ways to make sport of the locusts. They fashioned paddles of wood or metal or other hard materials and held contests to see who could swat the most locusts in the shortest time. "You could hear the *splats* of locusts hitting the paddles all over the place, and the heavy swingers counting, 101, 102, et cetera."

There were also scorpions, a danger because of their poisonous tail stinger. The creatures liked to burrow inside shoes and piles of clothing at night. Men who failed to shake out their clothes and examine their shoes in the morning often got a painful surprise.

Some men captured the scorpions. They poured a circle of gasoline on the ground, lit it, and tossed them in the middle. The scorpions would try to escape but could not get through the wall of flame. It became a sobering and gruesome game to watch the insects sting themselves to death with their own tails. And it reminded the men that they were waiting to take off on a mission that could end with their planes, and themselves, consumed by fire.

There was not much to see in the desert—sand and sky, a few clusters of palm trees, the occasional scruffy camel, and, to the Americans, some scruffy natives. The view extended for miles, except during sandstorms, but there was little to look at. Around the airfields, there were heaps of German and Italian planes in various stages of decay, but one couldn't sustain interest in them for long. There were piles of German ammunition, much of it live, which occasionally provided a diversion. Major Ardery of the 389th recalled the foolish chances they took.

> We took 88mm shells back to our tent and cut the tops off them to make ash trays. We tore the ends out of shells and set fire to the powder. We stacked up 20mm shells and shot at them with a .22 rifle to set them off. Once while we were enjoying the latter pastime Hank got slightly wounded. Paul, Del, and I were crouching behind our jeep while we shot at a pile of 20mm shells. Hank sat in the jeep haughtily denying that they would go off. When the explosion did occur it was something more than we expected. Though we had thought ourselves at a safe distance, a bit of shell whizzed by and cut Hank's leg. It was nothing serious—just another laugh.

The nearest town to the airfields was Benghazi, which had little to offer in the way of distractions. The town of 50,000 had been hard hit by the war and had changed hands several times. For many Americans, including Red Cross worker Margaret Cotter, Benghazi provided their first glimpse of a war-torn city.

"Parts of collapsed buildings littered the streets. Old staircases, pieces of marble flooring and ceilings, and bits of furniture were strewn here and there. Along the shoreline, where once stood beautiful villas, there was nothing but crumbled debris."

The Red Cross delegation moved into one of the few large villas still reasonably intact, though the doors and windows had been destroyed by bombs exploding nearby. The building had no water supply or electricity, and not a single piece of usable furniture remained. Nevertheless, it was the best place available for a Red Cross club.

The Red Cross "girls," as they were called, cleaned and painted the premises, and begged, borrowed, and appropriated furniture. When they could find only a few chairs, they made some out of the crude wooden boxes that had been used to protect the tail fins of bombs during shipment. When the women were finished, the villa that had been in such a sorry state boasted "our recreation room, our library, and our lounge, the walls of which were covered with murals of hometown scenes of cities from coast to coast of the United States."

The Red Cross club became the only place within a thousand miles where the air crews could always find coffee and doughnuts, Ping-Pong tables, and wholesome American girls to dance with. "There were never any dull moments," Margaret Cotter said. "We held dances with the odds of boys to girls never falling below a thousand to one. Naturally no girl could take more than two steps before she was cut in on, but we all danced until we could hardly stand up, and the boys somehow managed to have a good time. That was all that counted."

But other than the club, the town seemed like a slum, with widespread poverty and illiteracy. No more than 20 percent of the local people could read. Camels and donkeys plodded through hot and dusty streets, vendors at tiny stalls sold home-made baskets, woven rugs, and smaller items, none of which interested the Americans.

The only thing that reminded them of home was the fresh fruit, especially the tangerines and grapes. One corporal said, "Everybody eats tangerines all the time. You carry them in your pockets and bags and keep them in your room. In the cargo planes there is always a crate [of fruit] open for anyone to dip into." However, all of the local fruit had to be boiled in water to sterilize it, as a precaution against typhus.

Other than the Red Cross "girls," the women in Benghazi were Arabs, and Italians and other Europeans of mixed ances-try. The Arabs sported tattoos on their faces and the Americans quickly learned to leave them alone. An anonymous writer of an article on life in North Africa, published in the magazine *Air Force* in 1943, explained why. "The standard horror story of what the natives did to a couple of the boys who made passes at their women had been thoroughly spread around, so all is quiet on that front."

One complex of buildings in Benghazi that had not been bombed by either side during the fighting comprised the best hotel. The place was so comfortable, attractive, and large that each side took care not to bomb it so they could use it again as headquarters when they recaptured the town.

Over the course of the back-and-forth fighting in North Africa the hotel "had served for Italians, British, Germans, and Americans time and again. The same guest register started by Axis personnel was still being used. On a flyleaf a departing German had hurriedly scrawled: 'Keep this book in order. We will be back.'"

But by the summer of 1943, the Germans had been defeated; they would not be back. The hotel became headquarters for General Ent, chief of Bomber Command for General Brereton's Ninth Air Force.

Obviously, Benghazi was not an exciting or inviting place. For men who could get leave and manage to hop a ride aboard a plane heading east, the best places to visit were Palestine and Egypt. Capt. Robert Adlen of the 98th Bombardment Group wrote about them in his diary.

He saw Tel Aviv in April 1943 and declared it "by far the finest city in the Middle East that I have ever seen." He was less complimentary about Jerusalem. Although he enjoyed accommodations at the King David Hotel and appreciated the city's rich history, for which he had hired a tour guide, he declared that it was "plentiful in dirt and filth."

Alexandria, Egypt, was more inviting. Although it was not precisely a tourist haven, the women and wine were plentiful. "Bill and I spent the day acting like tourists," Adlen wrote, "shopping, book stores, and arguing with the vendors and yelling at the pestering wogs [natives]. What a perfectly stinking country. Everyone bullsheeshes you to death." But that evening, as Adlen described it in elliptical fashion, "Bill took off with Edith, and I went with the men [to a brothel] to pour a little coal. Mission was successful and I made three runs on the target."

Cairo was also a place for a good time but was more expensive because so much high-ranking brass was stationed there. The presence of so many senior officers alerted the MPs to crack down on junior officers and enlisted men who appeared to be having too much fun in public.

Cairo was also rumored to be a den of spies, especially from Brereton's office. "Security around this headquarters is practically nonexistent," wrote an officer to General Arnold in Washington. "All the typists and file clerks are hired locally and I suspect every one of them. The city is full of people gathering and selling information."

It was said that strangers openly approached American flyers on the street and asked when they were going to bomb Ploesti. B-24 pilot Herbert Light overheard two RAF officers talking openly at a Cairo bar about a planned raid on Ploesti. He had heard the same rumor at his base, started by replacement crews newly arrived from England. They reported that they had been told by London prostitutes that their next target would be Romania's oil fields.

And the rumors were not only in North Africa. Robert Lehnhausen, another Liberator pilot, had been wounded on a mission to Italy and was recuperating in a British hospital in Malta, where his plane had landed. "I was visited by a lieutenant colonel from the air force who was on duty at an advanced base on a small island off Malta. 'Did you people come here to bomb the Romanian oil fields?' I was startled. I had no knowledge of what our ultimate target would be."

The only thing that was not clear in all the rumors was when the raid would occur. None of the American airmen knew it yet, but it would be sooner than they expected.

On July 20, 1943, the crewmen assigned to the Ploesti mission were suddenly removed from operational status. They were given no explanation as to why they would stop flying combat missions. They had bombed several targets on Sicily and the Italian peninsula, including Rome and the famous monastery atop Monte Cassino, and had lost several planes and crews.

The men were pleased to be relieved from combat status but not so happy about a new order that restricted them to their bases, which had been placed under heavy guard, effectively sealed off from the outside world. There were no more excursions to Tel Aviv or Alexandria, or even to nearby Benghazi. Leaves were cancelled. Armed guards were detailed around a nondescript green building so small it was little more than a hut or a shack.

The green hut, part of a cluster of buildings in General Ent's on-base headquarters compound, was declared off-limits to all unauthorized personnel which, for a time, included almost everyone. One of the men who took a turn guarding the mystery shack was Gerald K. Geerlings, the architect who had prepared the drawings, maps, and models of Ploesti.

Geerlings had brought his planning aids from England in a B-24 called the *Exterminator*, piloted by Capt. Hugh Roper. The Ploesti material was packed in unmarked boxes, which contained something else as well that the crewmen were not told about: sticks of thermite, an extremely volatile explosive. Geerlings was taking no chances that any of his material would fall into enemy hands. Thus, if the plane took a hit, the thermite would explode, obliterating the ship and its contents—including the crew.

On the same day the men were restricted to base, the five bombardment group commanders—Leon Johnson, Addison Baker, Killer Kane, Keith Compton, and Jack Wood—were summoned to General Ent's office. There they were told the purpose of their mission—and that it would be carried out as a low-level bombing raid. Colonel Kane wrote in his diary that General Ent, "with great secrecy, swore each of us to keep our mouths shut about what he was going to tell us. We were not to give out a word to anyone until he released us from our oath."

None of the commanders, including Ent, liked the plan for the mission. They all continued to oppose it until Brereton made it clear that any man who continued to voice his objections would be relieved. But that did not stop the grumbling in private. One writer later reported on Killer Kane's reaction. "It was suicide, Kane snorted. Nobody, other than the starry-eyed planner who wouldn't be there, was enthusiastic about it."

On July 26, just six days after Ent disclosed Operation Tidal Wave to his commanders, another voice of opposition was heard. Sir Arthur Tedder, the RAF's air chief marshal and head of allied air forces in the Mediterranean theater, had previously endorsed the plan but with reservations. By late July, however, with preparations well under way, he changed his mind.

General Brereton recorded in his diary that day his account of a meeting with Tedder and General Spaatz, head of American Air Force units in Europe. "Tedder indicated," Brereton wrote, "that he was in favor of postponing or canceling Tidal Wave."

Tedder and Spaatz seemed to prefer to focus on industrial and aviation targets in Europe. They considered the Ploesti mission to be a needless diversion of their slim resources, and one not likely to produce results commensurate with the cost. Brereton, now fully committed to the operation, disagreed. He wrote:

> I opposed Tedder's view because I believed that the Ploesti refineries are more important to the Axis war effort than the Messerschmitt factory and because training has almost been completed for Tidal Wave and to call it off now would seriously impair the morale of the entire Bomber Command.

The following day, July 27, Brereton, Ent, and the other high-ranking officers involved in the preparations for the raid received news of such significance that it could have led to the cancellation of the raid. And perhaps it should have.

A Romanian air force pilot, Sgt. Maj. Aviator Nicolae Teodoru, took off on a test flight in a German JU-88 on July 22. Once airborne, he flew a lot farther from his base than his flight plan indicated. He actually had gone to Cyprus where he landed at an RAF base and surrendered. Teodoru had defected from Ploesti, a base Allied intelligence estimates insisted was poorly defended.

When first questioned, the Romanian pilot's responses supported everything Allied planners thought they knew about the defenses around Ploesti. He told them exactly what they wanted to hear, but when he was interviewed a second time, he changed his story and told them that the defenses were among the strongest in Europe. He told his interrogators that "the general feeling of Romanian pilots [was] that none of them would like the idea of attacking Ploesti."

Five days before Operation Tidal Wave was scheduled to be launched, there was no time to verify the defector's information, even if the Allies had had agents within Romania. Yet they remained adamantly opposed to sending reconnaissance flights over the target for fear of alerting the Germans to the imminence of a raid. They decided to keep quiet about Teodoru's information and proceed with the mission.

"The brass felt that since [the defector] had given two different stories in as many days, perhaps he wasn't telling the truth about either. They also pointed out that he hadn't actually been in Ploesti since April or May. The brass filed the report and hoped for the best."

A sandstorm envelops *G. I. Ginnie,* an aircraft of the 376th Bombardment Group's 514th Squadron. (*376th Bombardment Group Historical Association*)

5

WE DREADED THIS MISSION

B EGINNING AROUND JULY 20, every ship that could fly was
in the air every day. But not very far up in the air. "For
days," Killer Kane wrote, "you could look around almost anywhere on the desert and see formations of B-24s skimming
along the ground, just missing what few palm trees there still
were. In open spaces they swooped still lower until they barely
missed the ground. The sheepherders on the desert really had a
rough time! One lieutenant actually flew so low he scraped off
his bomb-bay doors, kicking up a lot of dust, and blew down
three tents. It was really fun!"

There was serious talk about what kind of target these low-
level fliers could bomb from only 20 feet high and how they
could bail out of a plane so close to the ground. Of course they
knew the answer to that last question. There would be no bailing out, no escape, if they were hit while flying so low. That was
a sobering thought, but the low-level practice runs themselves
were, as Colonel Kane said, a heck of a lot of fun. For some
pilots, however, it took some time to master the technique, especially flying in close formation. After all, they had been trained
to fly at 15,000 feet and higher.

With the hot air currents rising from the desert floor, and the powerful propwash from the planes ahead of them, there was little margin for error in keeping a B-24 stable at an altitude of 20 feet. The Liberator was difficult enough to maintain in level flight at 25,000 feet and so much harder in the turbulence over the desert. Even Colonel Smart, the architect of Operation Tidal Wave, had trouble in the initial practice runs. He recalled that he lost weight in the constant struggle to control his plane so fast and so low. "Flying a B-24 is so intense," he wrote. "You worked hard to control it, and at low altitude you certainly had to be keenly alert."

The men were brought down gradually in altitude, flying first at 500 feet, then at 200, and then 20 feet and lower. The experience took many back to their days as cadets, where low flying could get them washed out of flight school and end their careers before they had begun. But to some, it had been worth the risk.

It was considered great sport to scare farmers and their livestock, or the guys back at the airfield, by buzzing them. Typically it was the hot-shot pilots who liked to push the limits, to see how many rules they could break without getting caught. And, inevitably, some who took that chance got killed. But now, not only were they allowed to fly low and buzz anything they wanted, except perhaps General Ent's headquarters, they were officially ordered to do so.

Colonel Kane wrote:

> Many of our high-level pilots instinctively refused to endanger their B-24s by flying on the deck in the propwash of the preceding planes. Since our main defense was to get down as low as possible, too much altitude would be

deadly. We spent hours on lectures and demonstrations trying to drive home to the pilots that they had to fly low and stay low, only to find that on the next practice mission the pilots would simply not force their Liberators down into propwash.

Flying so low seemed an unnatural act; the pilots knew that the higher they flew, the safer they were from enemy fire. Now that habit had to be erased. Also, they were flying aircraft specifically designed for optimum performance at high altitude. That was where the unique narrow Davis wing provided maximum value. Gradually over the coming days, the pilots began to find the experience exhilarating. Capt. Philip Ardery of the 389th recalled a heightened sense of speed. "When you go 200 miles per hour, at an altitude of eight feet, you really know you're going 200 miles per hour."

There were other benefits of flying low, such as knocking down your buddies' tents or roaring over the men relaxing on Benghazi's beaches so that the swimmers ducked under water for safety. Sunbathers jumped up and scattered, kicking sand in all directions.

The local inhabitants made good targets. Richard Britt, a navigator for the 389th, described how the pilots deliberately headed for Arab villages while flying at about six feet off the ground.

> After passing a village, the planes would pull up sharply and the tremendous propwash would blow tents, wives, children, camels, sheep, goats and donkeys in all directions. Looking back we could see the men angrily shaking their fists at us. Those antics were firmly discouraged by our commanders, but we did them anyway.

Low-level practice may have been fun, but it was also dangerous. There were several close calls but, amazingly, no one was
killed, though a few planes were put out of commission. On one
practice run, turbulence caused an airplane to lose altitude,
dropping it perilously close to the ship directly beneath it. The
lower plane only had a few feet clearance from the ground and
dragged its belly across the sand for 200 yards before the pilot
managed to pull up. "I guess I hold the all-time distance record
for taxiing a Liberator on the ground with the wheels up," the
pilot said. He made it back to base, but some of the bulkheads
in the fuselage were so severely bent that the plane was no
longer safe to fly.

Colonel Johnson, commanding officer of the Flying Eight
Balls, lost an engine while close to the ground. Only a calm,
experienced pilot could have reacted so quickly to level the
plane in seconds. Lt. Robert Stine, a navigator aboard the B-24
Victory Ship, had a close call with a buzzard.

> [The bird] hit the center section of the nose glass. It
> sounded like a cannon went off. It shattered the glass,
> went through the nose and all the way back to the bomb
> bay. We got some glass splinters but nothing serious. The
> biggest thing was that the front of the airplane didn't smell
> too good after that.

After flying low over the desert most mornings, the afternoons
and evenings were spent studying the models, drawings, and
maps prepared by Gerald Geerlings. In addition, the men were
briefed on details of the target, though the name was still secret.
"I guess we received the most complete and detailed briefing of
any air raid in history," Colonel Kane wrote. "Each of our five
groups was assigned one of the thirteen oil refineries [and] each

one of the five waves in our group had a certain area. Every airplane had a specific building or part of a building on which the bombs were to be placed. Our target was the left end of a boiler house; the ship behind us was assigned the right end."

The crews initially did their low-level training in small formations of three and six planes, then squadrons of ten or more. Later they practiced in group formations of approximately 40 planes. They started off by flying lower and lower over the desert, but then something new was added.

South of Benghazi, the 835th Engineering Battalion constructed a full-size replica of the Ploesti refineries using whatever materials they could find. The complex was laid out in the sand with "each vital pinpoint target marked with a furrow of lime mixed with the engineers' urine. No water was available." The mock-up was still not identified by name except to the five group commanders. Oil drums filled with sand marked the buildings, and tall wooden poles simulated the smokestacks the pilots would have to skirt. At first the engineers tied rags atop the poles to help identify them, but the local residents stole the rags during the night. The rags were replaced with empty crushed gasoline cans.

The crews practiced attacks on the target, roaring in low and fast to drop dummy bombs. They made the runs time and again, in larger, more complex formations. Capt. Ardery wrote: "We practiced coming in one flight after another, the first flight making a run straight over, the second coming in from the left, the third straight over, the fourth from the right, the fifth straight over, and so on. It was a precise pattern and required precise flying."

Col. Jacob Smart, the man behind the plan, took part in the daily practice runs. As the training progressed, he was pleased with the way his ideas were being implemented and increasingly optimistic about the outcome. "The charm of the plan," Smart said, "was that the planes would go over in waves only a few seconds apart. The entire force would pass over the target in a matter of two, three, or four minutes and would be in the heavily defended zone only about fifteen minutes."

The men did realize that bombing this model target was hardly the real thing. Maj. Robert Sternfels, a pilot in the 376th, wrote some years later:

> There were major differences between "training" and actuality. The approach to the actual targets would be over the plains, rivers, and forests of Romania, not the flat sands of the Libyan desert. There was no similarity whatsoever to the ever-changing terrain of the Balkans. Another omitted factor was the absence of defensive fire, fighter attacks, and even worse, the barrage balloons with the dangling steel cables attached to impact explosives designed to blow the wing off an airplane.

There was concern among the men about those dangers, especially the question of how vulnerable they would be to machine gun fire from the ground. That, of course, had not been an issue on high-altitude combat missions. On those raids, they had flown well out of range of those kinds of weapons. But flying at 20 feet or so about the ground at about 200 miles per hour, no one knew whether machine gunners would be able to hit them.

There were British warships berthed at Benghazi's harbor, and someone suggested finding out if the experienced machine gunners aboard those ships could swivel their guns fast enough to get a bead on a low-flying B-24. It turned out that they could, quite quickly, when the planes made a practice run. The British gunners joked about how easy it was to line up a B-24 in their sights and stay trained on it. They said they would have had no problem shooting down the planes.

It was a sobering lesson, but the mission planners ignored the results and did not alter their plans. Their decision was helped by an additional test of the effectiveness of machine gunners against fast, low-level aircraft. This time the test, led by Geerlings, was performed by a group of untrained, inexperienced men pretending to be gunners. He later wrote that "probably the most discussed question among all the ranks was what losses would be due to small-arms fire."

Geerlings and several volunteers dug foxholes in the sand and hunkered down to wait for the Liberators. They carried broomsticks to simulate machine guns to track the planes flying low overhead. "It's something beyond belief," Geerlings reported, "when from nowhere there is a sound of power and fury, coming and going before one's reflexes can do anything but duck. I swallowed a lot of sand and never got a satisfactory shot." Considering that Geerlings and the others were untrained, the results are not surprising.

Fuel consumption was another concern for the planners. Could a B-24 with a full crew and a full bomb load complete a 1,900-mile mission? Could they carry enough gas to reach the target and return to Benghazi? Five crews were selected for a test, and they proved it could be done. They covered 1,900 miles in thirteen and a half hours with an average rate of fuel consumption of 202 gallons per hour.

As the date for the mission drew nearer, the pace of activity on the five desert bases increased. Modifications were made to the planes, including the installation of extra machine guns in some of them. Despite the inability of Geerlings and his volunteers to track low-flying aircraft with their broomsticks, the planners agreed that the ships needed more firepower to deal with machine-gun fire from the ground. They wanted the lead planes in every unit to have enough firepower to overwhelm machine-gun ground units before the entire formation reached them.

Four extra machine guns were mounted in the bombardier's already cramped compartment. The guns were stationary and aimed forward; they would be fired by the pilot. He could tilt the plane's nose slightly and press a button. The guns would then lay a pattern of fire to destroy everything in the plane's path. The other planes were modified to carry a single .50-caliber machine gun in the nose to provide suppressing fire. Many of the radio operators and engineers were given submachine guns to use on ground targets at their discretion. All the extra armament gave the planes as many as 12 to 14 guns.

The precision–built, highly secret Norden bombsight the bombardiers had been using for their missions were useless at low altitudes. In its place, engineers crafted a simple reticule device. Bombardiers were trained to peer through it the way they would to aim a rifle. As soon as the target was in the sight, the bombs were released. One pilot said it was as simple as "lobbing basketballs onto the court from the bleachers."

To carry the additional fuel for the long-range mission, two extra 400-gallon tanks were installed in the forward section of the bomb bay. To stretch the fuel as far as possible, anything not absolutely essential was removed the planes. In many instances this reduction in weight was more than offset by the extra armor plating added to cover the floor of individual crew positions. Heavy pieces of armor found in the wreckage of German and Italian planes strewn around the airfields were refashioned for the B-24s. They were thick enough to protect the men from machine-gun fire, but would be of limited value against antiaircraft shells.

Ground crews worked day and night. Engines were torn down and overhauled; any that could not be made perfect were replaced. Automatic cameras were installed in some planes so that pictures could be taken from the rear, once the plane had passed over its target.

The bomb load for each plane was a little over 4,000 pounds. Cases of incendiary bombs were also placed aboard. The idea was for the waist gunners to toss them out the windows like confetti. Since the planes were to pass over the target in waves, with some later than others, the bombs for the first waves had delayed-action fuses set to go off from five minutes to two hours after they were dropped. This would allow sufficient time for the next waves to pass over before the bombs exploded. The bombs in the last waves had regulation 45-second delay fuses. Thus, the planners believed that everything that could be done to ensure success had been done. Or so it seemed.

On July 24, the target was revealed to the officers in their first major briefing for the mission, although some had already guessed. When the name "Ploesti" was announced, they hooted and shouted, and when Tex McCrary's training film opened with the shot of the naked woman, some ribald comments were heard. They quieted down when President Roosevelt appeared on camera to emphasize the importance of their mission to the defeat of Germany.

After the movie ended, everyone agreed that it had provided one of the most thorough pre-mission briefings they had ever received. The crews were led to the model that had been constructed of Ploesti and the oil refineries. They were shown the most important buildings which, once destroyed, would stop oil production for months. The briefing officer then pointed out an electric power station and advised the men that it would be very hard to recognize on their final run.

> You will be on a southeast heading on the bomb run, so each one of you go to the far end of the table and sight along the model's ground. Pick out some tall structure behind and in line with your target: a smokestack, a cracking tower, etc. This will aid you in lining up when you are on the bomb run. Close your eyes and see if you have a mental image of the silhouette. If you don't, then repeat the process.

The men spent hours hunched over the model, lining up their targets to memorize how they would look when approached at 200 miles per hour. There would be no time then to look around, searching for something familiar. They had to be able to recognize the target and its identifying landmarks in seconds. They would be no chance to go around a second time.

They interspersed their careful study of the model with additional flights over the life-size replica of Ploesti in the desert. The more practice missions they flew, the more confident they felt. Col. Leon Johnson of the 44th claimed that "we could hit a target not much bigger than the door of a house without much difficulty at all, so we knew that if we could get to the target we could hit the target."

Some days later—and the various recorded recollections do not agree on precisely what day that was—all five bombardment groups took off for a practice run with their planes loaded with live 100-pound bombs. Their mission was to blow up the desert target, and do it exactly as planned, in no more than a few minutes. This was the final opportunity to test whether their preparations had been adequate.

They took off, assembled off the coast, and flew over several unoccupied islands that served as checkpoints for the navigators. The gunners fired at targets placed there for the mission and then the armada, which stretched across the sky for five miles, headed for the shore.

They were forced to make difficult adjustments in their flight paths to get into proper battle formation, just as they would have to do over Romania. Some flights crossed over others, some flew beneath others, and the formation as a whole had to execute a three-mile turn at the rate of one degree per second. All the while, they had to maintain a tight formation. This meticulous, demanding maneuver kept the pilots sweating, and swearing, every second of the way. "To the observer on the ground it was a sight to behold, almost beyond belief. Wave after wave of dune hugging B-24s flashed over and dropped their bombs 'on time, on target.' The 5-mile wide bomber front had wiped the target off the desert in less than two and a half minutes."

The mission was considered a dazzling success. The planners and leaders of Operation Tidal Wave were ecstatic, and so were the men. But once they landed and the adrenaline wore off they were subdued, realizing it was almost time for the real thing, over mountainous terrain with enemy fighters above and machine gunners below. And by July 31, the day before the mission, tension was high.

Each man was given a survival kit that contained a handkerchief map of the Balkans, a British gold sovereign or a $20 U.S. gold piece, 10 $1 bills, and $6 worth of Romanian drachmae and lire. Also included were pressed dates, water purification tablets, biscuits, sugar cubes, and chocolate.

The crews were also issued revolvers, carbines, and small compasses to use if they were shot down over enemy territory. However, most of the men left the guns behind. They knew that if they were captured, any attempt to shoot their way out would probably be futile.

A few hours later on Saturday afternoon, headquarters received a surprising cable from Gen. Hap Arnold, Army Air Force chief. It ordered General Brereton and Colonel Smart not to go on the mission themselves, as they had firmly intended to do from the beginning. Arnold was concerned that both men knew about too much about too many other forthcoming American and British operations to risk their capture.

Brereton, in turn, told his chief operations officer, Col. Ted Timberlake, that he was too valuable to risk capture and thus could not go on the mission. Gerald Geerlings recalled that "Timberlake's face became grim and he cursed softly, but vehemently. There were tears in Timberlake's eyes. 'God, my men will think I'm chicken,' he said."

At almost the last moment before the mission began several crews had to be reshuffled, and crews that had trained together as a unit were now faced with substitutes in their midst. Brereton had been scheduled to fly with Col. Keith Compton in *Teggie Ann*, the command ship for the 376th, the lead group. General Ent took Brereton's place as mission commander. His seat in the cockpit would be a stool behind Compton and his copilot. Ent had originally planned to fly as Kane's copilot, but now Kane was forced to select someone else to occupy the seat to his right. Colonel Smart had expected to fly as copilot for Maj. Kenneth Dessert of Ted's Traveling Circus, leaving another vacancy to be filled, and a replacement still had to be found for Colonel Timberlake.

This reorganization of the crews continued well into the night. In addition to the changes dictated by headquarters, as many as one of every three airmen had become ill with dysentery, and many, including Colonel Smart, had been hospitalized. Smart overheard several men say openly that they hoped they would not have to go on the mission; three flatly refused. Despite the large number who had reported sick, only two were grounded for medical reasons. One was Leon Johnson's copilot. To compound the manpower problem, ground crews managed to make three additional Liberators airworthy, which unexpectedly called for 30 more men.

By morning the vacancies were filled and every plane was fully manned, but some of the men who had volunteered (or who had been ordered to volunteer) had already completed their tours of duty, or had little or no combat experience. No ship was left behind for lack of a crew, but the staffing problems had increased the tensions and doubts about the mission's outcome well before takeoff.

"There was a growing pessimism at all levels," Gerald Geerlings wrote. Many men had come to believe that the Germans would be waiting, that surprising them was impossible and the odds of returning were stacked against them. It appeared to be a suicide mission that might—though this idea was becoming increasingly doubtful—succeed in disrupting German oil production, but at a horrific cost. If flak, and fighters, and balloon cables did not bring the Liberators down, then machine gun fire from the ground certainly would. "We dreaded this mission," Killer Kane recalled. "Tension was building up in the entire group. It was getting to where I couldn't sleep [and] the knowledge that the mission might turn out to be a suicidal one with disastrous results turned my sleeping moments into nightmares."

General Ent was equally pessimistic about the outcome, despite the impressive results of the attack on the replica of the Ploesti complex constructed in the desert. He had opposed the mission since its inception and had seen no reason to change his mind. In a letter to Brereton, Ent predicted that fully half the attacking force would be lost.

When General Brereton arrived in Benghazi from his Cairo headquarters on Friday, July 30, he was far from certain in his own mind about the mission's success, despite what he would tell his men. In a note to his aide that day he wrote, "This is where the Ninth Air Force makes history or wishes it had never been born. Hap Arnold has handed us a tough one."

The commanders of Operation Tidal Wave feared the worst—perhaps even expected it—by that last day before take-off. But although they revealed their doubts in their diaries, or to a trusted aide, they did not do so in front of their men. In the final briefings to the crews, all speakers were optimistic and positive about the outcome. It was their job as leaders to inspire their men to believe that the undertaking was vital to the war effort, and that they had the ability and training to carry it out—and to survive.

General Brereton opened his briefing on a note of stirring rhetoric.

> Tomorrow, when you advance across that captured coun-
> try, you will tear the hearts out of them. You are going in
> low-level to hit the oil refineries, not the houses, and leave
> your powerful impression on a great nation. The roar of
> your engines in the heart of the enemy's conquest will

sound in the ears of the Romanians—and, yes, the whole world—long after the blasts of your bombs and fires have died away.

Brereton went on to declare that if the crews destroyed the refineries, they would probably shorten the war considerably; what they could accomplish in minutes over the target would otherwise take a huge land army many months of fighting.

But his closing remark jolted everyone. "If you do your job right it is worth it, even if you lose every plane. You should consider yourself lucky to be on this mission." Leroy Newton of *Hadley's Harem* recalled the reaction to Brereton's final comment. "We sat stunned in the truck coming back to our base after the briefing. I don't think anybody said anything for a half hour. It's the worst thing they could have said."

Lt. Harold Korger, the bombardier aboard *Hail Columbia*, Killer Kane's ship, never forgot what he felt when Brereton said they were lucky to be going on the mission. "A strange silence seemed to descend upon the almost 1,800 crew members assembled for the final briefing; it is possible that at least 446 of the young Americans, average age slightly under 21, would not have agreed if they knew that in less than 24 hours they would be dead."

General Brereton had no awareness of the terrible impact of his words. That night he wrote in his diary, "There was universal high morale among everyone." But a later entry that night was more honest. "There was nothing to do now except to pray for them."

There were many prayers that night, following a dinner that had the opposite effect of what had been intended. Someone at headquarters decided it would boost morale to prepare a special meal for the aircrews, so steaks were flown in from Cairo. Most of the men had not seen steak for months, but it was not now seen as a cause for celebration. Lt. Korger echoed the thoughts of many when he wrote: "Our Saturday evening supper was quite out of the ordinary. I found it difficult facing up to my steak. I could only equate the quite delicious repast with the 'last meal' usually associated with death row."

Hundreds of men visited their chaplains, for spiritual guidance and consolation, and to leave personal effects for safekeeping along with letters to their loved ones for the chaplains to mail if the men did not come back. Colonel Kane was convinced he would not return. He wrote farewell letters to his wife and his parents. He tried to sleep but could not. Finally he got up and walked through the camp among his men. He recalled,

> There was a quietness quite unlike the usual buzz. Some crews were quietly giving away their belongings. I sat on my favorite perch on an old engine and stared for a long time at the stars. In my short lifetime, the stars had stayed in their places as they have for countless lifetimes before mine. They had remained unaffected whether I and the men with me lived or died. Whether we died in the near future or years later from senility mattered not in the great scheme of things. Yet the manner of our dying could have far-reaching effects. I have a young son I may never see again, yet, I shall be content if I felt that his freedom is assured.

Lt. Walter Stewart, a 24-year-old pilot in the 93rd, had named his plane *Utah Man*, so that no one would mistake where he was from. Before the war, Stewart had been a Mormon missionary in England. He held brief prayer meetings every night for his fellow Mormons and anyone else who wanted to come. On the night before the mission, a larger-than-usual group showed up. "We talked about death, resurrection, and the life to come," Stewart said. "I told the boys that no Nazi gunner could end that which has always been—the soul and intelligence of man. I was convinced beyond question that this life was just part of a great, everlasting, progressive existence that ruled before we came here. This testimony was much appreciated by the warriors of the 93rd."

Lt. Jesse D. "Red" Franks. (*Jesse D. Franks family*)

After the service, Stewart's commanding officer, Col. Addison Baker, looked at Stewart and said, "This is the biggest mission we've been on yet. I intend to go over that target. If I go over it in flames, I'm going over it! Stewart, you are my deputy lead. If I can't take us over, you take us over."

Lt. Jesse D. Franks, known as "Red" because of his flame-colored hair, was a 24-year-old bombardier from Columbus, Mississippi. Son of a preacher, like Killer Kane, he, too, had been a hell-raiser when he was growing up. After college he entered the seminary to train for the ministry but the Japanese attack on Pearl Harbor changed his plans. Franks could have stayed home (being a seminary student was a legitimate deferment), but he chose to join up, telling his father he could not let others do his fighting for him.

The crew had asked Red what to name their plane. He put the question to his father, who suggested a Biblical name, *Euroclydon*—the Storm, taken from the New Testament. It refers to the strong Mediterranean wind that blew the Apostle Paul's ship ashore on Malta.

The night before the mission Red wrote to his fiancée, Dottie, and to his father.

Dearest Dad,

I want to write you a little note before our big raid tomorrow. It will be the biggest and toughest we have had yet. Our target is the oil fields which supply Germany with three-fourths of her oil. We will get our target at any cost, and on a raid we cannot foresee all that will happen.

If anything happens, don't feel bitter at all. Please stay the same. You are the best Dad in the world, and always too good to a boy who was a pretty bad little redhead at times.

I am glad I am in this group and will get a chance at this important target. I know that it will save many lives from the results, so at any cost it is worth it. So, Dad, remember that, and the cost, whatever it may be, will not be in vain.

Hope you don't get this letter but one never knows what tomorrow will bring.

PART III
THE RAID

Brewery Wagon getting a final check at Benghazi before taking off for Ploesti. (*U.S. Air Force*)

6

NOT HERE! NOT HERE!

Sgt. Walter Patrick, a tail gunner in the 44th, had a dream about Ploesti. It happened one night after a low-level practice run over the desert. Some 61 years after the mission he said, "that dream was embedded deeply into my mind, and it is still there today."

In his dream, Patrick and Sgt. Walter Hazelton, another gunner aboard *Lady Luck*, were "outside the plane looking in. We saw that everyone else on board was dead. [It] was as if a snapshot had been taken of the crashed plane, the dead crew, the target area in the midst of being bombed, and Hazelton and I standing there at the scene of the crash. As it turned out, Hazelton and I were the only survivors of *Lady Luck*. We did not go to Ploesti."

When the men of *Lady Luck* went out to their ship at around six o'clock on the morning of August 1, 1943, the pilot, Lt. Thomas Scrivner, saw gasoline pouring out of one of the wing tanks. *Lady Luck* would not be making the raid on Ploesti. Nevertheless, its crew was assigned to another airplane, *Scrappy III*. As they prepared to board, Lieutenant Scrivner asked Sergeant Patrick a surprising question.

"Pat, are you going with us on this mission?"

Both gunners, Patrick and Hazelton, had flown 27 missions, two more than the required number of 25. Consistent with official Air Force policy, neither man could be ordered to fly any more; they had done their share, and then some. "Lieutenant Scrivner," Patrick said, "this is what I'm gonna do. I'm gonna flip a coin. 'Heads' I go, 'tails' I stay." Tails it was, and so, at the last minute, a new tail gunner was found. Hazelton also chose to stay behind. And more than 60 years later, Patrick said, "I still mourn for my lost comrades."

There were other changes in aircrews and planes that morning of the raid. Lt. Richard Britt, a navigator in the 389th, joined his crew boarding their plane, *Pistol Packin' Mama*, only to find that one of the engines had developed a problem. They were quickly reassigned to *Chattanooga Choo Choo*, which was in poor shape. Britt recalled: "Our first look at the plane was discouraging. The previous crew had written their opinions [inside]: 'You'll never get back in this crate,' and 'The Flying Coffin.' Nice cheerful sentiments to add to our nervousness."

Lt. Ernest Fogel, a pilot in the 376th, was assigned to a plane called "*Let's Go!*" He hoped it would not. He remembers pushing the starter button and thinking, "I hope the son-of-a-bitch doesn't start." But it did, and he taxied into position for takeoff.

A number of men who had been scheduled to fly were still suffering from the debilitating effects of dysentery, and should have been in the hospital instead of on the flight line. The copilot of *Thundermug*, Lt. Russell Longnecker, was wondering if he would ever get the chance to be a pilot when his own pilot, just released from the base hospital, declared that he couldn't make it. Another copilot was rounded up and Longnecker, who had never taken off a fully loaded ship before, was now in command.

Some men opted to fly the 13 or more hour-long mission despite their weakness from dysentery. One bombardier told his pilot he wanted to go even though he needed to carry along his own toilet. "I had no objection," the pilot said, "so he took along a 50-caliber ammunition box, which was metal lined, for an obvious use."

The belly turret gunners were not going on the mission, both to save weight and because they would not be needed since the planes were flying so low. All four gunners in one crew showed up to fly in *Heaven Can Wait*. None wanted to be left behind while their buddies went, despite their belief that this could be a suicide mission.

The radioman, Tech. Sgt. Donald Chase, watched as the gunners drew straws to see who would stay behind. "Young waist gunner Ralph Knox drew the 'unlucky' straw. He complained and cursed. Feeling abandoned, he withdrew from the rest of the crew, not to speak until just before takeoff, when, woefully, he wished us luck."

One man was not allowed to go on the mission as punishment. A gunner aboard Red Franks's ship, *Euroclydon*, he had made the mistake of getting caught stealing a bottle of bourbon from a neighboring tent. To set an example, the thief could not be allowed to get away with his crime. He was temporarily reduced in rank from sergeant to private and sentenced to 30 days' KP on the garbage detail, to begin immediately. "It was an odd punishment," one observer wrote. "Many of the men would grab at the opportunity to avoid this mission; they were looking for a way out, and KP duty might have been a blessing and a lifesaver." In this case, it was.

The wayward sergeant was replaced by a willing volunteer, who often managed to join combat missions even though he was a ground officer whose job was to train gunners. First Lt. Howard Dickson was only too happy to occupy the top turret, and he brought along a book to read on the long flight—*As You Like It*, by William Shakespeare.

Killer Kane was flying *Hail Columbia* with Lt. Johnny Young as his copilot. Kane wrote in his diary:

> At 0655, Johnny turned over number one engine as I fed it gas to get it running. One by one we brought the four engines to a steady roar. Those engines had to be treated with gentleness and care, for that day our lives depended on them. Everything checked out in fine shape. I gave the thumbs-up signal for the crew chief to pull the wheel chock and slowly moved out of the parking space onto the taxiway, then onto the end of the runway. I looked around in the peculiar reddish glare and saw billowing clouds of dust swirling into the sky to color the sun a bloody red. At 0710 sharp, we began our roll down the runway, on our way to Ploesti.

Lt. Richard Britt, navigator of the *Chattanooga Choo Choo*, took off from one of the other fields. He too remembered the huge clouds of sand created by all the engines revving up to maximum speed. The prop wash churned the loose sand and clay into an intense sandstorm. Only the first plane had clear vision; the rest were "flying blind into the billowing, dirty-brown night we had created."

All the planes were overloaded. They had not been designed to take off with over 3,000 gallons of fuel and more than 4,000 pounds of bombs. Most of the planes weighed in excess of 64,000 pounds, the maximum weight the B-24 was built to handle and still get airborne. At least that was what the manuals said, and few, if any, of the pilots had ever taken off in a Liberator so heavily laden.

It required almost a full mile of runway to reach the takeoff speed of 130 miles per hour, and even then they lifted off very slowly from the packed sand. At four of the five fields, a B-24 took off every two minutes. At Killer Kane's field, which was wider than the rest, they took off three abreast. The sea of dust and swirling sand rose as high as 3,000 feet and spread some 50 miles across the desert.

Not all of the planes made it. The *Kickapoo* of the 376th lost an engine shortly after getting airborne. The pilot tried to turn back to the field but the plane caught fire as he banked. He lined up on the runway but one wing was lower than the other and the airspeed was too great. "With a sickening jolt the *Kickapoo* hit the runway, bounced twenty feet into the air, hit again, skidded down the extreme edge of the field, smashed into a concrete telephone pole, and exploded." Only two of the crew survived, one with horrible burns over most of his body. Men in the other planes who saw the crash and the column of black smoke knew what it meant. It was a sobering sight. Colonel Kane wrote, "That was a bad omen for our mission, a plane lost before we even assembled."

It took the better part of an hour for the groups to form up in their proper places. They assembled in the following order:

1. The 376th, the Liberandos, 28 planes led by Col. Keith Compton with Gen. Uzal Ent on board as mission commander;
2. The 93rd, Ted's Traveling Circus, 37 planes led by Col. Addison Baker;
3. The 98th, the Pyramiders, 48 planes led by Col. John R. Kane;

4. The 44th, the Flying Eight Balls, 36 planes led by Col. Leon Johnson; and

5. The 389th, the Sky Scorpions, 29 planes led by Col. Jack Wood.

This magnificent armada, extending five miles in length from the first plane to the last, appeared unstoppable. Surely nothing could deter such a massive, powerful, and deadly force.

They flew in the familiar V-shape of three planes each, interlocking so that the pattern of gunfire would overlap, with each ship covering the others, leaving no gaps for a fighter to attack. The formations were so tight that no plane was more than 25 feet from the next. Each bombardment group flew slightly higher than the preceding one. The view from the front was like a series of steps ascending to the heavens.

The sky was clear of clouds, the visibility unlimited. Lt. John McCormick, flying *Vagabond King* in the 389th, recalled how they "got into formation and headed across the bluest Mediterranean you can imagine. Things were running smoothly. The air was full from starboard to port, from top to bottom with the Lib[erator]s. Everything looked good. Things never look dangerous when you have so much company."

But all too soon some planes turned back toward Africa with mechanical problems. The crew of *Jack Frost* from the 376th saw gas leaking from both wings. There was too great a risk of fire to keep going, so they dropped below the formation and turned around, praying there would be enough fuel to get back to base. They jettisoned their bombs into the sea and landed safely only to discover that there was no fuel leak after all. The tanks had been topped off just before takeoff, and the wind from their forward speed was siphoning off gas from around the tops of the overfull tanks.

The flight engineer of *Lil Joe* found a real leak. The plane had already lost 800 gallons, which meant they could not reach Ploesti and have sufficient fuel to return to Africa. The pilot, Lt. Lindley Hussey, remembered all they had been told about the mission's importance, and how it could shorten the war, so he made the decision to stay on course, knowing there was no way to make it back safely.

Ten, or possibly eleven, planes (the records differ) dropped out of formation and headed back. Capt. Will Bank of Kane's outfit, the Pyramiders, wrote that "every once in a while I would look off and see one or two Liberators feather a prop, wheel out of formation and start for home." The departing crews waved and gave the thumbs-up signal to the men they were leaving behind. One gunner said, "Those guys look too happy about it."

Seven of the planes that dropped out were from Killer Kane's 98th. "This percentage seems out of line," one historian later wrote, "and may have been caused by the fact that Kane often strongly advised his people to fly beyond their operational limit [of 25 missions]. It is known that in this mission, especially, he had exerted great pressure, even to the point of delaying certain men's stateside leave until their return from Ploesti." Ten days before the mission Capt. Robert Adlen, who had completed his 25 missions and would be grounded for medical reasons before the Ploesti raid, observed in his diary: "Looks like we're getting screwed again. Colonel Kane says we have to fly this next mission if we want to go home." For whatever reason— simply bad luck, or resentment against Kane—the Pyramiders lost 7 of their 48 planes long before reaching the target, a higher proportion than any other group.

They had been flying for three hours when something went wrong with *Wongo-Wongo*, piloted by Lt. Brian Flavelle of the

376th. This was the lead plane of the Liberandos and thus the first plane of the entire formation.

Aboard *Utah Man*, Lt. Walter Stewart heard his copilot yell, "Look at that," as a Liberator crossed downward in front of his ship. Red Franks, in *Euroclydon*, saw it too, and like everyone else, wondered what had gone wrong.

"As we approached Corfu, I glanced at the lead ship," wrote Lt. Richard Britt, a navigator in the 389th. "One second it was there, the next it disappeared in a cloud of black smoke. Seconds later, we saw a burning oil slick on the blue Adriatic." In not much more time than it takes to tell the tale, *Wongo-Wongo* and its 10-man crew were gone.

The pilot of *Vagabond King*, Lt. John McCormick, saw it go down but remembered it differently.

> Then, out of a blue sky, without warning, the lead plane of another group up front spun sickeningly out of formation and exploded against the sea, burning so as to leave a black tomb marker. The second ship had gone down before we had even reached enemy land.

Suddenly, *Wongo-Wongo*'s wingman, Lt. Guy Iovine, put his ship in a dive in violation of the orders given at the final briefing to remain in formation no matter what the circumstances. Iovine intended to check for survivors, not that he could have done anything for them. He could not land on the water to pick them up, he had no life raft or supplies to drop, and he could not even radio British air-sea rescue for help because that would break radio silence and give away their position to the Germans.

There seemed to be no survivors of *Wongo-Wongo*, and after circling the crash site a few times, Lieutenant Iovine started to climb to rejoin the formation. However, his ship was so heavily overloaded that he could not climb fast enough to catch up to them. He had to turn back to the coast, leaving yet another airplane lost to the mission. Now 175 bombers remained.

As they passed near the Greek island of Corfu, another crew realized that their plane could not return to base even if they survived the bombing run over Ploesti. Aboard *Chattanooga Choo Choo*, the flight engineer, Sgt. Frank Kees, worked out the figures on their fuel consumption so far. He consulted the navigator, Lt. Richard Britt. It quickly became clear that their rate of gas consumption was much greater than that of the plane they had been used to flying, but which had refused to start that morning. "We were in serious trouble," Britt recalled. He reported the problem to the pilot, saying that "with luck, we might get to Turkey after the bombing." Turkey was neutral, so the worst that could happen, they believed, was a period of internment—if they could remain airborne long enough to get there.

Shortly after *Wongo-Wongo* went down, the formation passed Corfu and turned to the northeast. That was when their problems became more serious: the formation had become split. The dangers started with a mountain range and high thick clouds. The Pindus Mountains of Albania rose to a height of 9,000 feet. Mission planners set the altitude for that leg of the journey at 11,000 feet, allowing a reasonable safety margin above the tallest mountain peak.

If there had been only the mountains to consider, there might have been no problem, but on the day of the mission the impenetrable cloud cover extended in places as high as 17,000 feet. When Lt. Edwin Baker, a pilot in the 93rd (no relation to the group's commander, Col. Addison Baker), saw the clouds, he recalled, "A cold chill went down my spine."

> It was obvious we were going to have to fly through there.
> We loosened up the formation, spread out, noted the
> compass heading and headed straight in, climbing. At
> 10,000 feet we put on our oxygen masks. We finally broke
> through at about 15,000 feet and leveled off. It was a great
> feeling to see the other ships around us and in a fairly
> good order. We quickly squeezed into our "V" elements of
> three ships as before and crossed the mountains.

Everything seemed to be in order once they passed through the
clouds and over the mountains. Except that the bombers in the
first two elements of the formation—the 376th and the 93rd—
could no longer see the three groups that had been behind them
before they reached the mountain range.

And the latter three elements—the 98th, the 44th, and the
389th—no longer saw any planes ahead of them. Yet, they were
all still flying the same course. The groups had become separated by some 60 miles, and neither knew for certain where the
other was.

The groups had started to become separated before they
reached the mountains, but they had retained visual contact.
When they reached the coast, the gap was only five minutes.
The growing distance resulted from a serious tactical difference
between Killer Kane and Keith Compton, who disagreed over
the power settings for the engines during the long flight to
Ploesti.

Compton wanted to use normal power settings until they
reached the mountains and then increase power to get above
them. Kane argued, instead, for saving power all the way to
Ploesti, then "pouring it on" at the last minute, to cross the target area as rapidly as possible. They had reached no agreement
before the mission, and General Ent, their commanding officer,

seemed incapable of demanding that they both use the same power settings, which of course would have kept the groups together.

Compton and Kane each followed his own instincts, Compton in the lead at 175 miles per hour, assuming that everyone behind him would follow his lead at the same speed. Kane, however, out in front of the last two groups, maintained a speed of 160 miles per hour.

There may have been a personal element in this dispute as well, based on their mutual personal loathing. Maj. Robert Sternfels, a pilot in Kane's outfit, wrote: "Knowing Kane, he was not about to submit to what Compton wanted to do, so he used less power as he always had." Kane continued to do things his way, though surely he knew that his group, and consequently the groups following him, would gradually fall farther and farther behind the groups that were maintaining the airspeed set by Compton. The results were inevitable: Compton would eventually pull ahead of Kane, particularly when they had to climb to cross the mountains.

When the planes emerged from the cloud cover, Compton's tail gunner reported that the other three groups were nowhere to be seen. Compton reduced his speed to 160 and made a series of gentle turns to give Kane and the others a chance to catch up, but by then they were lagging too far.

Subsequently, one historian laid the blame for the separation of the formation squarely on Colonel Kane, "who insisted on flying slower than Compton. It was Kane's responsibility to keep his place in the formation. He failed to do so. Compton gave up on rejoining the two halves and set to the task at hand. He pushed his throttles forward and increased his airspeed to 190 miles per hour."

The Germans knew the Americans were coming long before the planes reached the mountain range. Some time before the raid, German code experts in Greece had broken the American military codes. The Germans were aware that the massive bomber force was taking off from Benghazi before the last of the Liberators was even in the air. They did not know, however, where the planes were heading. The target could have been anywhere within the range of the B-24, and that included much of Italy, Greece, Austria, Yugoslavia, and Romania. Accordingly, the military commanders in those areas were notified.

Spotters first sighted the formation as it neared Corfu. When they plotted its direction they were able to narrow down the list of possible targets, ruling out those in Italy. Then a German radar site in Yugoslavia detected the planes as they crossed the mountains but lost them when they reduced altitude. But by then their bearing suggested only one target. In Bucharest, the Luftwaffe air defense commander telephoned General Gerstenberg, who was spending the weekend in the mountains.

"It is unclear what is developing," he told Gerstenberg, "but we think the objective must be Ploesti."

Gerstenberg left immediately for his headquarters. He ordered all fighter pilots and antiaircraft gunners in the area to maintain alert status. Barrage balloons were winched up into the air above the refineries, as well as certain parts of the city, and everyone else put on alert. Gerstenberg was ready for the Americans. He had been waiting for this day for a long time.

The formation's leading planes were no more than an hour away. Their altitude was only 150 feet when they crossed the fabled Danube River. The men were disappointed. The water was not blue like the famous waltz had promised. "Like that

Kentucky bluegrass," reported Tech. Sgt. William Leonard, the radioman aboard *Hadley's Harem*, "it just ain't blue." It was an ordinary brown.

Colonel Kane was also disappointed. "I wondered when I saw the Danube, what had happened to the beautiful blue. The muddy water seemed like any other large river, the Nile or the Mississippi." But Kane had time for only a quick glimpse of the river. He was too busy searching the skies; the two groups behind him were still in view but where had the others gone?

Kane had veered slightly off course in an easterly direction in order to pass through the clouds, so now he turned west to trace a path along the Danube. The others in his group, and in the latter two groups, dutifully followed his course change. Later Kane wrote:

> After several minutes of agonizing time I realized that we would not join the others and that I had to carry on without them. I was heartsick about being separated from the other groups, but I did not know what else I could have done, and at least two other group commanders agreed with me in following the course. Now we were committed to hitting that target alone, which was a dread that had been haunting Leon [Colonel Johnson of the 44th, commanding the group behind Kane] and me for days and nights. Well, we were on our way, on course and according to schedule, even if we were reduced in strength.

The bombers of the two separate formations scooted fast and low over the Romanian countryside. The crewmen gawked like tourists at the sights. The land looked so peaceful, beautiful and prosperous, the fields full of green wheat and rows of corn, with giant sunflowers shooting up between them. Farmers working the fields dropped their implements to gaze at the armada above them. The planes passed over some kind of festival. Girls in bright dresses waved at the airmen. The crews waved back.

Colonel Kane recalled how fertile the soil appeared and how well cultivated the farms seemed. "The houses were brightly colored, jewel-like in contrast with the green fields. Tall hedgerows separated the small farms. The roads were improved and the mud was rutted by the wheels of horse-drawn wagons." It had probably looked just the same a hundred years before.

It was Sunday and people in the small towns, dressed in their best clothes, were walking along the dirt roads to church. They stopped to stare, the roar of the engines ringing in their ears long after the planes had disappeared. Some elderly people dropped to their knees to pray as the planes roared over. They had probably never seen an airplane before. Others ran away, terrified. A man in a buggy shook his fist. "A girl beside him pulled her skirt over her face. The radio operator in Lieutenant Stewart's *Utah Man* saw a woman stop her wagon and dive underneath it as the bombers passed. When the plane shot by, the horses bolted, leaving the woman lying exposed and face down on the road."

As one plane passed over a lake the crew noticed some girls sunbathing in the nude. The men whooped and whistled, forgetting the war for a few seconds. But with every minute, every mile, they closed in on their target.

Aboard Red Franks's ship, *Euroclydon*, the men were quickly startled back to reality when their flight engineer announced that the fuel pump that transferred gas from the bomb-bay tanks to the permanent tanks in the wings no longer worked. Thus, all the fuel in the specially installed bomb-bay tanks was now useless. Everyone knew what that meant; they no longer

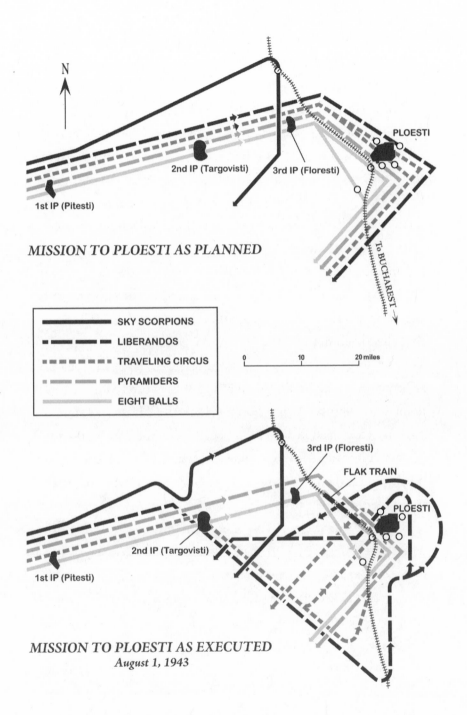

MISSION TO PLOESTI AS PLANNED

SKY SCORPIONS

LIBERANDOS

TRAVELING CIRCUS

PYRAMIDERS

EIGHT BALLS

0   10   20 miles

MISSION TO PLOESTI AS EXECUTED
August 1, 1943

had enough gas to return to Benghazi. They would have to go to Turkey where they would be interned. This is, assuming they survived the bombing run.

The scenic countryside became a target for the gunners in *Hail Columbia* long before they expected it. As they flew over a small airport, the gunners asked Killer Kane if they could test their guns on a couple of old biplanes that were parked there. Kane said no, but shortly after that, he gave permission for them to open fire on a moving freight train. "When my gunners began to shoot," Kane said, "all the guns in the formation poured bullets into that train. After we had passed on, the tail gunner reported that smoke was rising from several of the cars and the engine was standing still, spouting clouds of steam." The first shots had been fired on the mission to Ploesti.

In air force parlance, an IP, or initial point, is a well-defined location on a map and on the ground that is used as a starting point for a bombing run. For the Ploesti raid, three IPs had been selected, each of which had been studied from the model, the drawings, and the maps. Navigators and pilots had spent so much time and effort memorizing the IPs that, it was said, they could identify them in their sleep.

The first was the town of Pitesti, 100 miles west of Ploesti, where the pilots were to drop altitude to treetop level and increase speed. When the first two groups, the 376th and the 93rd, reached Pitesti, they identified it immediately, just as if they were checking the model back at the green hut in Benghazi. The three other groups, led by Killer Kane, were 20 minutes behind, still unaware of the position of the leading groups.

The third IP was Floresti, a town 15 minutes' flying time from Ploesti. At Floresti, the bombers were supposed to turn right, over railroad tracks, which would put them on course to approach the target from the northwest. They maintained a speed of about 200 miles per hour. A light mist and rain were falling, making it impossible to see Ploesti's distant smoke-stacks.

It was up to Colonel Compton of the 376th to identify the IP. When he saw a small town with the familiar road running through its center, a bridge over a river, and railroad tracks leading to the right, just the landmarks he expected to see, he shouted "Now!" to his pilot, who dutifully banked to the right. And so did the rest of the formation.

It was the wrong place, the wrong turn, the wrong town. They were over Targovisti, the second IP, about 13 miles from Pitesti. They had turned too soon and were heading straight for Bucharest. Compton's navigator, Capt. Harold Wicklund, warned them over the intercom that they had turned too soon, but Compton and General Ent, who was sitting behind the pilots, ignored him and stuck to the new course.

Pilots in other planes broke radio silence, yelling "Not here! Not here!" and "Mistake! Mistake!" but Compton and Ent could not hear them because their radio was turned off to maintain radio silence. All the careful, thorough, detailed, and precise training, planning, and preparation for the mission to Ploesti had just been rendered useless.

"We're going to Bucharest," said one of the pilots, who instantly realized the error. "What a hell of a waste of money."

"Killer" Kane's Pyramiders roaring toward their target area. The fireball in the background is a gas explosion from a downed B-24. (*National Archives*)

MY GOD! WE'RE SITTING DUCKS!

BREWERY WAGON WAS A jinxed airplane. Some ships were like that, just plain unlucky. It was plagued by mechanical problems on the ground and in the air. During combat missions, if a single antiaircraft shell burst nearby, it was a good bet that most of the shrapnel would strike *Brewery Wagon* while the planes around it would not receive a scratch. Although the plane had already been hit several times, however, it always managed to limp back home.

On that August morning over Romania, when the other aircraft in the groups turned to the right, heading toward Bucharest, *Brewery Wagon* was the first one to leave the formation and go back on course for Ploesti.

The pilot, 1st Lt. John Palm, from El Paso, Texas, had not been happy to be assigned the *Brewery Wagon* for such a long and dangerous mission. He knew the plane's reputation. Before he climbed aboard he threw stones at the fuselage; it was not a gesture of affection.

When Colonel Compton executed the wrong turn, Lt. Palm trusted the advice of his own navigator rather than the group commander. The navigator, Lt. William Wright, had called him on the intercom when he saw the other planes turning. "If this is the correct turn, I'm lost," he told Palm. "This heading is all wrong."

Palm turned *Brewery Wagon* back to the east and caught a glimpse of Ploesti in the distance. He lined up with a refinery on the perimeter of the target area and aimed for it, but *Brewery Wagon* never made it that far. A German shell exploded in the nose, killing the navigator and bombardier instantly. The force knocked out one engine and set two others on fire.

The ship did not have a chance; it had been mortally wounded and quickly became impossible to control. "Tramping the pedals was like fighting a bucking horse," Palm remembered. "I was not getting much pressure on the right pedal. I reached down. My right leg below the knee was hanging from a shred of flesh."

Palm jettisoned the bombs and banked away from the refineries and their antiaircraft guns. A Romanian fighter pilot flying an ME-109 attacked him from the rear, above the wounded B-24. A stream of bullets tore into Palm's plane from the tail forward.

Brewery Wagon could not take any more. Palm knew he couldn't keep it in the air any longer. When the plane came to rest in a field southeast of Ploesti, eight of the crewmen were still alive. Lt. Palm, fighting the severe pain in his leg, ripped out the cockpit window with one hand, "something I couldn't do under normal circumstances with both hands in a week."

The men fled from the burning plane and hid in a cornfield but German soldiers quickly surrounded them. One whipped out a knife and cut off Palm's wristwatch. Suddenly a lone Romanian soldier appeared and pointed his rifle at the Germans, gesturing for them to move away. The Germans left, giving custody of *Brewery Wagon*'s crew to the Romanians. The men of the jinxed B-24 couldn't know it yet, but they would be among the more fortunate of those captured.

The planes of the 376th and the 93rd continued on toward Bucharest. Colonel Compton and General Ent were still unaware of their incorrect course heading, but others were beginning to suspect that they were all going the wrong way. The pilot of *Utah Man*, Lt. Walter Stewart, listened to the frantic voice of his navigator. "We're going wrong. We're going wrong! Look at the tracks.

1st Lt. John D. Palm, pilot of *Brewery Wagon.* (*John D. Palm*)

We're heading for Bucharest." Stewart glanced down at the railroad tracks they had been following and noticed that they were rusted, an obvious sign of disuse. The tracks they were supposed to be flying over were in frequent use, part of a working rail line. Clearly, these were not the right tracks.

Over the intercom Stewart heard his rear gunner shout, "Look at nine o'clock, Lieutenant, smoke stacks to the rear. That's Ploesti!"

Stewart waggled his wings and waved to attract the attention of Col. Addison Baker, CO of the 93rd, who was aboard *Hell's Wench*. By then, Baker had also realized they were off course. He had made the decision to risk court-martial by turning away from the lead formation.

Baker could not radio his intentions to the other pilots in his group but had to act on his own, hoping they would follow him and not collide in the process of executing an unplanned 90 degree turn to the left.

Lt. Russell Longnecker, flying *Thundermug*, directly behind Baker's, later wrote: "There was no doubt about his decision. He maneuvered our group more eloquently than if he had radio contact with each of us. Ploesti was off there to the left and we were going straight into it and we were going fast."

To the German spotters on the ground, it appeared that the Americans were making a two-pronged attack, going after both Ploesti and Bucharest. A member of General Gerstenberg's staff expressed his admiration for the planning of the attack, calling it "damned cleverly done." He assumed that the bombers heading for Bucharest were intended as decoys to attract German and Romanian fighters, leaving the other group free to hit Ploesti.

The men of the 93rd saw the split in the forces for what it was, a monumental foul-up that would give Ploesti's defenders more time to prepare and would bring the bombers over the target from a different direction than had been projected. The flyers' concern now was how they would recognize the targets they had so carefully studied. The new course would also bring them over the target at that point where the defenses were strongest, exactly what the American planners had tried to avoid.

Suddenly, "all hell was breaking loose," recalled Lt. Edwin Baker, copilot of *Little Lady*.

> Anti-aircraft guns, ground fire and the pursuit ships had shown up. We leveled off and opened our bomb bay doors. Straight ahead of us was a row of eucalyptus trees. From underneath, antiaircraft guns started shooting point blank at us. You could hear the swish and feel the shells go by us. My God! We're sitting ducks.

It was a maelstrom; it was chaos; it was carnage. The planes of the 93rd, now only 10 miles from Ploesti, approached the target at a speed of 245 miles per hour, 65 miles per hour faster than their normal cruising speed. And they were a mere 50 feet off the ground. Everywhere the crews looked as they closed in on the refineries, they could see enemy guns firing. Ordinary haystacks in farmers' fields unfolded to reveal quadruple antiaircraft weapons. A chicken coop had become the hiding place of a deadly 88-mm gun.

The German defenders cranked the gun barrels down almost level with the ground to take aim at the low-altitude bombers. Barrage balloons soared high above the planes, but their deadly steel cables dangled to the ground. The crews could not escape them.

Giant concrete towers rising higher than the planes were topped by gunners firing down. Explosions and machine gun bullets crisscrossed to fill the air. The ships tried to evade the dangers by dropping even lower, some down to 20 feet, scraping the corn stalks in the fields with the leading edges of their wings.

In the lead element were *Euroclydon*, *Utah Man*, and *Hell's Wench*. Aboard *Utah Man*, Lt. Stewart shouted, "Fire at anything you see!" Every gun aboard the ship opened up. One of his gunners "riddled an enemy soldier raising a barrage balloon and saw them disappear in a puff of smoke. He swung his gun towards a locomotive and opened fire as the B-24 sped over it. He looked down to see a flak gunner cradling a shell and staring up with a gaping mouth." This was a strange air war at close quarters, not unlike the infantry where you saw the man you killed. Or the one who was about to kill you.

Up front in the vulnerable Plexiglas nose of *Euroclydon*, the navigator and bombardier, Jack Warner and Red Franks, felt as if every gun was firing directly at them, and they were not far from wrong. Warner was so overwhelmed for a moment that he froze, unable to fire back with his single .50-caliber machine gun until the pilot yelled at him through the intercom, wanting to know when he was going to shoot. He fired, swinging his gun from side to side, finding no lack of targets over the countryside. At the same time, Red Franks began to line up on the refineries ahead of them.

They were an estimated three minutes from the target when Lt. Stewart's copilot shouted, "Look at that!" *Hell's Wench*, Colonel Baker's ship, was on fire. The plane had hit the cable of a barrage balloon and snapped it in two, but part of a wing was left shredded. A shell exploded in the nose, killing the bombardier, and at least three more explosions rocked the plane. One shell hit a bomb-bay gas tank. The flames enveloped the cockpit and spread quickly.

One man, probably the navigator, though no one knows for certain, was spotted jumping from the nose wheel hatch. He fell so near the other ships that their crews could see the severe burns on his legs. Colonel Baker, who had vowed to his men that he would lead them over the target, even if his plane fell apart, was doing just that. He kept *Hell's Wench* flying, ignoring the flat field below on which he could have tried a crash landing.

Utah Man was to the right and slightly behind the doomed ship. Stewart saw two engines on fire, with flames streaming all the way back to the tail. "We pulled up on the colonel," Stewart later wrote. "We waved at him, trying to get him to belly land or pull up so his crew could get out."

Baker's copilot, Maj. John Jerstad, had volunteered for the mission, even though he had already flown more than the 25 needed to return stateside. The two men held the plane on course even after they jettisoned the bombs. There was no need to go on to the target then, except to lead the formation there. And for that, they somehow kept *Hell's Wench* going. A crewman on a nearby plane remembered:

> Baker had been burning for about three minutes. The right wing began to drop. I don't see how anyone could have been alive in that cockpit, but someone kept her leading the force on between the refinery stacks. Baker was a powerful man, but one man could not have held the ship on the climb she took beyond the stacks.

Baker and Jerstad pulled their plane up in a climb to about 300 feet. At that point, a few men—variously reported as three or four—jumped out, their bodies afire, flames spreading out in the wind. The plane slued over on its right wing and plummeted to the ground, missing a bomber in the second element by a mere six feet. That pilot saw *Hell's Wench* flash by, a flaming torch. "Flames hid everything in the cockpit. Baker went down after he flew his ship to pieces to get us over the target."*

Euroclydon, flying to the left of *Hell's Wench's* position in the formation, dropped its bombs and took a direct hit in the bomb bay. As flames engulfed the ship, another shell exploded near the nose. Neither the bombardier nor the navigator was

---

*Addison Baker and John Jerstadt were awarded the Medal of Honor posthumously, over spirited opposition from some Air Force brass. They argued that Baker did not deserve the honor because he had broken formation when he chose not to follow Compton when he made the wrong turn. They felt that Baker had disobeyed his orders to follow the mission commander and had instead made the independent choice to carry out the mission and lead his planes to Ploesti, even though everyone else was heading for Bucharest. The controversy continued for more than six months until, finally, other airmen in Baker's group who had witnessed his courage and determination prevailed.

wounded, but the hot raging fire was spreading toward the nose. "I tried to use the intercom," Jack Warner, the navigator, said many years later, but there was "no response."

> I reached up under the flight deck and tried to tug the pilots' legs or rudder pedals to signal our problem. Still no response! The fire was getting pretty bad, and I figured it was time to try and get out. I pulled the nose wheel door release and only one door opened. I looked behind me. Red [Franks, the bombardier] was trying to get his chute on. Another shell exploded behind me, which shattered my shoulder blade and put shrapnel into my head.
>
> The concussion blasted me back through the tunnel into the flames. My feet were in the fire and one of my arms was hanging out the open nose-wheel door. I was lying there kicking and screaming with my feet in the fire and my arms in the slipstream.

As the fire spread throughout the ship, the pilots managed to pull up the nose and climb high enough to give the crew a chance to bail out. Lieutenant Stewart in *Utah Man* watched *Euroclydon* climb. He heard his left waist gunner shout, "Two men out, two men out!" They were the two waist gunners, but no one else jumped from the plane until it faltered in its climb and began to fall—"like a blazing star," one observer wrote. As the plane started to plummet, with flames flowing from the tail for some 200 feet, a pilot saw Jack Warner tumble out of the nose wheel hatch followed, an instant later, by Red Franks. "I immediately reached for my ripcord," Jack Warner recalled, "mere seconds seemed like forever before I actually found it and pulled. I was so close to the ground that I struck it before the chute blossomed over my head as I lost consciousness."

Warner was taken prisoner by Romanian soldiers. They brought him to the nearest hospital where doctors declared him "too seriously wounded to survive. [They] left him to die among the bodies of American airmen lying on bloodied parachutes in the 'dead corner.'"

Red Franks's chute did not open, but his death was cloaked in mystery for more than 50 years. At first, Warner said that Franks tried to pull him out when his feet were caught in the fire but was unable to manage it and so jumped himself. Shortly after that, Warner said, he was able to extricate himself and bail out. But in 1995 Warner contacted Red Franks's sister, Nancy Lee, and spoke to her for two hours, telling a different story about that day in 1943. "Red pushed me out of the plane," he told her, "and we were too close to the ground for his chute to open."

Red Franks had saved his friend's life. Warner never explained why he was telling Nancy Lee the whole story some 50 years later, but she believed he felt remorseful and guilty because he had survived and Franks had not. Warner's daughter said that her father "always spoke of Red with regret because he had been such a good friend. And he lived the rest of his life knowing he had survived because of a twist of fate and the helping hand of a true friend."

Utah Man was now the only plane left of the three in the lead element, and every German gun opened up on it. Lieutenant Stewart, looking straight ahead through the windshield, saw an 88-mm antiaircraft gun, its long muzzle almost parallel to the ground, fire directly at him. He saw the brief spurt of fire at the end of the barrel but could not hear the sound over the noise of his ship. The shell hit the tail, leaving a large hole in one of the stabilizers.

Stewart pushed the control wheel forward and lowered the plane to "cornstalk altitude," wings almost scraping the ground. Shells and bullets tore into *Utah Man* from every direction. In front of him, one wall of a chicken coop fell open to the ground revealing a 20-mm gun. A stream of shells poured into the damaged plane's left side.

The front bomb bay door had been partially ripped away, leaving it flapping in the 200-mile-per-hour wind. Cables and hydraulic lines had been severed, along with the cables that released the bombs. A moment later Stewart spotted another chicken coop. "Bartlett with his big top guns said, 'What'll I do?' I said 'Let her go!' He turned his guns and he hit it. Feathers, hens and eggs went in all directions." This time it had been a real chicken coop.

Since by then the planes were approaching the target from a totally different direction from what had been rehearsed, Stewart had no hope of hitting his assigned target. He sighted on two other refineries, which had been designated for the 98th and the 44th, two groups trailing so far behind that they had long since been lost to view. Stewart climbed to 60 feet to clear the refinery he had chosen and the bombardier announced "bombs away!" The plane took another hit on the left, but Stewart suddenly saw a new menace.

Directly ahead of *Utah Man* was a radio tower soaring 200 feet in the air. He couldn't climb rapidly enough to get over it, and even if he could, he would be an easy target for the ack-ack guns at that height. He had to try to skirt it at his present altitude of only 60 feet. "We rolled the left wing into the street below and stood the right wing [up] to miss the tower. Flak chewed off the high wing tip before we leveled off." The left wing edged its way down the center of the street some 20 feet from the pavement. It was an amazing bit of flying.

But *Utah Man* was still not out of danger. As Stewart flew on over Ploesti, the number three engine was hit. A wide stream of gasoline blew out of the wing tank. Stewart told the gunners to cease firing to avoid setting the gas ablaze, and he ordered everyone to take their positions for a crash landing. He looked around for a place to set the ship down. Someone yelled to him over the intercom. "Don't look now, but we still have two bombs on this airplane!" The bombardier denied it, saying that he had dropped all the bombs. The other crewman said no; those two big bombs were still in place. That changed everything. Stewart could not attempt a crash landing with live bombs on board, but he could not remain airborne longer than an hour because that was when the bombs were armed to explode.

He turned the plane toward another refinery target and ordered the bombardier to drop the bombs there. The bombardier tried but the bombs did not release. Stewart spotted a railroad bridge and headed for it, telling the bombardier to try again. But as Stewart closed in on it, he was horrified to see that it was not a working railroad bridge but an ordinary crossing, over which a girl was driving some cows. She looked up and waved at the plane. It was too late to warn the bombardier. They roared over the bridge—and instantly Stewart was relieved that he did not feel the usual lift when a plane drops its bomb load. He heard the tail gunner say, "Hey, there's a little girl back there waving at us."

Although it was fortunate that the bombs had not dropped on the child and her cows, they remained a deadly threat to *Utah Man* and her crew. They had to get rid of the load before they exploded and blew the plane out of the sky. The bombardier and the flight engineer made their way onto the narrow catwalk to try to tackle the problem by hand. Finally their persistent hammering freed the stuck bombs. They dropped in an empty field and exploded.

Utah Man was the first plane to bomb a target at Ploesti. It flew safely past the refineries, beyond the reach of the German guns. Now all Stewart and his crew had to do was cover the 1,300 miles back to North Africa, with one engine out and the wings and fuselage riddled with holes, hoping no enemy fighters spotted them.

The rest of the planes in Baker's 93rd approached the target straight on, without altering course, despite what they had seen of *Hell's Wench* and *Euroclydon* ahead of them. Only one of the first V-element had made it. Flames and smoke from antiaircraft fire hovered over the ground, along with exploding bombs and gas tanks and burning B-24s. Ed Baker in *Little Lady* saw a gasoline storage tank erupt in a huge ball of fire. He managed to miss it, but the plane on his left flew straight into the flames. "I never saw him come out," Baker recalled.

Little Lady had taken considerable damage and had not yet reached the refineries. "Our number 3 engine was on fire and gas was pouring out of our belly tank from flak holes." They dropped their bombs and extinguished the engine fire after feathering the engine, but the gas fumes inside the ship were so strong that Baker opened the cockpit windows. He told the bombardier to open the bomb bay doors to clear out the fumes.

> We zigzagged through columns of black smoke and fire. We still were not out of it yet. Suddenly we popped out of the hell hole of fire, flame, and smoke into the clear sky and green fields beyond. We were clear and still flying

although badly damaged, but not fatally. Wilkie [pilot Ralph Wilkinson] and I looked at each other and smiled.

Little Lady had a chance of making it home.

Lt. Russell Longnecker, the pilot of *Thundermug*, remembered seeing a Liberator "sliding down a street, with both wings sheered off."

> A plane hit a barrage balloon and both disintegrated in a ball of fire. We saw bombs dropped by other planes skipping along the ground, hitting buildings, and passing on through, leaving gaping holes in the brickwork. The tracers were so solid in front of us that it looked like a fishing net woven of fiery cords. I thought the flight was over for us.

It wasn't. *Thundermug* dropped its bombs, and Donald R. "Deacon" Jones, the copilot, spoke up for the first time. "Let's get the hell out of here!" he said.

Lucky, flown by Harold Kendall, was not living up to its name. Just as Bill Fitzsimmons, the bombardier, released the bombs on their refinery target, German shells pounded the ship from nose to bomb bay. "Wires snapped, hydraulic lines ruptured, oxygen bottles exploded and a fuel tank spurted gas from holes in the side. Thick, choking, electrical smoke curled from behind the insulation in the nose."

Kendall alerted the crew to prepare to bail out, while three men raced forward and tried to douse the fires. Another went to the bomb bay to try to plug the holes in the gas tank. If he could stop the leaks—and if nothing else hit them, and if the engines kept running, and if no more fighters jumped them— then they might have a chance of surviving.

Huge gasoline storage tanks ringed the refinery area. They were hit repeatedly by incendiaries the B-24 waist gunners tossed from their open windows and by machine gun fire from both American and German guns. When those tanks exploded, their massive circular lids blew off sending a bolt of flame a hundred feet high, enough force to cut a plane in two. A few of the bombers were caught in those cauldrons and never seen again.

One plane roared over the town of Ploesti, chased by a small Romanian fighter that flew upside-down beneath it, spraying the fuselage with bullets. It brought the bomber down. Unfortunately, and this was the greatest tragedy of the raid to the Romanians, that B-24 crashed into a prison housing about 100 female prisoners. "Flaming petrol flowed through the cell blocks and down the stairs," wrote one eyewitness. German firemen rescued 40 of the women but the rest perished, trapped in their cells, while the 3-story building burned. Screams were heard throughout the day and night; the fire was not extinguished until the next morning.

Another Romanian pilot, Lt. Karol Anastasescu, flying a German ME-109, shot down two of the Liberator bombers. He was not supposed to be on duty that day but had volunteered so a friend could attend a wedding. When his squadron took off from their base near Bucharest, it did not take long to find the American planes. "They were practically flying wing next to wing," he recalled, in 2004, "like they were at a parade. I ordered the attack. When we got close to the bombers, a stunning tracer barrage unleashed. I had the impression that all of them were aimed at my forehead and I felt cold drops of sweat on my back."

Anastasescu dove toward one B-24 and opened fire at the left wing, where a fuel tank was located. He missed and quickly dove under the American formation, putting him perilously close to the ground. He managed to regain altitude but by then the bombers were taking heavy antiaircraft fire. Some of the refineries and storage tanks had already exploded and were burning furiously.

"It was like hell," Anastasescu wrote. He went after the same B-24 again once it passed beyond the ack-ack fire and this time shot it down. His fighter was damaged by return fire and flames trailed from the engine. Flying too low to bail out, he began climbing slowly.

> [He expected] to simply blow up in any second. I saw a B-24 coming at me, probably to give me the final blow. I was passing through horrible moments and couldn't bear anymore. I didn't have any way out, so I decided to ram him and finish it quickly. He tried to avoid me, but it was too late. I felt a powerful heat and then I woke up in the hospital.

The American bomber named *Jose Carioca* was ablaze from nose to tail, a flying torch. German gunners on the ground stopped firing; there was no need to shoot at it anymore. They watched it approach and pass overhead. It carried a crew on its first mission. The ship flew on through the smoke toward a refinery and crashed into the side of a building. Gasoline squirted and ran in licking flamelets across the refinery grounds. From the other side of the building came *Jose Carioca*, in level flight, without wings. The fuselage penetrated another refinery building, where it remained, lifting a cloud of brick dust and new fires.

Lt. Kenton McFarland, the pilot of *Liberty Lad*, was flying toward the rear of the formation of the 93rd. He watched several planes ahead of him explode in the air and others dive, flaming, into the ground. "A guy hit a [barrage balloon] and he went right up to that balloon-barrage cable, and it caught on the tail and just snapped the tail off, and he went down," McFarland recalled. He maneuvered *Liberty Lad* in among the other cables and at one point pulled up sharply to clear a smokestack. His ship was riddled by cannon fire, wounding the radio operator and damaging an engine, controls and cables, and the tail. They dropped their bombs, climbed a little higher, which gave them a good view of the destruction around them, and headed out of Ploesti. "We got away from the target, and we didn't see any other airplanes. We thought everybody had been shot down."

One of the last planes over Ploesti from the 93rd was *Honky Tonk Gal,* flown by Lt. Hubert Womble. The ship was hammered before it even reached the target. One engine was destroyed by a shell, another on the same side was running on reduced power, and the right side of the fuselage was full of holes.

"We weren't going to make it all the way home," Womble said. "Oil tanks blowing up, planes going down and others on fire or smoking. The Germans were shooting 88s like deer rifles and we were the deer."

The bombardier, Lt. Bill Little, dropped the bombs, and *Honky Tonk Gal* made it to the northern edge of Ploesti, where it sustained another hit. Another engine went out and a shell exploded beneath the flight deck, at Womble's feet. The force of the explosion knocked him straight up out of his seat and twisted his body to the right side. "I knew I was hit, but there wasn't any real pain. I couldn't put much pressure on the rudder pedals so Larry [copilot Lawrence Lancashire] did most of the flying from that point. With three engines out we had to come down."

They spotted a wheat field and lowered the landing gear. As they glided in, they bounced hard. The ship hit railroad tracks,

snapping off the landing gear. The plane slid through the vege-
tation and ground to a halt. Womble tried to get out of his seat
but he could not stand up. "I lifted my leg to try again, and my
foot was gone. It was still in my boot near the rudder pedals."

In less than ten minutes, the 93rd, what was left of it, had
cleared the Ploesti area. Of the 32 ships that bombed the target,
only 19 were still flying, and most were damaged. Not all would
make it back to their base.

Aboard *Utah Man*, Lieutenant Stewart noticed that everyone
had become quiet. After every other previous raid there had
always been happy, nervous chatter over the radio, once they
headed home. But not now. Today, no one said a word.

A Liberator flying low over the Astra-Romana refinery. (*National Archives*)

THE FURNACE OF HELL

W HEN COL. KEITH COMPTON, leading the 376th, saw the buildings of Bucharest up ahead instead of the oil refineries of Ploesti, he finally realized he had made a wrong turn. He later wrote,

> I turned to General Ent and told him we had turned too early and had missed the target. There was little choice as we could not get back on the planned bomb run heading. I asked him for permission to bomb any other target. Ent agreed, so I then went on the Command Channel and ordered all other aircraft to "bomb targets of opportunity.

The target that had been assigned to Compton's group was important for political and public relations reasons. It was the Romana Americana refinery, which had been the property of Standard Oil of New Jersey until all American business interests in Germany and the countries it occupied were confiscated.

If all the other refineries were bombed, some of which had been owned by French and British companies, and the American refinery was spared, it would prove embarrassing to the United States. And so that particular refinery had been assigned to the 376th because they were the most experienced of the five groups. As it turned out, however, the refinery would escape damage.

Colonel Compton turned his formation to the left and headed north toward Ploesti. His situation was now more difficult and confusing. Like the 98th, he was approaching Ploesti from a completely different direction from what his bomb group had planned and rehearsed. Consequently, the chance of hitting the assigned target, or even recognizing it from among all the other refineries, was extremely small.

Neither Compton nor Ent knew the whereabouts of the three formations led by Killer Kane. They did not know if those bomb groups had also made a wrong turn, or if they were still on course but lagging behind, or even if they had turned around and returned to North Africa.

All Compton knew for certain was that the overall attacking force had been greatly reduced. Thus, the amount of firepower that could be brought to bear on the German antiaircraft defenses was far less than the planners had called for. And that meant a greater likelihood that Compton's force would sustain severe casualties. Both Compton and Ent had initially opposed the idea of a low-level raid because of their belief that it would result in heavy losses.

Worse, as Compton and Ent neared Ploesti they saw huge columns of smoke and flames. They were unaware that the 98th had broken away and attacked Ploesti on their own, causing some damage but also raising the defenses to their maximum level. There was, then, ample reason to abort the mission and head home. One historian later noted, "Ent would not allow the mission to continue unless he firmly believed that there was a chance to hit the target and come out with as few casualties as possible." As for Compton, he "could see that all the planning, practice and work had gone down the tubes. At the moment Compton felt betrayed and abandoned."

The question looming for both men was whether they could, or should, press on with the attack and risk annihilation or break off and return to base to bear the disgrace of not even having tried to bomb at least some of the targets.

They made their decision shortly after they came under fire over the outskirts of Ploesti. Deviating from their southeast course, they swung in a semicircle some 20 miles wide around the edge of the refinery area, hoping to approach from the north where the defenses were weakest. As they closed in, however, they noticed that the antiaircraft fire was not abating.

The pilots had been instructed to bomb targets of opportunity. Thus, they dropped their bombs independently, on anything that looked suitable. And as a result, the bombing was haphazard. Many planes did not even unload near the refineries at all; one historian sarcastically referred to the raid by the 376th as their "grand tour of Romania."

Colonel Compton, with Ent on the flight deck behind him, dropped his bombs, but it is not known if he was aiming at a specific target or just getting rid of the bomb load. He did not wait for his bombardier to salvo them but pulled the emergency bomb release control himself in the cockpit. "With the bombs gone," he recalled, "I could then get a course to take us home."

Unfortunately, Colonel Compton had failed to open the bomb bay doors. The released explosives broke the doors with their weight and left them flapping in the wind. No one ever knew (and the question was asked at many of the group's reunions) what the bombs hit or if they even exploded.

Maj. Lynn Hester, Compton's bombardier, said when interviewed many years later, "I was not called upon to find a target nor to drop the bombs. I never saw the intended target nor did I see the bombs explode."

A copilot in Compton's group added, "It was a mess. We weren't dropping as a group, of course, or even on our planned targets. If one or two planes were over a likely looking target, they'd drop on it." Many jettisoned their bombs over the Romanian countryside after they had pulled away from Ploesti, except for five planes that did what they went there to do.

Before the war Maj. Norman Appold had been a chemical engineer in Michigan. Now he was the pilot of *G.I. Ginnie*, leading a section of four other ships. Having flown so far to get so close to so many targets, he was determined to find a good one and bomb it. His plane had already taken several hits. Both wings and an engine nacelle had been damaged and hydraulic lines had been severed. Both waist gunners had been wounded. No matter. Appold would not be deterred. "Let's tuck in now," he radioed the others in his section. "Stay with me and keep close."

As he flew along Ploesti's eastern edge he saw what he wanted, a large refinery called Concordia Vega. It had been Addison Baker's designated target, but now he was dead and the refinery untouched. Appold led his group in a sharp left turn, dropped altitude, and lined up his sights on the target.

Fires flared up at them. Thick columns of smoke erupted from the refinery forming pillars in the sky. A bombardier from the 98th had dropped delayed-action explosives around the refineries that were just now detonating. It was too late for Appold to change course, and he was flying too low to clear the raging fires.

At 200 miles per hour, *G.I. Ginnie* was covering about 290 feet with every tick of the cockpit clock. They were committed to hit this target in spite of the new dangers exploding into view. Appold could see they were too low to clear the stacks. There was no room to bank around them. They could only fly straight ahead and hope to clear the towers somehow.

The five airplanes passed over the target and dropped 500-pound bombs, which ultimately reduced the facility's production capacity by 40 percent. Appold's attack turned out to be the most significant of the entire mission.

Even before Major Appold reached the target, however, he saw small green shapes approaching his little formation from the far side of Ploesti. The planes were remnants of Addison Baker's 93rd trying to get out of range of the German guns. Then Appold spotted yet another group of bombers heading for him from the right. It was Killer Kane leading the other three formations. They were late, but they were on course and on target, and Appold's group was directly in their flight path.

Appold's group and the fleeing planes of the 93rd were racing toward each other at the same altitude at a closing speed of well over 400 miles per hour, skimming the rooftops and weaving to dodge antiaircraft fire. Appold pulled up a bit but the ships led by Colonel Kane were higher still and coming ever closer. At that instant Ploesti was "roofed with three layers of interweaving Liberators. In the open street below stood Gen. Alfred Gerstenberg, in awed admiration of the galaxy of bombers maneuvering precisely at top speed without colliding. He had no suspicion that it was all a horrible foul-up."

A gauntlet of German fire riddled nearly every ship, but Appold's five planes kept flying. He led them to safety by following a river bed and flying under the radar, but there was one more obstacle, a flak tower atop a bridge. It was bristling with guns. He lowered the nose of G.I. *Ginnie* as much as he dared so the top turret gunner could bring his guns to bear on it. Within no more than five seconds, tower, guns, and gunners disappeared. Major Appold led his men home.

Colonel Kane was puzzled. He was leading the formation to Ploesti but he could see up ahead that everything was dark. He wrote in his diary:

> In the distance toward Ploesti the sky was the ominous black of a threatening thunderstorm. It would be our luck to arrive there during a heavy rainstorm so that we could not see ahead of us. I tried to fit the steel helmet over my radio headphones but could not get it on. As I was looking toward Ploesti, I saw all hell break loose, the whole area burst into flames. With that view of the target, a cold hand seemed to reach inside my breast and grip my heart.

He immediately realized what had happened, that the two groups ahead of him had already dropped their bombs. A surprise attack was no longer possible. The Germans were fully alerted and ready for them. The situation was critical.

They were approaching Ploesti very fast, thanks to a tail wind, and Kane had only seconds to make his decision: proceed with the attack as planned, though fire and smoke would quickly surround them, or abort the mission and head for home.

A writer later noted, "To this day many people believe that Kane should have turned back. The dangers to bomb- and gas-laden planes flying into high-reaching flames, barrage balloons and billowing smoke at such low altitudes was enormous." Besides, the target had already been attacked. Was it worth the risk to try to hit it again?

Aircraft of the 98th Bombardment Group race through the smoke and fires of the bombed Astra-Romana refinery at altitudes of just a few hundred feet. (*National Archives*)

"I did not think it was possible for us to get through that blazing wall without serious damage," Kane recalled. Nevertheless, this was the mission they had practiced, the mission they had been told might shorten the war, and so he pressed on.

As they started on their final run after turning at the third IP, Kane and the others with him noticed a ragged formation of B-24s pass beneath them, heading away from the target, the survivors of the 376th. "I thought I was low," Kane wrote, "but those planes were *really* low. I hoped my pilots would learn the lesson from them and get down low like that. I thought, 'Well, here we go, boys, there it is in all its glory, right ahead of us.'"

The Germans called it *Die Raupe*, the Caterpillar, a special, very deadly train. At first glance it looked like an ordinary string of freight cars pulled by a locomotive, the kind seen hauling goods and supplies throughout Europe. But the freight cars contained several dozen antiaircraft guns of various calibers. *Die Raupe* was heading west, toward Ploesti, on tracks that ran the length of a long narrow valley, and it was moving at top speed.

Before they entered the valley, the last of Kane's groups, Col. Jack Wood's 389th, veered northwest to attack a refinery some 18 miles distant. Colonel Kane's 98th and Colonel Johnson's 44th assembled side by side, nine planes wide and five rows deep to head down the valley, traveling on either side of the railroad track. As they approached the train, the tops and sides of the freight cars peeled open and German guns started firing. "We had to shoot our way in," Kane wrote.

The gunners aboard the train let loose with everything they had, hardly needing to aim. The American bombers were so big, so close, and so low that they were difficult to miss. Even worse for the Americans was that the speed of the train made the relative speed of the bombers appear preposterously slow. The duel with the train was a slow motion nightmare.

Every .50-caliber machine gun that the planes could bring to bear began firing at the train. Kane's ship, *Hail Columbia*, was equipped with twin 50s in the nose, which he aimed and fired from the cockpit. He lined up on the moving train and kept his finger on the firing button until the guns stopped. He yelled to the navigator, Lt. Norm Whalen, to clear the guns and reload, but they were out of bullets. Kane had fired the entire nose gun supply of 2,500 rounds in about 90 seconds. It did not take much longer than that to destroy the train, but in that short time many of the bombers were damaged.

Kane pulled up to 200 feet for the bombing run. The 98th was on course and on target, if a bit late. His bombardier trained his sight on the Astra-Romana refinery, the one assigned to his group. Some of its buildings were already burning from the bombs dropped by the 93rd.

Hail Columbia released its bombs and Kane immediately dropped altitude, as low as he could, but at the same time some of the delayed-action bombs dropped earlier by the 93rd started exploding beneath them. "I didn't think I was going to live through it," recalled Norm Whalen, the navigator.

> I knew I was going to die in the antiaircraft fire, in the flames shooting up from the refineries, from the bombs exploding from the groups that had been there before us and had dropped indiscriminately. It was like the Charge of the Light Brigade. We knew it was a disaster, and that in the flames shooting up from those refineries, we might be burned to death, but we went right in.

"Suddenly," Kane wrote later, "we were enveloped in flames. My left elbow, which was resting on the edge of the open window, had the hairs singed off, and the cockpit filled with the odor of burned hair. We were out of the flames in a flash, through the target and past the far side of the refinery."

A shell hit the right outboard engine and oil began to spew out. Kane reached up to the panel above the windshield and pushed the big red button on the right end of a row of four, feathering the engine. The ship was taking hits from German gunners and with one engine out, was slowing dangerously.

Kane glanced around and saw that he was now in the middle of the formation he had been leading. He could not keep up with the other planes, which were passing him by on maximum power. Then his copilot, Johnny Young, reached over and pulled back the throttles, reducing their speed and making them an even easier target. Kane asked him what he was doing.

"We must save the engines," Young said.

Kane laughed aloud.

"Boy, howdy," he said to Young, "this is no place to save anything other than our own hides. We can save the engines later after they save us."

Kane quickly jammed the throttles forward but couldn't get up an airspeed greater than 185 miles per hour. By the time they reached the far side of Ploesti, *Hail Columbia* was all alone; the rest of the formation had outrun them. Kane tried contacting the rest of the group but the radio no longer worked.

He asked Whalen to plot a course to the predetermined point where crippled planes that could not make it back to Benghazi were supposed to assemble. Kane reached the position but soon veered away, realizing they would never make it back to North Africa. He would try for Cyprus instead.

Kane cut the airspeed to 155; now it was indeed time to try to save the three remaining engines. Three other crippled planes joined up with *Hail Columbia*, each crew grateful for the sight of the others. They all knew it would be a long way home.

Hadley's Harem had stuck close to *Hail Columbia's* left wing as the group approached Ploesti. Kane liked Gib Hadley, the hotshot young pilot of the *Harem*. Perhaps Hadley reminded Kane of himself at that age. Before they reached the flak train, Hadley flew so low that he scraped the treetops, spreading twigs and leaves through the plane. "Quit trimming the hedges," his waist gunner, Leroy Newton, shouted over the intercom.

Hadley remained in position as they flew over the train and approached the target. The bomb bay doors were open. They were no more than 60 seconds from their objective, flying at 200 feet above the explosions from the delayed-action bombs of the 93rd. Flak exploded all around them; flames and thick smoke hovered like ground fog. "It was just like a movie," said radioman Bill Leonard.

An 88-mm shell tore into the *Harem*'s Plexiglas nose. The fierce explosion jolted the plane from nose to tail. It tore open the chest of the bombardier, Leon Storms. The navigator, Harold Tabacoff, beside him when the shell went off, saw pieces of shrapnel rip into his arm. "They got me too," Tabacoff yelled over the intercom. "Can you send someone down with first aid?" Before Hadley could answer, Sgt. Russell Page, the flight engineer, reported that the number two engine was on fire. Bright red flames leaped across the wing, trailing off behind them in the wind. *Hadley's Harem* was in serious trouble.

Hadley told Page to go forward and help the wounded navigator. But before he could do so, he remembered that the bombs had not been dropped; the bombardier had been hit before he could release them. Page pulled the emergency release and the bombs fell away. The sudden weight loss caused the plane to buck like a horse out of control, forcing Hadley and his copilot to use all their strength and skill to keep the plane in the air. Finally Page reached the nose and saw the bombardier whose chest had been torn apart. "I never want to see a mess like that again," he recalled.

The navigator was dizzy from shock and loss of blood. Page bandaged his wounds and dragged him out of the wind roaring in through the shattered nose and carried him up to the flight deck.

Hadley feathered his number two engine. The plane lurched and dove so close to the ground that Sergeant Leonard started to pray out loud. Hadley and the copilot pulled up just in time to avoid a crash. They leveled the ship, but another shell buckled the floor of the fuselage, twisting the metal in the shape of a V.

The force of the explosion knocked Leroy Newton, the right waist gunner, off his feet. He pulled himself up but was so dazed that he grabbed the gun and opened fire at a flock of birds overhead, believing for an instant that they were German fighters. He did not report whether he shot them down.

Hadley kept the *Harem* skimming over the treetops as they cleared the target area. They passed through a cloud of smoke so dark and dense that it shut out the sun. They emerged in time to see two Liberators, both on fire, crash-land. They couldn't tell if anyone made it out alive.

The crew spotted another B-24 that was beginning a slow climb. The entire plane, from wingtip to wingtip, was engulfed in flames. The pilot was trying to gain enough altitude for the crew to bail out safely. Inside, they were most likely burning alive. Suddenly, perhaps mercifully, the ship disappeared in a brilliant flash of flame and smoke leaving a trial of debris raining down to the ground. "For a split second I saw that," recalled Sgt. Christopher Holweger, Hadley's left waist gunner. "It was the most horrible thing I had ever seen. It is stamped on my mind."

It could just as easily have been *Hadley's Harem*, and everyone on board knew it. As it was later described in the *New York Times*, "By this time, the *Harem* was staggering along at 25 feet altitude beyond the target area. Her hydraulic system was shot out and there was nothing the engineers could do about it. Gasoline was leaking badly from the number one engine into the bomb bay, so [flight engineer] Page transferred the fuel from the dead number two engine to number one."

Gib Hadley turned the plane south, heading toward Bulgaria, holding formation with four other crippled B-24s. The pilots were trying desperately to gain altitude in order to clear the 6,000-foot mountain range ahead. As they began their slow, tedious climb, they flew over a train. They could see the passengers leaning out of the windows to wave, as if they were all off on a holiday.

The B-24 named *The Sandman* was in the fourth wave of Killer Kane's 98th. As *Sandman* approached the target the pilot, 1st Lt. Robert Sternfels, and his copilot, 1st Lt. Barney Jackson, were having difficulty keeping the ship level because of the fierce prop wash from the planes in the three waves ahead of them. It was so great, Sternfels remembered, "that I had the control yoke over so hard that I could read the metal warning sign: THIS CONTROL WHEEL IS UPSIDE DOWN. I was too low to turn and had no room to maneuver out of that rough air."

When they reached their assigned target, visibility was zero because of the dense smoke. At no more than 20 feet of altitude the bombardier, Lt. David Polachek, dropped the bombs. "Full throttles, Barney," Sternfels said to his copilot. "Let's get the hell out of here!"

They flew past a smokestack that towered above them, leveled off, and spotted the thick steel cable of a barrage balloon not far in front of them. Sternfels stomped on the rudder pedals and swerved enough so that the cable caught the number three engine instead of the nose. "When we were in [the smoke]," Polacheck wrote, "there was that balloon with steel cables hanging down from it. Anyway, we hit one of them with the engine, the propeller wound up the cable and finally it snapped and hit the side of the plane." Copilot Jackson, said, "I guess we were lucky there. The prop chewed {the cable] up and below where I sit it looked like a knife had dragged down the side of the fuselage. We were fortunate. The charge attached to the cable never got to us."

Sandman emerged from the clouds above the target. An automatic camera in a nearby bomber snapped a picture of it flying low over buildings and smokestacks. (That photograph has achieved the status of an icon, representing the fury and daring of the Ploesti mission; it has been reprinted in almost every book about the raid.) Once in the clear and away from the antiaircraft guns, Sternfels joined with *Hadley's Harem* and *Hail Columbia* to head south.

All the planes were badly shot up. The crews were tossing overboard everything they could to reduce their weight, but even so they were barely making 140 miles per hour. And the mountains lay ahead.

In the last wave of the 98th, *Baby*, flown by Francis Weisler, with Francis McClellan as copilot, began to vibrate violently as it approached the target. One engine was shrieking so wildly it could be heard over the roar of the others. The cause was a runaway prop resulting from a sudden speed-up of the engine. The danger was that the propeller would fly apart and strike the fuselage or the other engine. Weisler yanked back the throttle for that engine to feather it, making them slow so rapidly that they fell behind the rest of the formation. "Suddenly and without warning," wrote waist gunner Sgt. Paul Joyce, "our forward progress decreased drastically, and within seconds the rest of the group left us far behind and quickly disappeared. It was like dropping an anchor. We found ourselves alone, 200 feet over a forest of trees, crippled, and 1200 miles from home."

As *Little Joe* approached the refineries, several explosions went off beneath them, sending flames high above their flight path. The copilot, Bill Berger, recalled that the target "looked like the furnace of hell as we entered." Thick black smoke obscured everything. They were flying blind, the gunners firing almost randomly at the ground, and they flew on through an inferno of German shells exploding in the air and American bombs detonating as they hit the ground.

The pilot, Wesley Pettigrew, flew *Little Joe* right into the flames. Berger said,

> When we got there it was just like an inferno, it was hot as hell. The airplane got so hot that it felt like the airplane would snap apart. Over the target, when I saw all those planes go down, I just got a "don't-give-a-shit" attitude and didn't care if we went down or not. Be out of the war and all its misery.

The B-24 called *Raunchy* flew directly into a steel cable attached to a barrage balloon. The cable held firm as the wing of the plane caught it and dragged it forward and down, until the explosive at the end hit the edge of the wing and detonated. That wing buckled and the other pointed skyward. *Raunchy* tumbled sideways toward the ground.

Sgt. William Schiffmacher, a waist gunner aboard *Raunchy*, remembered the sight of flak bursting all around them and the feeling of release when the bombs were dropped.

> The next thing I knew we were on the ground. I was lying between the two broken halves of the plane. It was on fire. There was a body under me, one of the gunners. I could- n't tell who it was. The flesh on my hands was turning black, popping like a cooked chicken. No pain. I was par- alyzed from the waist down. There was a large hole at the base of my spine, large enough to put my four knuckles in

it. No sign of life around me. I crawled out, the fields were on fire but I managed to crawl through a clear spot. Pulled myself through a barbed wire fence and rolled down a hill into a small stream. The water put out the fire on my burning clothes. I must have fainted then.

There was only one other survivor from *Raunchy's* crew.

A formation of B-24s moving across the burning refineries. (*National Archives*)

9

WE WERE ALL DEAD ANYWAY

"WE FLEW THROUGH SHEETS of flame, and airplanes were everywhere, some of them on fire and others exploding. It's indescribable to anyone who wasn't there." So wrote Col. Leon Johnson, commanding officer of the Flying Eight Balls, the 44th bombardment group.

Flying as copilot in *Suzy Q*, Johnson was heading toward Ploesti on the right side of the tracks that carried the flak train. Killer Kane's 98th was on the other side, taking the brunt of the train's antiaircraft fire. The 44th was spared the worst of it because their flight path took them closer to the train, which meant that the German guns would have to be elevated higher to hit them.

In addition, the planes of the 44th presented a smaller target; only 16 followed *Suzy Q*. The remainder of the group, led by Lt. Col. James Posey, had already turned south to attack their designated target five miles south of Ploesti.

Colonel Johnson was wrestling with the same dilemma Kane had faced. Should he continue with the mission even though his target had already been attacked, or seek another target in the few seconds left to him to decide? The pilot, Maj. William

Brandon, glanced at Johnson, silently asking whether they should turn back. "William," Johnson said, "you are on target!" But Johnson could not yet see the target. He recalled:

> Ahead the target looked like a solid wall of fire and smoke. It appeared that we would have to fly through it. When we got closer to the target we could see that the smoke was staggered a little. Our individual targets were in the center of a clearer spot so we were able to get through.

The break in the smoke also allowed them to see how many planes from previous waves had been shot down. One crewman reported that "the ground was littered with charred and still-burning bodies of fallen comrades, many racing desperately for cover to avoid capture." One of the ships being consumed by raging fires was Addison Baker's plane, *Hell's Wench*.

Johnson led the 44th into the smoke, as though maneuvering his way through an obstacle course. "We found that we could weave around the fires like we weaved over the trees and over the high-tension wires because the fires were not a continuous line across."

They were no higher than 130 feet when they jettisoned their bombs, low enough to see them hit. The tail gunner, William Brady, was snapping pictures and saw one bomb strike an industrial plant. Two others took a couple of bounces and crashed into a boiler house. Then Brady saw a lone German soldier crouched beside a house. He raised his rifle and took aim at the plane. Brady shifted position to put away his camera just as a bullet crashed through the turret's Plexiglas precisely where his head had been. He had escaped death by a fraction of an inch and no more than a second in time.

The planes of the 44th flew on past the target but not yet out of danger. Johnson spied an 88-mm gun aimed directly at *Suzy Q*. He swung the ship left and right and passed over the gun as it fired. A shell went through one wing, leaving a gaping hole. Fortunately it did not explode; had it gone off at that low altitude, no one would have survived.

So it was for many of the bombers, life or death by an inch, a second, a turn to the right, a swing to the left. Perhaps a difference of a few feet in altitude, or because something went wrong with a shell and it did not explode where it was supposed to. The crew of *Suzy Q* was among the lucky ones.

Calaban was lucky too. Piloted by James Hill and Ed Dobson, the ship was in the second three-plane element behind *Suzy Q's* lead element. As they headed into the bomb run, Dobson pushed himself upright when he realized what was in front of them. "Balloon cables!" he shouted, knowing there was no time to take evasive action. Some 50 years later, Dobson's son described what happened.

> A cable whipped past *Calaban's* nose and sliced into the right wing a foot from the fuselage and Lt. Dobson. It missed the inside propeller, a hit which might have been fatal. It cut the deicer boot and the air speed indicator tube, but the main spar held. The cable snapped instead of the wing, and it snapped before any of the affixed contact bombs hit the wing.

As the plane approached the target, a huge fireball erupted from the smoke and flames already filling the sky, caused by the delayed action bombs of the 93rd. *Calaban* dropped its bombs and flew clear. Watching from the rear, Hubert Womack, the tail gunner, saw a Liberator from another group bearing down on them. Two of its engines were on fire and it was angling downward from the right, apparently out of control. Womack struggled with his throat microphone to try to warn the pilot, but Dobson, the copilot in the right-hand seat, saw it in time to turn *Calaban* out of the way.

Then Womack spotted several German fighters, "at least a hundred fighters everywhere I looked and so many of our own ships behind us that I couldn't shoot at any fighters. Our own ships were being shot down behind us so fast that I didn't think we'd ever make it through."

Dobson added, "*Calaban* got away from Ploesti but the ship was all shot up." Their bomb bay doors were open, waving in the wind. The pilot took the plane down so low that it lopped off the tops of corn stalks, but he was more concerned about burning out the engines by going too fast. The barrage balloon cable had destroyed the air speed indicator, so he had no idea how fast they were going. He told Dobson to watch the engine RPMs and the manifold pressure. "Don't worry about the speed," Dobson answered. "Just drive it."

Years later Dobson recalled dryly that "the irony of driving a B-24 through cornfields took the edge off for the moment."

In the element following *Calaban*, Worden Weaver's plane, *Lil' Abner*, was not so lucky. (There was also a *Lil' Abner* in the 376th Bombardment Group.) The navigator, Walter Sorenson, recalled his thoughts as they flew toward Ploesti. He knew "this would be a day for the history books. If the raid was successful, it would be hailed as a brilliant idea. However, if unsuccessful, it could go down as one of the U.S. Air Force's biggest blunders."

Lil' Abner made it over the target and dropped its bomb load, but the ship had been riddled by ack-ack fire. Three engines were damaged and most of the flight controls destroyed. Barely able to stay airborne, Weaver realized he had no choice but to crash-land in a field some 40 miles from Ploesti.

The impact was so severe that the nose ended up beneath the fuselage. The top turret broke loose (as often occurred in crash landings), crushing to death William Scheltler, the flight engineer. Fire broke out behind the flight deck, trapping both pilots and the navigator in the cockpit. Six other crewmen fled from the rear of the ship before the flames spread.

Weaver managed to break through the windshield to try to escape, with Sorenson, the navigator, pressing close behind him. But Sorenson's parachute snagged on the shattered windshield, leaving him hanging halfway out of the plane and trapping the copilot, Robert Snyder. The fire was spreading forward and there was no other way out.

The bombardier, Lloyd Reese, had escaped from the rear but when he saw what was happening at the cockpit he plunged through the fire to cut Sorenson's parachute free so that he and Snyder could get out. Then, Sorenson recalled, he saw "a German fighter plane circling over our wrecked plane. I guess he was reporting our position. We all ran to a nearby farmhouse where some women treated our burns as best they could before enemy troops showed up and took us away."

Wing Dinger, flown by George Winger, was damaged so badly as it passed over the target area that it was knocked off course and forced to fly under cover of another ship. By the time Winger got the plane beyond the target, it was orange with flames from nose to tail. The fuel tanks in the bomb bay were afire and the flames were spreading rapidly. Winger had already flown 27 missions and was officially finished with combat, but when he learned how important the Ploesti raid was to the war effort, he volunteered to go one last time.

The two waist gunners jumped from the burning *Wing Dinger* and parachuted to safety. Bernard Trout, 17 years old, was so tired from not sleeping the night before the raid that he found some bushes for concealment and promptly fell asleep. He was *Wing Dinger's* only survivor.

John Harmonoski, a bombardier aboard another plane nearby, later said that he "saw Lieutenant Winger salute him just before he pulled his plane upwards." Winger must have known that he was not going to make it but he was trying to gain altitude to give his crew a chance to bail out.

Horse Fly dropped its bombs through the smoke and fire surrounding the target area and headed into the clear. The flight engineer, Leo Spann, recalled:

> We then went down on the deck as low as we could, as those picturesque haystacks opened up and then revealed their guns. And these guns started giving us hell! They shot out the number four engine and a shell exploded between the two waist gun positions, wounding both gunners in the legs.

Horse Fly collided with a balloon cable, snapping it, and the ship flew on, but by then it was on its own. With one engine dead, it could no longer keep up with the formation. German fighter planes pounced on the stricken plane.

> With the two waist gunners out, [the fighters] came in so close to us it seemed we could almost touch them. We figured that we had shot down four of them, and they finally left us, but the number four engine had frozen up and with a flat propeller, it caused a hell of a drag. The propeller would not feather.

The crew of *Sad Sack II* was in worse shape by the time they dropped their bombs. (There was also a *Sad Sack* in the 98th Bombardment Group.) Henry Lasco was the pilot; the copilot was Joe Kill, "for whom crew members erected a sign in the plane that read 'Kill, the Copilot.'" Kill had been sick with dysentery prior to the raid but found that his severe intestinal cramps miraculously disappeared as the plane made its final turn toward the target. "This proved to me," he joked later, "that one can be 'scared shitless.'"

Before *Sad Sack II* reached the target, however, Charles DeCrevel, a waist gunner, was wounded in the thigh. He strapped on his parachute, ready to bail out, but changed his mind when he realized they were flying level with the treetops rather than above them. Before they could drop their bombs, someone shouted over the intercom that the tail gunner had been killed. Then, as the bombardier yelled "bombs away," the navigator took a fatal hit in the chest. He managed to crawl to the rear of the plane before he collapsed. At the same time, the number two engine was crippled.

When the plane cleared the target area the antiaircraft gunners were waiting. This time they got the radio operator and the top turret gunner. DeCrevel, the wounded waist gunner, recalled that he "began to have grave doubts if anyone was alive on the flight deck. Wherever he looked he could see holes as big as his fist, and the left wing was almost scraping the ground. *Sad Sack II* was vibrating badly and extremely rough to handle."

As many as nine German fighters lined up to attack *Sad Sack II* from the rear. DeCrevel shot down the first one and Al Shaffer, the other waist gunner, scored a few hits even though one of his legs had been nearly torn off by an enemy shell. Lasco and Kill were having great trouble controlling the ship. *Sad Sack* was shaking to pieces. And if that was not enough, some of the ammunition on board had caught fire and was going off in all directions.

DeCrevel took a second hit. He said it felt like fingers were plucking at his clothes. "I received shrapnel wounds in the back, head and knee, and was floored by a 13-mm. in the butt. The parachute pack in that area saved me."

A German fighter circled the crippled B-24 and attacked head on. The American pilot remembered:

> We were very low to the ground, probably 50 feet, when an ME-109 circled around us and came in very shallow at ten o'clock on my side. I saw his wing light up and felt a tremendous sock on the jaw. I was shot through both cheeks and upper palate. I had no strength. I couldn't see anything.

Sad Sack II was dropping into a cornfield with Lasco sprawled over the control wheel. Kill, the copilot, was still desperately trying to lower the flaps by hand and level the ship by pushing hard on the right rudder pedal. In back, DeCrevel heard someone scream.

> The navigator was kneeling on the catwalk and holding on to the open door to the bomb bay. He looked like he had caught an 88 right in the chest. The flesh was stripped away and I could see the white ribs. I wanted to help him but there wasn't time. We were all dead, anyway.

The next thing DeCrevel remembered was the crash. "I tumbled head over heels in flame and tearing metal and hit the forward bulkhead with a sweet, black thud. [There was] no plane to speak of, just a pile of burning junk."

He hauled himself out of the wreckage and tried to run on his wounded leg. Something made him turn to look at the plane and he saw Shaffer trapped in the burning debris. He went back, pulled the gunner free, and dragged him 50 yards away from the plane.

Both pilots were trapped in the cockpit. Kill later recalled how Lasco, who had been shot in the face,

> was blindly thrashing around, pinned in his harness. All I could do was to tell him I couldn't get out. Both of my legs were broken and the right foot was out of the socket at the ankle. Lasco somehow got loose and unfastened my legs from a tangle of wires and cables. He grabbed me under the arms and dragged me through a hole in the side of the fuselage.

The four crewmen who survived *Sad Sack*'s mission to Ploesti, seriously wounded and in great pain, were left sitting in a cornfield in Romania awaiting help, or perhaps to be killed on the spot.

The rest of the 44th, 21 planes led by Lt. Col. James Posey, were on course for a refinery five miles south of Ploesti. Their portion of the mission was going flawlessly, just as they had practiced, rehearsed, and drilled back in Benghazi. They were the first over their target, so it was free of smoke and flames, but it quickly turned out not to be safe from antiaircraft fire.

The bulk of the formation roared over the target in four five-plane waves. Colonel Posey was the copilot for *V For Victory*, second from the left in the first wave. Its gunners kept up a steady fire as the ship pulled up to chimney height to drop its bombs. The unrelenting return fire from the ground was strong and accurate, and a shell that shattered a portion of the tail also killed one of the waist gunners.

After the first wave dropped its bombs, Posey led them back down, flying as low as they could get. "People ask me what I mean by low level," wrote David Alexander, pilot of *Flak Alley*, on Posey's left. "I point out that on the antenna on the bottom of my airplane I brought back sunflowers and something that looked suspiciously like grass."

Satan's Hellcat bombed its target even though one engine, hit by flak, was trailing smoke. The pilot, Rowland Houston, was able to keep up with the rest of the formation, but once they got beyond the target, they were hit by German fighters. Set ablaze, *Satan's Hellcat* began to fall, taking with it an enemy plane that had been flying beneath it. The two planes plummeted to the ground, exploding on impact. The German pilot, Wilhelm Steinman, was thrown clear, but all aboard *Satan's Hellcat* perished.

Avenger, flown by Bill Hughes and Willie Weant, had brought an extra passenger, as usual. Rusty, a cocker spaniel, belonged to Robert Peterson, the navigator. Rusty enjoyed flying and spent the journey to Ploesti asleep on the nose wheel doors, but once the action started, he took up his favorite post in the nose to bark at the flak exploding ahead of them. After dropping their bomb load on target, Avenger was pounced on by four German fighters. The American gunners quickly shot down three of them before they could inflict any serious damage.

Timb–A–A–AH, in the third wave over the target, also had a dog on board. Eightball, a black terrier, had been found in an airplane hangar in Ireland two months before. He crept under the pilot's seat when the firing started over Ploesti and remained there, apparently asleep, until the plane and its crew were safely home.

Earthquake McGoon was a barrel-chested wrestler in the popular comic strip "Li'l Abner." It was also the name of a B-24 in the second wave, flown by Walter Bunker and Dick Butler. As they passed over a large building with a red cross painted on the roof, the recognized symbol of a hospital, no one aboard noticed that an antiaircraft gun was also on the roof until it started firing at them. The plane took a hit in one wing, and another shell struck the fuselage near the bomb bay, destroying electrical and hydraulic lines.

After *Earthquake* dropped its bombs, a shell caught the number three engine. As Butler, the copilot, reached for the button to feather that engine, the ship snagged a steel cable from a barrage balloon. The cable snapped, but in the confusion, Butler pressed the control for the number four engine. With both engines suddenly gone, *Earthquake McGoon* tipped sharply to the right. Loy Neeper in the top turret "glanced sideways and watched the right wingtip barely clearing the cornstalks while the other wingtip pointed towards the clear blue sky." Bunker struggled to level the ship while Butler corrected his mistake. He unfeathered number four and feathered number three.

On the run to the target, Dale Lee, a waist gunner in *Southern Comfort*, saw on the ground "a German sergeant [who] had three rows of troops all lined up in formation. I just wanted to even the score for them having wiped out so many of my good buddies. In my anger and frustration I opened my 50-caliber guns and mowed right down their lines. At the time it seemed so justifiable and right."

As they got closer to the target, Lee saw something else, a sight that stayed with him for a long time. "An old lady stood right out in the middle of all this commotion. She was calmly pumping water into a bucket." After the plane passed over her,

Lee spotted some oxcarts in the middle of a cornfield. "Those poor oxen went berserk from all the noise and the excited farmers were in hot pursuit, trying to bring them under control."

Glen Hickerson, *Southern Comfort's* tail gunner, opened fire at a gun partially concealed in a haystack, but he did not notice, until it was too late, that several civilians were standing nearby. Everyone disappeared in a cloud of dust and smoke as his stream of bullets tore them apart.

Southern Comfort bombed its target but was seriously damaged in return. One shell knocked down a waist gunner. The impact sent the small incendiaries bouncing out of their box. The gunners picked them up as fast as they could, before they could catch fire. They tossed the explosives out the window, adding to the devastation on the ground. Another shell exploded beneath one wing. The plane pitched over on its side, with one wing high and the other about to scrape a furrow in the ground before the pilot brought it under control.

In the last wave of B-24s, *Old Crow*, piloted by James McAtee and Harold Lautig, flew over a B-24 that had crash-landed. Beyond it they saw an old shed. Suddenly the walls tumbled down to reveal an antiaircraft gun, but there was no one around to fire it. A German soldier appeared from across the field and raced toward it, but *Old Crow's* gunners were faster. They directed a withering fire at the man, raining bullets all around him. He fell to the ground, either wounded or pretending to be.

One of the waist gunners, Mack Morris, saw several civilians waving at the planes.

> I saw dogs, and I swear even some chicken running. In one picnic group the women even waved aprons. At one point a group of civilians were in an area between two gun

emplacements that were concealed in grain shocks. Suddenly some of them fell as our gunners swung from firing at one gun emplacement to the other.

Colonel Posey's group lost no planes over the target, and only two after the bombs were dropped, both casualties of enemy fighters. Compared with the groups that had already attacked the Ploesti refineries, Posey's men had the fewest losses and the greatest success. For them, the mission went much the way Colonel Smart had planned. The refinery that was their designated target was destroyed so completely that it could not be brought back into production for the rest of the war.

The 389th Bombardment Group, led by Col. Jack Wood, was assigned a target 18 miles northwest of Ploesti. When word of their target became known back in Benghazi, the men of the 389th took considerable kidding from the other groups about having such an easy mark, one far removed from the concentration of defenses in the Ploesti area.

The crews of the 389th were the freshest to arrive in England and had no combat experience prior to their departure for North Africa to prepare for the Ploesti raid. Because they were so green, they were out to prove that they could accomplish their task as well as their more battle-seasoned counterparts.

But as they approached the target, they were off to a shaky start. Colonel Wood, in *The Scorpion*, sat behind pilots Kenneth Caldwell and Otis Hamilton. Wood was acting as his own navigator. When *The Scorpion* crossed over a ridge and he spotted a valley seeming to lead in the direction of the target, he ordered Caldwell to turn right.

And as Caldwell executed the turn, all 28 ships in the flight behind him followed in synchrony, even though some of the other navigators immediately recognized that they were turning too soon. Colonel Wood had just repeated the mistake made earlier by Colonel Compton of the 376th. "Too soon!" shouted Stell Meador, Wood's navigator, into the intercom. "You're turning too early!" Navigators in other planes yelled the same warning to their pilots. Aboard the ship called *I-For-Item*, in the second wave, navigator Herbert Solomon told pilot Edward Fowble, "They've turned too soon. We are not in the right valley."

Although no one dared break radio silence to inform Colonel Wood of his mistake, Meador was soon able to convince him of the error. Wood then made a course correction to the left, leading the formation into almost a 180-degree turn, until they were back on their original heading for the town of Campina.

Once again they were approaching their refinery precisely as planned. The crews observed scenes of ordinary domestic life on the ground as they flew over—people having picnics, farmers in their fields, women waving, a little boy who tossed a stone in the air in their direction. As they neared the target, Wood led their descent to 30 feet, just as they had practiced over the desert. Now that they were on course, everything seemed as smooth as a practice run above the sand, except that this time people started shooting at them.

Maj. Philip Ardery, a command pilot occupying the copilot's seat in *I-For-Item* in the second wave, wrote:

> We found ourselves at that moment running a gauntlet of tracers and cannon fire of all types that made me despair of ever covering those last few hundred yards to the point where we could let the bombs go. The antiaircraft defens-

es were literally throwing up a curtain of steel. From the target grew the column of flames, smoke, and explosions, and we were headed straight into it.

In the first wave, Colonel Wood in *The Scorpion* spied the gun emplacements firing at them. As they roared toward the refinery assigned to them, Wood's ship dropped its four 1,000-pound bombs squarely on the boiler house, which exploded in a mixture of scalding steam and flaming gases. *I-For-Item* flew past with no casualties or major damage.

Chattanooga Choo Choo, flown by Robert O'Reilly, was also in the first wave. Up front in the nose, navigator Richard Britt grabbed the 50-caliber machine gun and fired into the trees. "We were on target," Britt wrote. "The noise was deafening with the bursting of the antiaircraft shells, machine gun fire and the *carumping* of some of the bombs. Thick black smoke was rising in tall columns of brilliant yellow-red colors of burning oil."

Britt watched in fascination as the bombs dropped from the plane beside his. He followed one as it broke through high-voltage wires, setting off sparks, leaving a 15-foot gap in the side wall of a brick building. He felt his plane lurch as the bombs fell and then jolt as it sustained several hits from ground fire. Control cables snapped and one engine was damaged, forcing the right wing toward the ground.

The pilot yelled through the intercom for the crew to prepare for a crash. At almost the same instant, someone else shouted that there was still a bomb aboard. Alfred Romano, the bombardier, rushed to the bomb bay to try to break it loose. If they crash-landed with it still on board, no one would get out alive.

Britt tore his navigation charts and maps into tiny pieces and tossed them out through the slits around the nose wheel door.

He made his way to the bomb bay to help and saw Romano and Frank Kees, the top turret gunner, perched on the narrow catwalk, working to pry the bomb loose with a screwdriver. Finally, it dropped through the open bomb bay door. Britt remembered:

> Roof tops and trees were blurring below us. Our speed was still 220 miles per hour. People were scurrying to get away from this huge monster dropping destruction on them. You could almost touch the houses. One had a porch swing like the one on my grandmother's front porch in Illinois.

Britt scrambled up to the flight deck as fast as he could, with Romano right behind him. Kees remained on the catwalk in the middle of the open bomb bay doors, fascinated by the sight of the trees and houses appearing to whiz by beneath his feet. Britt said, "Looking down at the housetops below, he knew he couldn't jump. He looked at us, then down below, and finally started to climb."

Chattanooga Choo Choo plunged toward a dry river bed. "The next few seconds seemed to last for hours," Britt wrote.

> The terrible crunching, grinding, scraping and buckling of metal against metal was deafening as we slid along the ground. It seemed we would never stop. I was braced between the radio desk and the wall between the flight deck and the bomb bay. Two pieces of metal began to squeeze my head in a vice-tight grip. Tighter and tighter they pressed as I slipped into darkness. For one brief moment, a mental picture of my father flashed before me. I felt no pain, just a numb feeling of weightlessness, making me giddy. "This isn't such a bad way to die," I thought.

By the time the second wave of the 389th Bombardment Group approached the target, the burning refinery was shooting up huge columns of flame higher than the planes. The ships bore into the inferno with bomb bay doors open and bombardiers zeroing in on their portion of the target. Just before *I-For-Item* plunged into the smoke, Philip Ardery glanced to his right at *Eager Eagle*, piloted by Lloyd H. "Pete" Hughes.

Gasoline was pouring from *Eager Eagle's* left wing in a stream so thick that no one in neighboring planes could see the waist gunners in their open windows. "Poor Pete!" Ardery thought. "Fine, religious, conscientious boy with a young wife waiting for him back in Texas."

> Hughes kept his place in the formation, aware that by staying on that flight path he would fly directly into the flames with all that raw fuel drenching his ship. He had only a few seconds to make a decision: try to save himself and his crew by pulling up and riding above the flames or stay steady on course to bomb the target. He flew straight ahead.
>
> A moment later we were in the inferno, dropping our bombs, Hughes along with the rest of us. Next I remember heat coming up into our bomb bay as the flames enveloped us.
>
> Emerging from the flames, I looked again at Hughes' aircraft. It was now a huge, flying torch. Hughes apparently cut the throttles to attempt a crash landing. For a moment, it seemed as though he might make it. He was headed toward a stream bed on our right. Then, just as the flaming B-24 was about to touch down, the whole left wing came off and a big ball of fire appeared where the aircraft had been.

The only survivors were two of the gunners.*

When *Scheherazade* approached the refinery in the second wave, Milton Nelson, the bombardier, told John Blackis, the pilot, that the bomb bay doors were stuck. The extra fuel tanks in the bomb bay had jammed them shut. Blackis ordered the flight engineer, Joseph Landry, to climb down into the bomb bay and pry open the doors, but they would not budge. Blackis made his decision quickly: if the doors would not open, then *Scheherazade* would drop the bombs right through them. The bombs struck their target. The damaged doors trailed low beneath the plane, snagging cornstalks and other debris, but the ship was fine. While Landry was at work in the bomb bay, David Rosenthal, the radioman, climbed in the top turret and shot down an ME-109. He had never fired the guns before.

For a variety of reasons, a few of the planes in the bombardment group had not been given names; one was 42-406-19-N. The tail gunner, George Fulton, habitually got airsick every time they practiced low-level flying in North Africa. Sure enough, he got sick again on the long flight to Romania. Another gunner, Brandon Healy, volunteered to take his place in the tail until they got close to the target. Fulton threw up in the bomb bay and settled down to sleep. He slept soundly throughout the raid and did not wake up until his plane was on its way home.

Aboard *Sandwitch*, in the fourth wave, no one fell asleep. A gunner one plane over, in *The Little Gramper*, saw what happened. Some crewmen from *Sandwitch* were waving at him when an antiaircraft shell struck the bomb bay fuel tank. In an

*Six months after the raid, in February 1944, Hughes was approved for a Medal of Honor.

instant, gas poured out of *Sandwitch* and the plane caught on fire. The pilot, Robert Horton, took the plane up to bombing altitude and dropped their bomb load squarely on the target, but *Sandwitch* was finished. It took several more hits. The gunner watching from *The Little Gramper* said, "It was a horrible sight watching the burning plane and knowing that the men in there were fighting for their lives and there was nothing we could do to help."

One of *Sandwitch*'s wings hit a tree and broke off. The fuselage plowed on through the woods and disintegrated into several flaming pieces. The top turret was thrown clear; the gunner, Zerril Steen, although badly burned, managed to crawl to safety.

Vagabond King, in the last wave of the 389th, became the last plane to bomb Ploesti. By the time it reached the target, all of the German guns were trained on it. The flames and smoke from the burning refinery were so thick that the crew could hardly see anything. John McCormick, the pilot, remembered, "Tracers, red, white, streaming up at the boys ahead and hitting them too. Then our cockpit exploded with sparks, noise and concussion. Tracers spat over my head. Wham! More bullets through the cockpit. The emergency windows blew open, giving us a 225 mph blast of air in the cockpit."

They dropped their bombs and McCormick brought *Vagabond King* as close to the ground as he dared and raced away from the burning refinery. Three minutes later, he said, "the boys told me we had been hit pretty hard, that Van [Martin Van Buren, the radioman] was bleeding badly. An antiaircraft shell had hit as he was turning on the automatic camera. [Paul] Miller, in the tail turret, called to say that the bombs we dropped had exploded, and our target was burning fiercely."

The crewmen of the 389th had done their job well. Four of the 29 planes in the group were shot down in the raid, but their bombs inflicted such extensive damage that the refinery did not resume production until after the war was over.

As the planes set course for Benghazi, "The sky was a bedlam of bombers flying in all directions," remembered Philip Ardery.

> Some [of them were] actually on fire, many with smoking engines, some with great gaping holes in them or huge chunks of wing or rudder gone. Many were so riddled it was obvious their insides must have presented starkly tragic pictures of dead and dying, of men grievously wounded who would bleed to death before they could be brought any aid; pilots facing the horrible decision about what to do, whether to make a quick sacrifice of the unhurt in order to save the life of a dying man, or to fly a ship home and let some crew member pay with his life for the freedom to the rest.

The mission to Ploesti was over. Now began the mission to survive.

Part IV
THE RETURN

A B-24 returning home from Operation Tidal Wave is destroyed by German fighter aircraft based in Crete. (*U.S. Air Force*)

10

A WING AND A PRAYER

T HE PLANES WERE STRUNG out for a hundred miles to the south of Ploesti like a great flock of wounded birds. Some were dying on the ground, others afire, others struggling on three engines and some with only two, desperate to remain airborne for another fifty miles, or ten, or even one. There were wounded aboard many of the ships and no medical aid beyond a tight compress or tourniquet and a quick, merciful stab of morphine to dull the pain.

Their fate was uncertain. They could die before reaching Benghazi. The plane could run out of fuel. The engines could stop turning. German fighters, Bulgarian fighters, Italian fighters might pounce at any moment.

Some planes flew on alone. Others had another B-24 or two along for moral and physical support, the greater combined firepower protection against fighters. The truly lucky ones were flying in formation with eight or ten others. But none of the crewmen knew whether they would make it home safely, or spin out of control and crash or dive into the sea. Or ditch somewhere in Turkey to be interned, or be carried to a safe haven such as Malta or Cyprus that offered medical help and fuel and repairs.

Regardless of what they told themselves, what hopeful view they chose to put on their situation, they still had hundreds of miles and hours to go before their mission to Ploesti was over. But in their memories—the sight of friends bailing out, of chutes failing to open, of bombers turned into flaming coffins, the sight of a buddy waving from the cockpit before disappearing in a ball of flame—the mission would never end. It would lodge in their consciousness for as long as they lived, be it another 15 minutes or some 70 years.

Daisy Mae was one of the planes heading home that day. Its pilot, Lewis Ellis, recalled:

> Quickly we looked around to assess the damage. Number three engine had been hit and was smoking. The nose wheel was knocked out. The hydraulic system was inoperative, fluid pouring into the bomb bay. The top turret was out, and one gun in the tail turret was inoperative. Flak holes were all over the fuselage and several were in the wings and engine nacelles. But we were still flying and no one was badly injured. Our chances looked pretty good.

Daisy Mae's crew spotted wrecked B-24s still burning on the ground. Ellis watched one damaged plane nearby try to climb, then go into a stall and plummet; at the same time he saw another crash-land in a field and a German fighter go down in flames. He was "amazed at the capacity of my subconscious to record so many details at a glance."

And as all this destruction registered, he was keeping *Daisy Mae* in tight formation with the others, as close as possible while scanning the skies for German fighters, searching for obstacles ahead, and skimming so low to the ground that the plane cut "corn, wheat, and sunflowers with the propellers."

The navigator warned over the intercom that one of the planes in their small formation had lost an engine and turned off course. He identified it as *Hail Columbia*, Killer Kane's ship. There was nothing anyone could do to help him. Ellis flew on, at 175 miles per hour, and the farther they got from Ploesti, the more ordinary sights he noticed on the ground.

> We buzzed over small villages and, invariably, people waved. We passed so close over a 2-wheeled hay wagon that three girls in brightly colored skirts jumped off, but nevertheless they smiled and waved. I wondered if they knew who we were. A farmer plowing in a cornfield saw us coming and left his horse and plow and lay flat between the rows, obviously frightened. He didn't wave.

Daisy Mae, and the other ships whose pilots thought there was a chance of getting back to Benghazi, were heading over Bulgaria and Greece, hoping to reach the Mediterranean Sea. They had the option of landing in Malta but would prefer to go all the way back to North Africa.

Crews who were less optimistic, whose planes had suffered greater damage, had less fuel and wounded men aboard, flew toward Turkey or to British-controlled Cyprus beyond. At least half the planes had sustained serious damage, many were low on ammunition, and all faced the mountains they had crossed on their way to Ploesti, to get over one more time, even with only two or three engines running.

And there were the fighter planes to contend with, first Bulgarians and then Germans. One formation of eight Liberators had climbed to 5,000 feet south of Sofia, Bulgaria, when they saw fighters. An American top turret gunner thought they were Italian planes. They made a few ineffectual attacks on the Americans and flew off, having inflicted no damage.

The B-24s were set on by biplanes that looked like relics of the last war, though in fact they had been built only 10 years before. These Czech-made Avia B-534-IVs were flown by Bulgarian pilots. They had been superior planes in their day, but with fixed landing gear, maximum top speed of 245 miles per hour, and four 7.7-mm machine guns, they were easily outclassed by the B-24s.

That did not stop the daring Bulgarian pilots from attacking. They swooped down on the disabled formation, guns blazing, but caused little harm because of their light armament. The Liberators' heavier guns inflicted far greater damage and shot down several of the biplanes. The Bulgarian pilots appeared eager to try their luck again, but their planes could not gain altitude fast enough to catch up to the Americans. A second group of Avias attacked, but they, too, could not get into position for a second strike.

Four other Bulgarian pilots, led by 30-year-old German-trained Lt. Stoyan Stoyanov, were flying ME-109s. Stoyanov's first pass met with withering return fire, causing him to miss completely. "It was so terrible," he recalled, "that I didn't have time to get scared."

After he pulled out of range, Stoyanov began to have second thoughts about attacking the planes he described as big fat birds. "I felt my heart starting to beat strongly, some cold sweat appeared on my face. My wish to attack was now becoming less eager. I felt that I had not sufficient strength inside me." Nevertheless, Stoyanov swallowed his fear and decided to attack head on. He swung around in a half circle and with the sun behind him roared in toward the lead bomber with his guns blazing. In a passage from a book written after the war, Stoyanov's son translated his father's account of his experiences.

I press triggers and watch how my gunshots are making fire traces and sink in the glass nose of the heavy bomber. From that end comes a reverse fire. This moment is like a wonderful play: I throw fire balls to the nose of the big plane which is approaching me and the same fire balls immediately come back on me. Some of them pass very close to my plane, but still do not touch it. This play last-. ed for a few seconds only and in some more seconds the winner will be known. The tension of my nerves is extremely high now.

The two planes approached at well over 400 miles an hour. Lieutenant Stoyanov's shells and bullets shattered the nose of the B-24. The bomber turned downward and Stoyanov passed overhead with a clearance of only 15 feet. The fighter issued a stream of bullets, tearing the larger plane open from one end to the other. Stoyanov's target was identified as *The Witch*, from the 98th Bombardment Group. Its pilot managed to crash land in a field; all the crew survived.

A fighter flown by Bulgarian pilot Petre Bochev shot down *Prince Charming* from the 389th. Only its tail gunner survived the flaming crash.

Daisy Mae and the other eight planes in its formation reached the southern tip of Corfu when they saw 15 ME-109s at three o'clock. "We either had to shoot them down," said the pilot, Lewis Ellis, "be shot down ourselves, or wait for them to run out of gas."

The American gunners fired first and hit two of the fighters, both of which exploded. But one B-24 was hit by the German pilots, setting the ship on fire; its crew was seen to bail out. Another Liberator went down, and a Messerschmitt, and then it was *Daisy Mae's* turn. Fighters zeroed in from all directions, wounding one crewman. They knocked out all the guns except the two waist positions. The crew rushed to shift ammo from the other guns to the waist.

A fighter roared in from behind. With the rear turret out of commission, the pilot could take the time to aim carefully. He sent a 20-mm shell into the left rudder, another into the flat tail surface, and two more into the fuselage, leaving Guido Gioana, the bombardier, with 35 shrapnel wounds. The shells cut the control cables and *Daisy Mae* slipped into a shallow dive to the left, out of control, drifting far away from the other bombers.

"Let's move back into the formation," warned the copilot, Calliste Foger, not yet aware that *Daisy Mae* was out of control.

"Can't do it," Ellis told him. "The controls are gone."

The German fighter broke off, low in gas, but *Daisy Mae*, down to 500 feet, was in danger of crashing. Ellis was trying everything to regain control but nothing worked until he switched on the automatic pilot. He was able to climb to 11,000 feet and level off, staying beneath the other B-24s in case more enemy fighters showed up. He wrote:

> The trip home was one of sweating out the gas. [Flight engineer] Sergeant Dillman figured we had enough to last until 7:00 PM. Lieutenant Klinkbeil [the navigator] said we would never make it by then. So we decided to stretch it as far as possible. We threw all the guns except two overboard and most of the ammunition and everything else we figured we wouldn't need if we were forced to ditch.

They cut back the engine rpms and prayed.

Utah Man was in big trouble, seriously damaged with two bombs still aboard. Crewmen clinging to the narrow catwalk in

the bomb bay worked frantically, using screwdrivers to try to
pry the bombs free of their slings. They had to be careful that
both the front and rear slings released at the same instant. If
they did not, then the bombs could get stuck in the racks, nose
first or tail first, and it would be impossible to dislodge them
while the plane was still airborne. And until the bombs were
gone, pilot Walter Stewart could not even think of setting the
crippled ship down. They would all be killed.

Finally both bombs fell free and Stewart began searching for
a place to land, in case his number three engine got worse. *Utah
Man* had been flying alone since shortly after leaving the target
area, but now Stewart spied a formation of nine other
Liberators. The crew was relieved to have company. One of the
bombers was Stewart's old plane, whose pilot was a close friend.

Stewart's gratitude at no longer being alone did not last long,
however, because he could not maintain sufficient speed to keep
up with the others. "Every time *Utah Man*'s speed approached
130 she would vibrate and shake like an old washing machine.
Sadly, Stewart watched his friend pull away."

Utah Man plowed on, but when Stewart crossed the coast of
Greece he asked the flight engineer, John Connelly, how much
fuel was left. Connelly said that one engine had no fuel and the
other three were "very low." Stewart demanded a precise
account. Was it enough to cross the Mediterranean? But the
fuel gauges had been badly damaged; it was impossible to get
exact readings. "Skipper," Connelly said finally, "I've never been
so out of gas, either in the air on the ground."

Stewart polled the crew. What did they want to do? Should
they try to make it home, knowing they might have to ditch in
the open sea if they ran out of gas or developed more mechanical problems? They knew that in open water, B-24s tended to

break apart and sink fast, sometimes before the crew could get out.

Before anyone could answer Stewart's question, Richard Bartlett, a waist gunner, spoke up. Before they all voted on a course of action, Bartlett said, he wanted to make a speech. "You call this an ocean?" he said, referring to the Mediterranean. "We got rivers in Montana wider than this. Let's go! Our skipper can set this thing down in the middle of the Med just like a kitten."

There was nothing more to be said. *Utah Man* headed for home. After some time flying alone over the sea, Stewart asked Harold Steiner, the radioman, to hang out the antenna wire to see if they could pick up some music from "Command Performance," the British armed forces program. They tuned in just in time to hear a popular song that seemed tailor-made for them at that moment. It was Dinah Shore singing "Coming in On a Wing and a Prayer."

Liberty Lad of the 93rd was also in bad shape. Its pilot, Kenton McFarland, faced a similar choice for himself and his crew: try to make it across the Mediterranean or bail out over land and risk capture by the Germans, assuming they survived the jump.

Their number three engine had been hit and was likely to freeze at any moment. Numbers one and two, on the left side, could not get any fuel transferred to them from the bomb bay tanks. When the gas tanks in the wing went dry, they would stop. McFarland decided he did not want to become a prisoner of war. He would try for North Africa, as near as his engines would take them. At least they were not alone.

Out over open water, the fuel for the number one engine ran out. McFarland and his copilot, Henry Podgurski, pressed hard on the left rudder pedals to keep *Liberty Lad* from skewing to the right. With that engine out completely, and number three still running rough, they quickly lost speed and altitude and could no longer keep up with the other planes.

About 15 minutes later, the number two engine stopped. The pilots pushed on the left rudder pedals with all their strength. They were at least 500 miles from Benghazi and now flying alone on one-and-a-half engines. McFarland ordered the crew to toss everything out of the ship that was not necessary, including the guns and ammunition, so he would have a better chance of keeping the ship in the air.

Liberty Lad limped on, trailing everything that was expendable behind it. The men had unclamped and disconnected every object they could and used fire axes to hack off everything else. But even with so much weight removed the ship dropped 10,000 feet to an altitude of only 5,000 feet, still high enough to bail out—if they had time.

McFarland exerted his full weight on the rudder pedal so forcefully that the back of his seat broke. Two crewmen propped themselves behind him, their backs against his, so he could keep the pressure on the pedal. The strain on him was so intense that the crewmen took turns crawling up front to massage McFarland's aching legs.

Little Lady was also hard to control, low on fuel with one engine out. Pilot Ralph Wilkinson and copilot Edwin Baker had trouble keeping the plane in the air. Every time they tried to climb, the speed dropped so much that the ship started vibrating and came perilously close to stalling. They could not reach an altitude higher than 1,500 feet, and they knew they were facing a 6,000-foot mountain range. If they could not cross the mountains, then they stood no chance of getting home.

Wilkinson spotted a valley up ahead. Since they could not climb, perhaps they could find an opening through the mountains. But as he explored the valley, he found that it did not provide a straight passage. It was like a maze with too many choice points, splitting in two or three directions at once. Wilkinson had to make split-second decisions about which way to turn, without the benefit of a map or any other indicator. Copilot Baker called it "the greatest game of chance in our lives," one played at a speed of approximately 140 miles per hour.

Eventually *Little Lady* made it through the mountains, based on not much more than luck and good guesses. But now they had no idea where they were. The navigator, Kenneth Herbert, was asked for a new course heading. He responded, "Hell, I don't know where we are with all that zigzagging through the mountains. Give me a couple of minutes to find something to orientate us."

Little Lady had just enough fuel to stay airborne for another hour. Then they would be forced to land. Herbert told the pilots there was only one airfield they might be able to reach. It was in Turkey.

Maternity Ward of the 98th was also trying to get as close to the North African coast as possible. One engine was out and the nose of the plane had been shot full of holes, so it was forced to fly at greatly reduced speed. By the time they left Greece and headed out toward open water, pilot John Ward and copilot Andrew Anderson had joined up with *Cornhusker*, another crippled ship.

Both planes were trailing by about five miles a formation of nine other B-24 survivors of the Ploesti mission. The leader of that group radioed the two stragglers that they would slow down to let *Maternity Ward* and *Cornhusker* catch up. Before the two could do that, however, they were attacked by a flight of eight German fighter planes. They rapidly shot down *Cornhusker* and closed in on *Maternity Ward*.

The plane did not have a chance. First the tail gunner, Robert Long, was hit as shells and bullets tore apart his guns and ripped through the plane all the way to the nose. The tail assembly was shattered and control cables severed. Fire broke out in one of the bomb bay gas tanks. The radioman, Leon Pemberton, and Anderson, the copilot, were also hit and the plane rolled over in a dive.

Ward sounded the alarm bell to abandon ship. The fires were spreading and *Maternity Ward* was rapidly losing altitude. He managed to pull out of the steep dive but the plane was already down to 3,000 feet and dropping at least 500 feet per minute. Ward moved out of the cockpit, intending to make sure the others were bailing out, but found that Pemberton's parachute was worthless, riddled by bullets, and the tail gunner was too badly wounded to jump.

He returned to the cockpit and, with Anderson's help, leveled the ship so it would hit the water at the smallest possible angle, to give the crew the best chance of getting out alive. When the plane struck the water, the nose broke off and the pilot, who had neglected to fasten his seat belt, was thrown into the sea and knocked unconscious. When he regained his senses, he surfaced just in time to see his airplane sink into the sea.

Copilot Anderson was trapped in the cockpit. He floundered underwater, attempting to save the wounded tail gunner who had braced for the crash by wedging himself behind the pilots' seats. The top turret had collapsed, trapping him. Anderson clambered through the opening where the nose had been and surfaced in the middle of a pool of burning gasoline.

He dove back underwater, swam clear of the flames, and met up with Ward about 50 feet away.

They were the only survivors. The life raft, which Anderson had managed to inflate before the crash, floated past and they hauled themselves aboard. Then there was nothing they could do but drift with the current and hope the British Air-Sea Rescue Service would find them soon. They had little idea of their location, somewhere between Italy and Greece. They had no water and little food. Their matches and flares were wet. There were no paddles on the raft and nothing to rig a sail with. Ward and Anderson spent 15 days in that condition, aboard the tiny rubber raft, freezing at night, baking in the blinding sun during the day.

One ship came so close on their third night at sea that the two men could hear voices from the deck, but no one saw them or heard their cries for help. Or if they did, then they deliberately ignored them.

On the eighth day, while they were having delirious visions of food, an injured albatross landed in the raft and hopped on Anderson's shoulder. Ward tried to grab for the bird, but Anderson said he did not think he could eat it. He said he felt "sorry for the bedraggled thing with the scared eyes." He cradled it for a short while then set it free. Ward was not happy to let any source of food get away but he was too weak to prevent it.

On the twelfth day, they were spotted by two British fighter planes, which signaled that they were sending help. And as promised, at dawn the next day, a fast-moving boat came in sight. But its crew never saw the life raft despite their shouts and waves.

On the fifteenth day, truly more dead than alive, Ward and Anderson landed on a tiny island and struggled ashore. As they lay on the beach they heard an unbelievable sound: singing! They rose to their knees in disbelief as a boatload of Italian soldiers landed, came over and picked them up, then gently laid them in their boat. After rowing to a nearby sheltered harbor, they carried Anderson and Ward to a building near an old castle and gave them food and water. The two men were put in beds and a doctor came to tend to their wounds. They became prisoners of the Germans, but they would survive the war.

For those waiting in Benghazi to hear about the raid, it was a long, hot, tense afternoon. For an ordinary mission, General Brereton would have been in constant radio contact with the mission leaders to follow the progress as the operation unfolded. But this was no ordinary mission. The strict radio silence, designed to prevent the Germans from learning that the bombers were coming and the route they were taking on their return, meant that Brereton had to sweat it out in the absence of any first-hand information.

Although no messages were received in Benghazi from General Ent, the mission commander, there was considerable radio traffic to them from the RAF, and it was all bad news. The British were relaying distress messages and SOS calls from an alarming number of B-24s. To judge by the many messages received, it was clear that a lot of planes were in trouble, a disturbing indicator of the possible outcome of the mission.

Outside the small building that housed the radio equipment, Gerald Geerlings, the architect who had prepared the drawings, maps, and models of the target, was trying to concentrate on pitching horseshoes. Several other men had joined his game, though none of them could really focus on it. One was Ted Timberlake, for whom the 93rd, Ted's Traveling Circus, had been named before he had been assigned to the planning staff for Ploesti. With them was Col. Jacob Smart, who had proposed the idea of a low-level attack on the refineries. He and Brereton had expected to be flying with the B-24 crews until Hap Arnold grounded them the day before. Now they could only join the many men waiting for some word.

General Brereton was inside the radio shack listening to the increasing number of distress calls passed on by the RAF. Finally, a full six hours before the ships were due to return to their bases in North Africa, Brereton received a two-word message from General Ent: "Mission successful."

At first there were cheers all around and an enormous feeling of relief, but it didn't last long. As one historian described the mood,

> A feeble attempt was made to play gin rummy and chess in the officers' club, but everyone realized that the message was, in itself, ambiguous and possibly in error. Furthermore there was the matter of survivors. How many fliers would get back? How many had already been drowned? Where and when would the remainder land, especially the crippled planes?

And how long would they have to wait before they learned what "Mission successful" really meant, and what the ultimate cost would be?

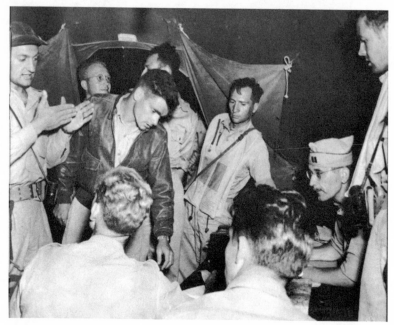

A weary survivor enters the debriefing tent. The airman on the left is describing a fighter attack. (*U. S. Air Force*)

11

THE LAST PLANE BACK

Hadley's Harem joined up with four other crippled planes including Killer Kane's *Hail Columbia*. Gib Hadley gently nursed his ship over a 6,000-foot mountain range, but his situation became critical once they descended on the south side of the mountains and reached the Aegean Sea. The five-plane formation's destination was Cyprus, which offered a short but serviceable runway and the chance to make repairs and take on fuel.

Just as they reached the coastline, *Hadley's Harem* lost another engine. They were now down to two and maintaining a speed of no more than 125 miles per hour. The other ships pulled ahead of them. This alarmed Colonel Kane, who had befriended the brash young pilot of the *Harem*. "Hadley called me," Kane wrote later, "and said he had lost another engine and was going to land on the coast. I called him repeatedly but could not get an answer. Our transmitter could not be repaired. We could only sit there praying that they would make it all right."

The supercharger on Hadley's number four engine caught fire and, no more than 20 miles from the Turkish coast, the number one engine began leaking oil. Within minutes the level on the oil gauge fell to empty. Both engines were in danger of freezing at any moment. Hadley switched on the intercom and briefed his crew on their situation. "Do you want to bail out or try to stick with the ship?" he asked. "Let's stick with her," they agreed.

Turkey's coastline was in sight but the *Harem* was losing altitude fast. The two remaining engines were barely turning over. The four other ships in their formation were now at least two miles ahead. The crewmen removed their shoes, standard preparation for ditching in the water. They were skimming the waves, too low to bail out or try for a landing on the beach, less than a mile away.

William Leonard, the radioman, broadcast their position for as long as he could. The flight engineer, Russell Page, perched behind the pilots on the flight deck, reached up and opened the top escape hatch. He braced himself against the armor plating behind the pilot's seat and waited.

Both engines stopped at the same instant; *Hadley's Harem* crashed into the sea. The crew described the shock as "paralyzing." Several of them were knocked unconscious. Page recalled that he "bounced back and forth like a spring." Water poured in through every flak hole and the open nose, slamming the escape hatch shut. The men of *Hadley's Harem* were trapped inside.

"My God," Sergeant Page thought, "am I going to die this way?" He tried to break through the escape hatch but it would not budge. He saw Gib Hadley and copilot James Lindsay unstrap their seat belts and flail around in the rushing water on the flight deck, searching for a way out. They also tried the top escape hatch but without success.

That was the last Page saw of them. As the plane filled with water, he was losing consciousness fast. He stuck his head up into the top gun turret, which still contained a small pocket of air. He inhaled as deeply as he could and dove underwater again. He made his way toward the rear of the plane where the tail had broken off in the crash. He swam free just as *Hadley's Harem* sank, taking both pilots and the body of the navigator, Leon Storm, who had been killed by the first bust of flak over the target.

When Page got to the beach he met up with Harold Tabacoff, the wounded bombardier, waist gunner Leroy Newton, who had a broken leg, and five other crewmen all with bruises, cuts, and broken bones. As they dragged themselves onto the sand and became aware of their surroundings, they saw 15 ragged but fierce Turkish men gesturing with ancient rifles for the Americans to kneel.

The Turks searched each man and confiscated flashlights and anything else that could be used as a weapon. They turned out to be friendlier than they had first appeared, but they spoke no English. They had no food and could do nothing to treat the injured, two of whom passed out from their pain. They did build a fire to try to keep the Americans warm through the night.

The following day a British air-sea rescue boat arrived with morphine, first aid equipment, and a translator. They moved on to a village some four miles inland where a local doctor treated the wounded as best he could. The villagers were kind and cooked fried eggs and beans for the men, their first meal since the previous morning.

The village elders were reluctant to release the American captives to the British but finally agreed. As they were ready to leave, a Turkish man who spoke English told the flyers, "We hear it was a big raid. Congratulations. It was a good job. Your enemies are also ours."*

Hadley's Harem was not the only plane to finish the Ploesti mission in Turkey. Some 78 U.S. airmen were interned there. *Little Lady* was forced to zigzag through the mountains because it could not climb high enough to scale them and made its way to a small airfield in Turkey, which had been built for fighter planes. None of the runways looked long enough to handle a B-24, but the pilots, Edwin Baker and Ralph Wilkinson, had no choice. They did not have enough fuel to go elsewhere.

"I told 'Wilkie' we had only one chance to make it," Baker wrote later. "There would be no going around. We had no electrical power for lowering the gear and flaps. I went to work hand-pumping our landing gear down." Baker finally lowered the wheels but he did not know if they had locked in place. If not, they would collapse as soon as *Little Lady* touched down.

Quickly Baker pumped the flaps down. The airspeed dropped, and Wilkinson pushed the throttles to the three remaining engines all the way forward. *Little Lady* was "coming in too steep and too fast," Baker said. "I grabbed the wheel and we both pulled with all our strength back, back as far as the column would go and tight against our chests, literally standing on the rudder pedals."

The ship came down on the nose wheel first. The main wheels hit with such force that the plane bounced high before dropping hard and settling onto the runway. The landing gear held but the brakes were gone; the hydraulic lines had been severed. Baker flicked off all the switches as fast as he could when

*They departed by boat from the same beach to which one of them, Leroy Newton, *Hadley's Harem's* waist gunner, would return 31 years later to find his plane and the bodies of Gib Hadley and James Lindsay.

they neared the end of the runway. They rolled onto a dirt field and up a slight incline, grinding to a halt in a shower of dirt, dust, and fumes from broken fuel lines.

Baker shouted for everyone to get out before the plane caught fire and exploded, then he pitched himself head first through the cockpit's side window. The crew scurried out and raced for safety at the top of the rise. They collapsed, exhausted, staring at their airplane, which did not catch fire or blow up. *Little Lady* had brought them through the hell of Ploesti and kept them alive. Baker sat transfixed, overwhelmed at how the B-24 had kept flying through all the flak, loss of an engine, and the roughest landing he had ever made. Later he wrote,

> As the dust settled I could see the holes in her. It was unbelievable. She looked like a sieve, yet not a man on board was even scratched. The landing gear cracked and slowly lowered the belly of the ship to the ground as the left wing buckled at the fuselage and sagged until its wing tip dug into the soft earth.
>
> *Little Lady* was dying and never would fly again. I almost expected her to make the final flutter of her wings. I started to choke up and shake inside not knowing whether it was finally realizing I was still alive, or that I was seeing an airplane that we had cared for and babied through all these months slowly die.

The crew of *Flossie Flirt* of the 44th Bombardment Group was also lucky to reach Turkey. The pilots, Charles Hughes and Sylvester Hunn, brought the ship in nose high because it had no brakes. They hoped to stop by letting the tail drag along the concrete runway. It seemed to be working. *Flossie Flirt* slowed, but then the runway collapsed under the plane's weight.

A B-24 with no name, Army designation 42-40744-S, flown by Harold James and Harold Schellinger, maintained formation with another damaged Liberator, *Hitler's Hearse*. Neither would be able to make it beyond Turkey. They were further encouraged to land when two American-built P-40s from Turkey's air force drew alongside and lowered their landing gear, the universal signal to land or be shot down.

The Americans knew that if the Turkish pilots were any good, the B-24s would not stand a chance in their condition. And so they lowered their wheels and hunted for a place to land. James brought his plane down at a fighter base, although the runway was too short for a four-engine bomber. The landing was rough and the brakes burned out in his effort to bring the plane to a halt.

When James and his crew emerged, they were surrounded by Turkish troops with fixed bayonets. An officer greeted them in a seemingly friendly manner then wheeled around and struck one of his own soldiers so hard he fell down. Other officers arrived. They rummaged through the plane as though they had never seen a big American bomber before. According to one recollection, they went "berserk with curiosity. They pulled the rip cords on the parachutes, emptied the first-aid kits, and unrolled the bandages."

Hitler's Hearse came down in a wheat field. The copilot, James Gerrits, landed it; the pilot, Robert Mooney, had been killed in the raid. Several crew members were wounded and needed medical assistance. As the ship landed, one of the P-40s tried to land nearby but ended up in a ditch, damaged beyond repair. The pilot survived but was court-martialed and imprisoned for 20 years for destroying government property.

The following day, the Turkish government arranged for the burial with full military honors for Captain Mooney of *Hitler's Hearse*, much to the dismay of the German ambassador. Mooney's crew, and the men of the ship that had flown with them, marched behind the coffin. It was borne on an artillery caisson covered by an American flag. When the graveside ceremony ended, an honor guard of Turkish soldiers fired a three-volley salute. It was as fine a memorial service as could be hoped for so far from home, and in a nation in which the survivors were to be interned.

Germany's ambassador to Turkey, Franz von Papen, expressed his indignation at this honor paid to an enemy of his country. He was also offended that the funeral cortege, with its American-flag draped coffin, passed in front of the German embassy. Worse, as far as von Papen was concerned, at one point the American flag and German flags on the embassy grounds almost touched. He lodged a formal protest, but the Turkish government declined to issue an apology.

The 78 crewmen from the Ploesti mission who landed in Turkey were treated well during their internment in Ankara. Housed in a nice hotel, they were paid their regular salaries plus a generous clothing allowance and were free to go almost anywhere. They liked to dine at Ankara's fine restaurants, often seated just a few tables away from von Papen and other German dignitaries.

Earl Zimmerman, a radioman aboard one of the unnamed B-24s in the 389th bombardment group, recalled their stay in Turkey.

Our time in the Yeni Hotel in Ankara did take its toll on the lads. After six months of dinner parties, beer busts,

picnics and dates with allied embassy secretaries, our guys
got a little bleary eyed. It was rough walking into Pop
Karpich's [the city's best restaurant], slipping him a pack
of American cigarettes, and getting caviar and oranges
sent to your table. The zither player in the back would
break out in an old favorite when he saw us enter.

The necessary political arrangements were eventually made for
the Americans to be quietly evacuated, a few at a time, using
clandestine routes through neighboring countries. All the men
returned to active duty.

Twelve planes were able to overfly Turkey to reach an RAF
base at Nicosia, Cyprus. The first to land was *Baby*, from the
98th, piloted by Francis Weisler and Francis McClellan. On
only three engines they were flying so low that the bombardier,
Joseph Nagy, diligently scanned the landscape ahead to make
sure they cleared the trees. The navigator, Paul Warrenfeltz,
remembered seeing "leaves blowing off the trees just 10-15 feet
below us."

Baby reached Cyprus after dark. The field at Nicosia was
ringed by mountains, and when the crew first saw the lights
from the houses, they realized that the villages were as high as
they were. As the pilot lined up on the runway, he heard distress
calls from other B-24s, including *Hadley's Harem*, about to go
down off the Turkish coast.

He also heard Killer Kane, who was flying somewhere
behind, trying for the same landing strip. *Baby* executed a
smooth landing but the airstrip was too short. Pilot and copilot
jammed their feet on the pedals until the brakes burned out,
and *Baby* and its crew were safe.

Vagabond King, flown by John McCormick, almost didn't
make it over the mountains in Turkey. The plane's altitude was

not much greater than the peaks. While transferring fuel from the bomb bay tanks to the wing tanks something went wrong; all four engines suddenly stopped. "I damn near died!" McCormick wrote. "We had only about 1000 feet of clearance, and there wasn't a flat spot within 50 miles."

The radio operator was wounded and could not bail out. The crew would not abandon ship and leave him. And then, "with a roar and a lurch, those good old Pratt & Whitney's took hold again." Relief! They might make it to Cyprus after all. But when the engines quit a second time the flight engineer, David Slattler, "moved faster than any man I'd ever seen," McCormick said. "He jumped down into the bomb bay and switched gas valves to break the air lock in the lines."

The engines ground up again and McCormick steered *Vagabond King* through the peaks toward Cyprus, 400 miles south. They had been flying for 10 hours, alone over mountainous terrain, and did not know whether they had sufficient fuel to reach the RAF base. The navigator was using a map torn from a child's schoolbook because they had long ago flown off the edge of their official Air Force map. It was already late afternoon and would certainly be dark before they reached the air base. McCormick recalled, "Our nerves were sure taking a helluva beating."

He was holding *Vagabond King* to as slow a speed as he dared in order to save gas; the gauges were showing that the tanks were close to empty. Down to the last 100 gallons, there was still no sign of Cyprus. McCormick worried that they were way off course. "We listened to our radio, hoping to get in touch with the air base at Nicocea, the only airport on the island. We could hear other planes in distress. One was going down near us, into the sea [most likely *Hadley's Harem*], but we couldn't help."

Three other distressed planes had joined up with McCormick. He searched for a beach or any spit of land on which to bring the ship down, but all he saw was water. Suddenly, through the darkness, he spied the airport's beacon. He needed to set down fast, while he still had fuel, and so his injured crewman could get medical attention. He radioed the tower that he had wounded aboard.

Vagabond King was given permission to land first. McCormick brought her in, coasted up the rise, and pulled off the runway so the other planes could touch down. He cut the engines. He had been flying fourteen and a half hours. "The silence was deafening," he recalled. "We were safe! We were the happiest, tiredest, hungriest boys you've ever seen. We all kissed the ground we landed on. I can tell you, there wasn't a man among us who will ever be the same after that."

Killer Kane's ship had suffered terrible damage. The main wing spar was bent, one engine was out and another running roughly, the fuselage was full of holes, and there probably was not enough gas to get them to Cyprus. "We have about as much chance as a snowball in hell to come out of this," he told himself, even while offering optimistic words to his crew.

After the plane cleared the mountains, Kane ordered his men to toss out everything but guns, parachutes, and what little food they had left. Quickly, all sorts of objects flew out of the plane from every opening. Even the bomb bay fuel tanks were jettisoned. The pilot of the B-24 to Kane's right radioed, "What are you doing? House cleaning?" With the extra weight gone, Kane could manage to keep *Hail Columbia* flying at sufficient speed to keep up with the three others in formation with him.

About 9:15, after more than 14 hours in the air, Kane reached the Cyprus airfield. The airport's green light was on, so he lined up on the runway for his final approach. He saw that he was coming in a bit low and would touch down before he reached the field's hard surface.

> I did not dare use more power or I might overshoot the short runway, and if I did I would have to go around the field for another try at landing. I was almost exhausted, too tired to fight the pull of the unbalanced power of the engines. Therefore, I tried to stretch the glide and float the plane on for those few extra yards.

Despite Kane's best efforts, *Hail Columbia* dropped just short of the edge of the runway and bounced about one hundred feet in the air, nose down and tail high. He pulled the control wheel hard into his chest, bracing both feet on the dashboard to push himself against the seat back, but the plane was almost standing on its nose. The tail crashed down but the plane's momentum took it fast down the runway.

Kane watched in amazement as pieces of the aircraft tumbled and rolled ahead of them: "A prop from the dead engine cartwheeled ahead and curved off to the right. Two tires were rolling straight ahead and disappeared into the darkness. *Hail Columbia* was groaning and scraping on the asphalt. She continued straight on down the runway for about 200 feet, then began to swerve to the right."

The ship spun around and ground to a halt. It was not the best of landings—*Hail Columbia* would never fly again—but Kane and his crew got out alive. Some knelt down to kiss the ground. Others collapsed by the side of the airstrip, sifting the dirt between their fingers, relieved to be back on the ground. "I sat down in a daze," Kane wrote in his diary, "and just sat there patting the ground. It was over; yes, completed. But what was the cost? How many of my brave men had stayed back there in that hell?"

The crew of *The Sandman* watched *Hail Columbia* leave a trail of sparks as it skidded down the runway below them. They were next in line to land, but the controller in the tower shot a red flare into the air; Kane's wreck had closed the runway. Pilot Robert Sternfels recalled:

> What a helluva situation. Out 14 hours, low on fuel, low on oil and at least three hours to the nearest friendly terri-tory. Not enough fuel or oil for that. We circle in the dark-ness, pondering our alternatives. Bail out over the field? Ditch the airplane off shore? Nothing sounded very good.

And if that was not bad enough, Sternfels felt a desperate need to urinate. "I haven't had time to go to the 'john' yet, but the real burning question: will the oil supply hold out along with my bladder?"

The crew had thrown out everything they could find to lighten the ship, and so far all four engines were still running, but the flight engineer warned Sternfels that the oil levels for all of them were too low. And if the engines ran out of oil, they would stop dead.

Sternfels circled the RAF field for 15 minutes trying to decide the best course to take when "as if by magic, a green flare soars into the sky and another runway is lit up." He landed without mishap, surprised to discover that the plane had a few gallons of oil left. *The Sandman's* crew survived the dangers of the mission to Ploesti, but that night, taking shelter in a local inn, they were bitten all over by a swarm of fleas.

In the morning the crews who had found a safe haven on Cyprus were eager to leave, to return to Benghazi and to find out how many of their buddies had made it. They checked over the planes to make sure they were airworthy and laboriously refueled them by hand. "There are no gas trucks," Sternfels said, "no gas pumps, just many metal 5-gallon size cans. Every can is carried up a ladder and poured into the wing tank. It was just damn hard work in the boiling sun."

Hail Columbia was not leaving with the others; Killer Kane and his crew would be passengers aboard the other ships. They would all make an overnight stop at Tel Aviv before going to Benghazi. Before they left Cyprus, Kane and his crew walked around the wreck of *Hail Columbia* to survey the damage and bid it goodbye. Two engines were crushed, the nose wheel and right landing gear sheared off along with one propeller, and another was bent with a bullet hole through the tip of a blade. Kane reported that

> the plane had been riddled by so many bullets it was a miracle no one was killed. I counted over 20 holes made by 20mm and 40mm shells. The smaller bullet holes were too numerous to count. One wing had serious damage from an explosive shell. It was unbelievable that we could have received so much damage and not been scratched ourselves, much less have flown all the way from the target, in such a damaged condition. *Hail Columbia* had earned her rest. Grand old girl that she was, she had taken deadly wounds but had brought us back safely. I patted her side for the last time and turned away so that the men could not see the tears in my eyes.

It was dark when the first planes reached Benghazi that night. Everybody was outdoors watching for them, from General Brereton down to the ground crews, each waiting to see if his ship was coming home. Two Red Cross women, Margaret Cotter and Madge Smith, joined them, ready to welcome the guys back.

> The first three planes buzzed the field so low that the women were tempted to fall flat on our faces. When they came in like that—boy, it's good news! But that was only the beginning. The rest of them straggled in minutes, and sometimes hours apart, with broken wings, flat tires, hacked fuselages, flapping bomb doors. I thought we were dreaming as we watched the pilots land those skeleton planes. We forgot for the moment that we were Red Cross girls, here to "bring them in with a smile." We were too stunned to say even a word of greeting.

Most of the planes were barely airworthy, with engines out, bodies and wings riddled with holes from enemy fire, and the dead and wounded on board. And it puzzled the observers that so many ships were blackened; it was rare to see a plane that had flown through fire.

One of the first to land was *Teggie Ann*, with General Ent and Colonel Compton aboard. General Brereton greeted them personally. He later noted in his diary that they both looked "downcast," and with good reason. They knew that their part of the mission was unsuccessful because of Compton's decision, taken with Ent's approval, to execute the turn too soon, causing them to miss the target. It is likely that because of that error, Ent persuaded Compton during the long flight home not to push for a court-martial against Killer Kane, whom he disliked, for falling behind the other groups on the way to Ploesti. Compton wrote about the events years later.

I originally blamed Colonel Kane for not maintaining his position in the formation in accordance with the mission plan. On the return trip to Benghazi I spoke to General Ent and asked him if he were going to initiate court martial proceedings against Kane for not following orders? His reply was, "I don't think we should as we did not stick to the mission plan either." I am still angry with Kane for not keeping up with us and permitting a single massive attack on the refineries.

Of course, if Kane had kept up with the first two groups led by Compton and Ent, he might also have followed them on the wrong course, in which case all five bombardment groups would have missed their assigned targets.

Walter Stewart's *Utah Man* reached the coast of Africa after almost 14 hours of flying. "It's the ugliest piece of real estate," he said, "but it looked beautiful to us then. We came straight in because we were out of fuel." The crew, who had listened to the song "Coming in on a Wing and a Prayer," on the long flight over the Mediterranean, were coming in on not much more than that. Stewart and his crew kissed the ground when they got out of the plane. Then the officers gathered in Stewart's tent to gave thanks to God for hearing their prayers the night before, asking for a safe return.

Shortly after, the crew chief informed Stewart that he had examined the plane and found flak holes in the top and bottom of one wing tank, which meant that a shell had passed through without exploding. And, he added, *Utah Man* was completely out of gas!

Daisy Mae's pilot, Lewis Ellis, wrote that "The trip home was one of sweating out the gas." His flight engineer, Blase Dillman, told him that the fuel would run out around 7 P.M., and the navigator said they couldn't reach Benghazi by then. And even if they did, the forward landing gear had been knocked out so any attempt to land would be extremely hazardous. In addition, the bombardier was unconscious from his serious injuries. The three wounded gunners were in back, looking after him and themselves, while the flight engineer worked to splice the severed control cables.

The sun set and there was still no sign of the African coast. Ellis knew that ditching at sea in the dark was more dangerous than ditching in daylight, but the crew could not bail out because of the condition of the bombardier; they would not even consider abandoning him with the plane. Their only option was to keep flying until they ran out of gas and try to ditch without any power.

"Finally," Ellis wrote, "we saw some red flares straight ahead and knew we were approaching the field. The engines were still going but couldn't last much longer; the gas gauges indicated zero. It was already 9:30 P.M. We only needed a few more minutes."

Dillman cranked down the two main landing gear by hand to save what little hydraulic fluid might remain for lowering the flaps. The nose wheel was so badly damaged there was no point in trying to use it. Because the radio was out, *Daisy Mae* was unable to contact the field except by firing a red flare to announce that there were wounded aboard. Ellis knew he had only one chance to bring *Daisy Mae* down.

> We could never go around if we missed the first time. The wheels touched, and she bounced several feet. I advanced the throttles, and she settled back to the ground as one engine cut out; she rolled halfway across the field, as we

lost speed, the nose began scraping the ground, and we came to an abrupt stop. It was 9:54 p.m., fifteen hours after takeoff.

The crew chief counted more than 150 holes in *Daisy Mae*. He found extensive damage to one engine and no fuel in any of the tanks. He told the pilot that he did not think the plane could have flown even five minutes longer.

In *Liberty Lad*, pilots Kenton McFarland and Harry Podgurski pressed hard on the left rudder pedals as the B-24 made its way across the Mediterranean Sea. The radioman was wounded. Their fuel was dangerously low, the vertical stabilizer bent, and the hydraulic system inoperative so wheels and flaps would have to be lowered by hand. *Liberty Lad* had been in the air nearly 16 hours.

McFarland spotted the coast of Africa and soon saw the airfield ahead. He allowed himself to think that they might make it. As he lined the plane up for the final run, the lights on the instrument panel blew out. A crewman quickly found a flashlight and focused it on the speedometer: it read 120 miles per hour. If their airspeed dropped lower, *Liberty Lad* would go into a stall and crash. If it went higher, McFarland would land too fast and might go off the end of the runway. As he described it to an interviewer:

> The ground crew lit up the runway with floodlights. And, as McFarland made his final approach, the engines sputtered out; the fuel tanks were empty. He brought the gliding bomber down from 2000 feet and hit the runway. Fire trucks and ambulances raced alongside the plane for a mile until it finally rolled to a stop. It was the last plane back from Ploesti.

Of course no one knew yet that *Liberty Lad* was the last plane back. People continued to wait throughout the night for more ships to appear. Surely there would be more. Where were all those planes that had taken off that morning? The ground crews thought their ships would still come back. When all hope was gone they waited still longer. Finally, the reality of the day's events began to sink in. They shook their heads and wiped tearful eyes as they turned and made their way back to their tent in choking disbelief.

Many of crew who returned from the Ploesti mission stayed awake for hours, unable to sleep, unable to forget the sights and sounds. They congregated in the mess tent, eating, smoking, and drinking coffee, cup after cup. The Red Cross women sat with them.

"Madge and I listened," Margaret Cotter wrote, "poured more coffee, and listened again. The majority of them confided that they had not expected to get back at all and couldn't believe they'd made it. Others of the boys were so quiet they seemed stunned. No matter what happens I'll feel lucky that I've been fortunate in this war, because I can look back in memory to that huge, smoky tent, crowded with men in flying suits covered with the dust and grease and sweat and even the blood of that day. I shall always remember that once I sat with heroes."

The men did not feel like heroes. They were too exhausted, benumbed with shock and grief over their losses and the horrible memories of planes on fire spiraling down. When Killer Kane and the others from the Cyprus airfield came back two nights later, they were, Kane wrote, "horrified at the blank spaces in the parking area. They would spot a vacant space and say, 'Oh, no! Not Hinch.' 'There, Taylor's gone too.' 'And Neely!' Each name was a sharp dagger piercing my heart. We seemed to be passing through a vacant graveyard. There were so few planes and no one was about. The whole place seemed dead."

The next day, recalled one of the gunners, "all the survivors were grouped together at the operations building and told that despite the casualties—five hundred personnel—despite that, the mission had been highly successful. But nobody made any comment. They all just shuffled away silently. They didn't seem to give a damn."

Part V

THE PRISONERS

A B-24 nose down in a cornfield south of Ploesti. (*Richard W. Britt*)

12

NIGHTS WERE NOT
HAPPY TIMES

I OAN GRIGORESCU WAS 14 years old when he witnessed the bombing of Ploesti. More than 40 years later he recalled those skimming bombers flying into the heavily defended refineries so low they were pulling the roofs off of houses. "I saw bombers on fire, with the young Americans trapped inside. I saw a river on fire from a crashed plane. I saw a dead American in a walnut grove looking up into the sky, not far from his burning bomber."

The boy also found a book near the wreckage of the plane, a copy of Shakespeare's *As You Like It*, the property of Lt. Harold Dickson, the ground officer who had volunteered for the mission. The downed B-24 was *Euroclydon* and the body nearby was that of Jesse D. "Red" Franks, who had written such a moving letter to his father the night before the raid.

Another Romanian boy watched the attack and also explored the plane's wreckage. A bolder lad, he rifled through the airman's uniform and took his belt and wallet. The wallet contained two photographs and a business card. The pictures showed a young, attractive couple, an Air Force lieutenant and a young woman, seated on the front steps of a house. The business card read: Jesse D. Franks, Jr., Lieutenant, Air Corps, Army of the United States. On the back of the card Red had written, "Send to Dr. Jesse D. Franks, Sr., Columbus, Mississippi."

Euroclydon was one of 35 B-24s shot down over Romania. Of the more than 300 crewmen aboard, only some 115 survived. The rest were killed in crashes or died soon after from their wounds. The German commander, General Gerstenberg, treated his fallen enemies with the greatest respect, ordering proper funerals with full military honors.

The Romanian women held wakes for the Americans, and on the caskets they placed special thin cakes, each with a small American flag made of colored candies. A German officer asked why these women did this and why they were crying for the Americans. One lady replied, "We cry, because we know American mothers soon will be crying for their sons."

Jack Warner, *Euroclydon's* navigator, whose life was saved by Red Franks, may have been the first American to parachute into Romania and live to tell the tale. The force of his landing knocked him unconscious, and when he woke up, he found himself in a shallow creek. Despite severe burns and a broken collarbone, he recalled that his "initial inclination was to walk to Turkey, which was only some 400 miles away." At that moment, it seemed better than the alternative: becoming a prisoner of the Germans.

He did not get far before realizing that he needed serious medical attention. Two Romanian soldiers found him and brought him to an aid station. Along the way, they stopped to watch the refineries burn. Warner found this upsetting because he knew that some of the bombs the planes had dropped had yet to explode. "I figured," he wrote, "it would be my luck to get blown up by my own bombs!"

At the aid station, the triage personnel shunted him aside, leaving him with some dead American crewmen because they did not expect him to survive the night. To their surprise, he was still alive the next morning. He was transferred, with about 60 other men, most of whom were suffering from horrible burns, to the Luftwaffe's hospital in Bucharest. Warner convalesced there for two weeks, receiving excellent care. Doctors found 35 pieces of shrapnel in his neck and left shoulder; the arm had almost been severed.

Other wounded crewmen were also brought to Bucharest, transported in ambulances, private cars, trucks, and horse-drawn wagons. General Gerstenberg had ordered that they receive the finest medical care, but for some there was no hope. Some 30 flyers were beyond help and clearly had only a short time to live. All the doctors could do was give them enough morphine to ease their suffering.

Only four men got out of *Sad Sack II*; all were badly wounded. Henry Lasco, the pilot, had been hit in the mouth and upper palate. His hair was burned and a piece of shrapnel had lodged in one shoulder. The copilot, Joe Kill, had broken both legs in the landing. The impact had yanked his right foot out of its socket. Al Shaffer, a waist gunner, had an injured leg and burns over a large part of his body, and Charles DeCrevel, the other waist gunner, had also been burned.

DeCrevel was able to walk and he made his way to a village where the inhabitants welcomed him, took him to a bar, and spent all the money from his escape kit on drinks for everyone. Once the money was gone, they put him in a horse cart, formed a procession, and started off for the next town as though on parade. Eventually he reached a hospital in Bucharest.

Shaffer and Kill were unable to move but Lasco crawled away from the crash site to seek help. While he was gone, some men found Kill in the cornfield where he had landed. Seeing an easy mark, they beat and robbed him.

> [They] jumped me and tore off my watch and ring, emptied my pockets and then belted me a beauty. I guess they figured I was about gone anyway, what with the legs, a cracked forehead and bad burns. Surprisingly, I didn't go out, although I prayed for unconsciousness.

Either those peasants or another group gathered in a circle around Kill brandishing pitchforks and other farm implements. They kept shouting "Rushky," until he realized they thought he was Russian. Once he was able to persuade them that he was an American airman, they hoisted him on their shoulders and carried him to a churchyard where other crew members were waiting for help.

Pilot Henry Lasco, wounded in the face, apparently was so disfigured that people ran away when he tried to approach them for help. Some even threw stones. "I must have scared them with my appearance," he said. But eventually the local people overcame their fear. "Before long, they grabbed me," he wrote. "They took my .45, rings, watch, Parker 51 pen, escape kit and money. Everyone looked at me and shook their heads or covered their eyes. Some even cried. I guess I looked grotesque."

He was taken to the churchyard where Kill and others were waiting and from there to a hospital for treatment. When he was finally given a bed, he found Al Shaffer from his own crew in the bed beside him. Making conversation, Shaffer said he was in Lieutenant Lasco's crew in *Sad Sack II*, and asked who the newcomer was. Lasco could not talk because of his mouth wound, but he wrote his name on a piece of paper and handed it to Shaffer. Lasco recalled that Shaffer "looked at the note and then looked at me again. He got a horrible expression on his face. 'My God, Lieutenant, I didn't know it was you.'"

John Palm managed to land his B-24, the severely damaged *Brewery Wagon*, in a field. Despite his nearly severed leg, Palm made his way out of the ship and collapsed amid the rows of cornstalks. Some German and Romanian soldiers found him. The Germans tried to claim Palm as their prisoner but the Romanians refused. They hoisted the pilot into the back of their truck and drove him to a hospital. Palm remembered: "There was a nurse and two orderlies. The nurse was standing over me, trying to hold on. Even though my leg was killing me, all I could think about was the nice view I had up her dress!"

He was transported to a larger hospital in Ploesti. Delayed-action bombs were still exploding but Palm was in such agony by then that he didn't care. "I just wanted something to kill the pain. A shot of morphine helped, but I watched them take off what was left of my leg below the knee." When he regained consciousness he asked the medic for his leg. He explained that he and his father owned a shoe store in El Paso, Texas. Displayed on one wall was a chart showing the bones of the foot. Palm thought it would be a nice idea to use the skeleton of his own foot instead of the chart. "The doctors and nurses said I was crazy," he said.

Worden Weaver and most of his crew got out alive from the flaming wreckage of *Lil' Abner* but all had suffered various injuries. Weaver had sustained burns along one side of his body from his leg to his face and large painful blisters were forming. He and two others set off in one direction to seek help, while the rest of the men took a different path. Weaver's group met a farmer's boy who led them to a village. The inhabitants clustered around them offering water. They gently soothed the flyers' burns by using feathers to apply some sort of homemade oil.

The men went on to a larger village that had an aid station staffed by a friendly woman doctor who spoke English. Shortly after, Romanian soldiers arrived and took them by truck to a military hospital six miles away, where they received additional treatment. Many local people came to visit and bring them food. The Americans seemed a bit surprised that everyone was so hospitable to men who had bombed their homeland.

Jerome Savaria, copilot of *Margie* in the 98th Bombardment Group, received a less warm welcome. He was not badly injured but was bruised and dazed from bailing out at a low altitude. He had hit the ground hard. In his confused state, he wandered about, trying to find a place to hide. He was spotted by a crowd of civilians who were convinced that he was Russian. They were determined to kill him.

With remarks and gestures he tried to explain that he was American but could not make them understand. He wrote:

> A big ox of a man pushed me down. He had an ax. [He struck Savaria in the leg and head.] When I came to they were still there, but were arguing with each other. One man had a rope, another had a shotgun, and there was the man with the ax. Some had pitchforks and clubs. They were arguing about which method to use to kill me. I was in shock, but the situation struck me as funny, so I started laughing.

His laughter made the crowd even angrier, but the situation changed abruptly when two German soldiers arrived. They menaced the crowd with their weapons and took Savarian away in an oxcart to Ploesti where he received treatment for his injuries.

The navigator on the *Chattanooga Choo Choo*, Richard Britt, was trapped in its wreckage. Unable to move, he held fast to an image of his father. He drifted off, thinking that maybe this was not such a bad way to die. He jolted awake about four hours later.

> I was still in the plane with two oxygen bottles in my lap, my left foot caught in the bomb bay wreckage, my right leg folded under me, and the Plexiglas dome of the top turret gun over my head. I felt no pain, but was unable to think clearly.

He called out for Ernie Poulson, the copilot, but got no reply. Then he noticed a body nearby and choked back his grief, thinking it was Poulson's. He looked up through the top turret. He saw "people peering down at me. I heard them chattering like magpies, but couldn't understand what they were saying. I called, asking if I was in an airplane. They didn't understand, but increased their chatter."

He called out the name of his pilot, Robert O'Reilly. Silence. He shouted "Romano," for Alfred Romano, the bombardier, which led to "an agitated reaction from the people looking down at me. They nodded and chattered faster and louder. I found out later they thought I was saying 'Romania,' and they were telling me I was right." Suddenly the crowd grew quiet. A woman's voice addressed Britt in fluent English.

"Are you an American?"

He replied that he was.

"We'll have you out of there in a jiffy," she said.

The woman who spoke to Richard Britt was the 50-year-old

Princess Ecaterina Caradja, and her actions would have a profound effect on him and on every other American flyer from the Ploesti mission whose plane went down over Romania. Many would become her "boys," as she called them, not unlike adopted sons, and would remain close until her death in 1993.

She had been at home, on her thousand-acre estate ten miles from Ploesti, having lunch, when she heard the thunder of the American bombers overhead. She and her guests ran outside in time to see the second wave of planes, the survivors of the 389th Bombardment Group, leaving their target. Some of the B-24s were on fire. *Chattanooga Choo Choo*, with Richard Britt aboard, had reached the end of its run. The pilot aimed for an open field and crash-landed, only a mile from Princess Caradja's estate.

She got in her car, a 1937 Plymouth, and headed for the crash site where she found Britt, trapped and apparently delirious, burned from the aviation fuel dripping on his body. It took almost an hour for her workers to cut him out of the wreckage. As he was lifted out and placed on the ground, he began to shake. "I felt no pain," he recalled, "but the shaking was severe. When the men were holding my ankles, I noticed my skin slipped around like a loose sock. I knew I had been scalded by gasoline leaking from the wing tank."

When Princess Caradja asked if he was all right, he mentioned the burns. She unbuttoned his shirt, saw huge blisters forming on his chest, and realized she had to get him to a hospital. As they carried him to her car, two armed German soldiers appeared from the woods and demanded to take Britt prisoner. Britt understood German and was amazed to hear the woman tell the soldiers "in the most impolite German, 'Go to Hell.' This started a heated argument and a tug of war, with me as the object."

Suddenly Princess Caradja stopped talking and left Britt beside the car, causing him fleetingly to think she had given up. "I thought the Germans had won. She ran around the rear of the car, opened the far back door, climbed in and grabbed me from behind, pulling me into the car. The Germans grabbed my feet. She pulled harder and gave orders for the driver to start the car. As the car began to move, the soldiers let go, swearing at her."

They drove to a hospital in the town of Filipesti, where Britt was treated for his wounds. Princess Caradja had saved him from the Germans, and shortly she would be responsible for rescuing all 113 downed American flyers. Without her courage and determination to help, their captivity would have been a far greater ordeal.

After making sure that Britt was receiving proper medical care, Princess Caradja rushed to Bucharest, to act on her impulse to keep the Americans out of German hands. She knew all the high-ranking men in Romanian social and political circles, and, more important, she knew their wives. The women were the ones she visited, persuading them to exert pressure on their husbands to protect the Americans instead of allowing them to be transported to prison camps in Germany.

The influential husbands, in turn, persuaded General Ion Antonescu to recommend to General Gerstenberg that since the airmen had been shot down over Romania, they should remain there. Gerstenberg agreed. Indeed, he may have been relieved to be freed of the necessity of caring for the prisoners and transporting them to Germany, where they would be a drain on German resources. As soon as Princess Caradja learned that Gerstenberg was willing to let them stay, she returned home to face another task, to arrange for the burial of

Chattanooga Choo Choo's flight engineer, Frank Kees, in her family's private cemetery.

On August 8, a week after the raid, the wounded Americans who were well enough to be moved were brought to Sinaia, a resort in the Transylvania Mountains that had been converted to a military hospital. The setting was gracious and idyllic. The summer palace of the King of Romania was located there, along with villas belonging to wealthy Bucharest residents. Britt wrote, "The houses were picturesque, made of white plaster or stones with heavy dark wooden beams accentuating the steep roofs. Fascias and beams were decorated with colorful hand painted designs. Flowers were everywhere, in gardens, flower beds, and window boxes. Pots of geraniums and petunias decorated balconies and stone ledges."

The main hospital facility was a large, three-story building that had once housed a luxury hotel. The entrance was framed by a huge impressive stone archway with gates 12 feet high. The interior was even more luxurious. As Richard Britt remembered, "The graceful spiral staircase made a quarter-circle as it descended. An elaborate crystal chandelier hung from the high ceiling. The herringbone parquet floor gleamed with a golden-brown luster. White paneled walls and arched doorways completed the picture. It looked like a setting for a Hollywood movie."

The American flyers received highly professional care and considerate treatment. It was not only the hospital staff who offered kindness. They also had many visitors to brighten their recovery, including Princess Caradja and an entourage of attractive, well-bred young women. They came in groups, bearing gifts of food, candy, and English-language books. But there was still much pain and suffering, and many grim reminders of the horrors of the mission. Again, the navigator Britt wrote, "Nights in the hospital were eerie. I began having horrible nightmares, reliving the crash over and over. I would waken suddenly, so glad to find I was only dreaming. Then, unable to get back to sleep, I could hear the mutterings and loud cries from other rooms."

An airman in a room down the hall hollered for the nurse several times each hour, pleading for something to relieve his pain. In Britt's room, William Schiffmacher, the rear gunner on *Raunchy* of the 98th Bombardment Group, "was in constant pain, but you would never know it by looking at his face. Sixty-six pieces of shrapnel had penetrated his back and head. Some had been removed, but others were pressing on nerve centers in delicate places. During the day, the smile was always there. But late at night, I could hear him sobbing. Nights were not happy times."

Although several of the men suffered acutely because of the nature of their wounds, most made good progress at Sinaia owing to the high quality of medical care they received. Henry Lasco, the pilot of *Sad Sack II*, who had been shot through the face, was horribly disfigured. Britt said that Lasco's face below the nose "seemed to be missing." Jack Warner said that Lasco's face was "torn almost from ear to ear." The doctors decided not to operate on Lasco, believing he would recover faster if the flesh healed on its own. His skin turned black and he could not chew solid food. For a time he was quarantined to prevent infection. But his spirits remained high and he talked and joked with the others. Within a few weeks his face started to mend and the quarantine was lifted.

James Waltman, a gunner aboard *Yen-Tu* in the 98th, was, according to Britt,

not a pretty sight. His face was mottled with red and pur-
ple skin and unsightly scar tissue. His eyes were sunken
deep in their sockets. He was over six feet tall, but
weighed less than a hundred pounds. Parts of his ears and
nose were gone. Both arms and hands had been burned by
fire. Metal cages were placed over them and then bandaged to keep the air from the seared flesh. Each arm was
in a sling so that the cages were crisscrossed in front of
him. He looked like a visitor from another planet.

One day the men did have a visitor who seemed to be from
another world, a Catholic archbishop who brought gifts from
the Pope, along with a German camera crew to record the pres-
entation. The film was to be shown to the German people to
demonstrate how well the wounded American prisoners were
being cared for.

The gifts, packed in large wooden boxes, were quarts of
cognac, enough so that there was a bottle for every two men.
They made quick work of them. And the brandy made quick
work of them! The men had not had any alcohol to drink in
several weeks and they were still in a weakened condition from
their wounds. The German film crew left long before the party
was over. Hubert Womble, pilot of *Honky Tonk Gal* in the 93rd,
was walking with crutches and although he had been managing
well, the "fool things" kept sliding out from under him, leaving
him sprawled on the floor. "These are the drunkenest crutches
I ever did see," he muttered to Britt.

Charlie Wallace, bombardier aboard *Boomerang*, removed all
his clothing and ran down a corridor shouting, "You can't catch
me; you can't catch me!" Three nurses and the hospital director
took off in pursuit. They chased him into a room but he circled
them and ran out. They followed him up and down hallways

but did not nab him until he went back to his room and climbed "a large, ornate clothes tree. A nurse grabbed his feet and the tree began to fall. With a shout of 'Timberrr!' Wallace rode the tree down and hit the floor with a thud. He was out cold. Two nurses picked him up and carefully put him in his bed, tucking him in securely." The others tiptoed past, being careful not to wake him. Suddenly he gave a shout and bolted from his room. This time no one ran after him. He had worn them all out, and the next day most of the men woke up with fierce hangovers.

When a patient at Sinaia was judged sufficiently rehabilitated, he was taken by bus through spectacular mountain scenery to the camp that housed the Americans who had not been wounded seriously. Britt remembered his emotional farewell and conflicting emotions when it was his time to leave. The men awoke early on the morning of their departure. The village women who did the hospital laundry brought their uniforms, neatly patched, cleaned, and ironed. When the men dressed and gathered downstairs, they no longer looked like "the sloppy patients we saw around the hospital. We were military men again. No more uncombed hair or scruffy beards. We stood proud and erect." They ate a hearty breakfast. The kitchen staff marched into the dining room carrying huge plates of omelets. "It was a festive occasion," Britt wrote. "We realized that our treatment had been exceptional. We had received the best medical care available. We felt great respect for the Romanian people."

As the men climbed aboard the buses that were to take them away, the entire hospital staff assembled outdoors to see them off. Many of them—the staff and the airmen—were crying as they waved goodbye.

Lagarul 14 prison in Timisul de Jos, Romania, the "Gilded Cage." (*Richard W. Britt*)

13

THE GILDED CAGE

T HE PRISONERS CALLED IT the Gilded Cage. One man
described it as "probably the best prison camp in the
world." Its official name was Lagarul 14, and it was located at
the top of a pass in the Transylvanian Alps, in a village called
Timisul de Jos.

There were two camps, because the Romanians insisted on
housing officers and enlisted men in separate quarters. The 39
officers lived in a three-story building that had been a hotel for
a ski resort. Before the war it had served as an exclusive retreat
for civil servants. The facilities included a large dining room,
two sizable baths, and 14 bedrooms, each equipped with a sink
and hot water. The well-maintained grounds provided pleasant
walking paths, tennis courts, a gymnasium with showers, and
spectacular mountain scenery.

The 71 enlisted men were assigned to the two buildings of a
former girls' school, located a few hundred yards away.
Although not as luxurious as the officers' lodgings, they were far
superior to any POW camp in Germany. There were dormito-
ries and a large washroom and kitchen, but the toilets were outside, as was typical of many European countries at that time.

Some of the airmen expressed amazement that the Romanians treated them so well. But the people considered the downed Ploesti flyers as heroes because they confined their bombing to military targets, not civilian areas.

The Romanians believed that the reason for the low-altitude mission was to spare civilian lives and property, even though it increased the danger to the American bomber crews. Such bravery, the Romanians concluded, deserved special consideration, as far as wartime conditions allowed. In contrast, men shot down over Romania in later raids on Ploesti, and in other parts of the country, were thought to be no better than gangsters because they bombed from high altitudes, killing many civilians. "Accordingly," wrote an American airman who flew a later mission to Ploesti, the Romanian dictator Ion Antonescu "imprisoned us as near to military targets as possible, namely the Bucharest Marshalling yards, as punishment for our inhumane deeds."

Therefore, the surviving aircrews of the August 1, 1943, mission to Ploesti were treated more like guests than prisoners. Except for the barbed wire fences, their quarters did not look like prisons. Nevertheless, they still meant confinement to those living behind the barbed wire. Soon boredom would become a major problem.

The men were paid approximately $225 per month—a portion was withheld for room and board—and received regular Red Cross parcels. With the money and items from the Red Cross, such as cigarettes, canned milk, candy, and concentrated foods, they were able to engage openly in a brisk business with civilians living nearby. Thus the men were able to obtain "fresh butter, bread, meat, wine and spirits, even champagne."

With white tablecloths, table napkins, cutlery, and Russian POW waiters, they ate in style. Newspapers were brought in by a local barber who came to cut their hair and keep them clean shaven. About twice a month they were permitted a bath. The Russian prisoners were detailed to heat the water and keep it coming until every officer had taken his bath.

A teacher came periodically from Bucharest to instruct them in the Romanian language. He began his first class by saying how much he missed Boston, where he had once lived. The Americans quickly learned how to ask for beer, plum brandy, and champagne.

They kept current with the war news by listening to the BBC on a console radio purchased by one of the officers. The Romanians allowed them to keep it with the stipulation that they not tune in to the BBC. The guards and the commandant's staff all knew they were listening to the British radio service, however, but pretended they did not. Every night at 9:00 the officers gathered around the set to wait for the chiming of Big Ben in London announcing the beginning of the news report. One man remembered: "For some strange reason, we all watched the radio. No one spoke during the broadcast, but there were cheers or groans depending on the news. When the news was over, the radio was turned off."

Even with the activities and facilities available for their use, the men still had difficulty filling the days and nights. Passing time and the lack of work weighed heavily; this led some of them to drink, sometimes to excess. When Richard Britt and the men with him first arrived from the hospital, they were caught up in five successive nights of heavy drinking and partying. By the end of the fifth night the revelers were "exhausted, grouchy and irritable." Something had to be done. One of the officers, a captain, called a meeting to discuss the problem. Britt recalled,

In a calm, fatherly, but firm manner, he said their parties were not only bad for our health, but bad for morale. Even the partygoers agreed it was time to stop. A motion was made that we ban alcohol except for holidays or special occasions. The motion passed. No more alcohol.

The next instance of excitement occurred the following morning when the Romanian army colonel in charge of prison camps arrived at Timisul for an inspection. As the American officers gathered and exchanged glances, they realized they were a sorry-looking bunch. They were still wearing the uniforms they had been shot down in. The enlisted men looked worse and they were in no mood for a full-scale regulation, spit-and-polish inspection. That had not been standard practice back in Africa when they were training. And when they saw the 5'2" officer in riding breeches, with a coat top-heavy with medals and ribbons, they were even less inclined to be respectful of military protocol.

When they lined up in front of the officers' building they looked like a gang of ruffians. Some were not even wearing shoes. As the colonel moved down the line to review the troops, he could hear them muttering snide remarks.

The colonel was livid at the lack of respect. He ordered the barefoot men to return to their quarters and when they did, everyone, including the colonel, heard their laughter. That was the final insult. Richard Britt wrote that the colonel

> exploded with a tirade: "I have never been so insulted in my life," he shouted. "I am Colonel Pitestu, a member of the Command Staff. I am the head of all Prisoner of War Camps in this country. You owe your very life to me. See these medals on my chest? I am the most decorated soldier

in the entire Romanian Army and you greet me like this with your sloppy clothes and lack of military courtesy."

Obviously, the Americans had to be punished for their insubordination. They would have to take the consequences for their arrogance. Colonel Pitestu paced up and down in front of them as though contemplating suitable revenge. Finally he announced that he was taking away their radio. Then he said, "I am taking your Ping-Pong table, and your cards, and your chess, and your checkers! I won't return them until you decide to show a little military respect."

The barefoot men who had been banished overheard the colonel's remarks and quickly gathered up the playing cards and hid them. The American major who owned the radio removed the inner workings and put rocks inside the plastic case to match the weight. He placed it back in its original box, tied it with cord, and turned it over to the Romanian guards.

As a result of his quick action, the men still had a working radio on which to hear the BBC news and the guards never found out what he had done. When the box was later given back to the Americans, the cord was still in place; the guards had never opened the box. Colonel Pitestu did not return, perhaps feeling assured that he had taught the prisoners a lesson.

Princess Caradja, a frequent and welcome visitor to the camp, brought not only her radiant presence but also news and gifts such as warm winter underwear, tennis rackets, golf clubs, clothing, and English-language books. She arranged for a shipment of gloves for the men whose hands had been burned or whose skin was painful to the touch. In addition, she had a personal request, and a warning. She expressed her concern for the prisoners to Richard Britt, whose plane had crashed on her estate,

I'm worried about you. I'm afraid you might do something foolish. The war is going well for you and badly for the Germans. Your raid did hurt Hitler. But I want you to promise me that you will not try to escape. You are safe here. If you were to get to a border and were caught, they would shoot you.

Fortunately, she did not ask Britt directly for assurances that they were not planning to escape, for such a plan was already under way. What had led to it was not so much a desire to escape or to return to the fighting, though both factors probably contributed to their urge to break out. The primary motivation for planning an escape was sheer boredom. Britt wrote: "One day began to merge into another. We began to suffer from being cooped up. We started to get on each other's nerves. We started snapping at each other." The men realized that they needed some kind of goal, a focus, a directed activity. What could be better than digging a tunnel, an escape route under the barbed wire that surrounded the camp?

The enterprise would bring everyone together, requiring them to work as a team toward a common objective. Also, it would require physical labor, which would help reduce the tension of living together in close quarters with so little to occupy them. After careful reconnoitering and measuring of the terrain around the building, the direction for the tunnel was chosen. Teams of four men each were scheduled to begin digging. They would take turns in two-hour shifts.

The work was slow, tedious, and difficult, one tin-can scoop at a time in a tunnel a mere two feet wide and two and a half feet high. While some men dug, others appeared to be taking leisurely strolls in the area between the building and the barbed wire. Their job was to listen, to find out if they could detect sounds of the digging. If they could hear the men at work, then so might the guards. The teams developed a system of signals to alert the men in the tunnel to stop because the guards were too close.

Once, when the tunnel had reached some 12 feet beyond the building, Princess Caradja arrived with some special items Richard Britt had requested. He had said the men wanted to put on a show and asked for electrical wiring, light bulbs, and women's dresses to use as costumes. The real purpose of the wiring and the lights was to illuminate the tunnel; the dresses were to be used for disguise once the escape was successful.

Princess Ecaterina Caradja was responsible for the survival of the crew of *Chattanooga Choo Choo* and helped all the U.S. airmen who were shot down over Romania. (*Richard W. Britt*)

However, the clothing selected by Princess Caradja was hopelessly outdated. The dresses were gaudy, bedecked with the beads and bangles popular with the "flappers" of the 1920s. They were perfect for a theatrical performance, but not for men trying to blend in with the local Romanian population in 1943. Britt was certain the princess knew what the men had intended to use the dresses for. "I looked at her," Britt said, "and saw a glimmer of humor in her eyes. She had out-foxed us." She warned him again about the dangers of an attempt to escape. "Should you escape," she told him, "you cannot trust anyone. People will betray you for a little money. You know nothing about treachery. This is not like the United States and you cannot understand this way of life."

The men continued digging. Progress was faster now that the tunnel could be lighted. The teams worked around the clock until the day two guards discovered that some stacks of wicker furniture stored in a basement room appeared higher than usual. And then they discovered the heaps of dirt from the tunnel that were piled beneath the furniture. The secret was out. The tunnel project was over. Britt recalled,

> A feeling of gloom descended on us. All that work for nothing. We felt doomed to waste our time here while the rest of the war effort went on without us. But, somehow, working together on the tunnel had improved our relationship with each other. We were more tolerant and started looking for other ways to pass the time.

One way they found to pass the time was throwing snowballs; the first snow of the year had just fallen. They tossed them at one another at first, and then tried to use the guards as targets. But that was no fun because the guards did not seem to know the game. They would not throw any snowballs in return. The airmen turned to the passing trains, packing stones in the centers of the snowballs, but the trains were too far away so most of their missiles fell short.

The camp commandant warned them that most of the passengers on the trains were Germans. If they got angry at being made targets, the POWs might be shipped to camps in Germany. The excitement of throwing snowballs faded quickly.

The trains had long provided another kind of diversion, however. For some time, the Americans had been observing each passing train and keeping records of those carrying troops and other vital supplies for the war effort. They passed the information on to a dentist from Bucharest, who regularly visited the camp to care for the prisoners' teeth. He, in turn, managed to send the information to British intelligence. At least in some small way, then, the flyers felt they were making a contribution to the war effort.

They did get occasional weekend passes to visit Bucharest, with the guards along as escorts. When they were able to get the guards sufficiently drunk, the prisoners could go off on their own for a night of carousing, rejoining the guards in the morning somewhat worse for wear. And in an odd experience for a prisoner of war, one officer was invited to give a talk at Bucharest's Rotary Club.

Christmas 1943 was extraordinary. One man recalled, "We were being paid salaries, more money was coming from the Red Cross, and the Pope sent 72,000 [Romanian] lei. We bought beer, wine and champagne. We were permitted to do anything we liked except dig holes." They listened to President Roosevelt's Christmas speech on the radio. Bing Crosby sang "White Christmas." They gave small gifts to one another, to the Russian prisoners who worked as cooks and orderlies, and even to those guards who had been especially considerate. The enlisted men prepared a lavish dinner for the officers and themselves. The camp commandant provided a 30-piece orchestra to entertain them.

The musicians were Russian prisoners, whose gaunt faces revealed their suffering and despair. The American airmen felt guilty partaking of such a feast in front of people who obviously did not get enough to eat. After a while, the Americans insisted that the Russians share their food. Happily, they agreed, and after eating, they played even more beautifully than before.

On New Year's Eve, the officers gave a party for the enlisted men. There was plenty of food and an ample supply of cham-

pagne, beer, plum brandy, and bottles of what passed for bourbon. The commandant and several guards were invited. One
arrived wearing a bear's head, which, they explained, was part of
a Romanian New Year's tradition, the dance of the bear.

Before long, everyone was dancing faster and wilder, until
they collapsed on the floor, exhausted. Although the dancing
was over, the drinking continued. Then one of the Americans
poured a bottle of beer over a guard's head. Taking offense, he
cursed at them in Romanian and left the party. He was discovered upstairs in the prisoners' quarters filling a pillowcase with
American cigarettes. "The party was over," wrote Richard Britt,
"and it had ended badly."

On April 4, 1944, nine months after Operation Tidal Wave,
American bombers took off for a mission over Romania. Their
target was the railroad marshalling yards at Bucharest. They
attacked with a large force from a high altitude and had ample
fighter escort from their new bases in Italy. The bombers hit
their target, but a number of bombs missed, killing 2,942 civilians and injuring more than 2,000.

The news of the deaths spread rapidly. People living near the
prison camp at Timisul vented their anger at the Americans,
shaking fists, making threatening gestures, and shouting epi-
thets whenever they saw the flyers from the Ploesti mission.
The following day, April 5, a force of 334 B-24 and B-17
bombers, again with a strong fighter escort, attacked Ploesti. In
contrast to the raid nine months earlier, only 13 planes of the
attacking force were lost. This mission marked the beginning of
a massive bombing campaign against Romania carried out by
the RAF at night and the American air force during the day.

Two months later the men learned of the military invasion of
Normandy. The news was brought to them by gleeful

Romanian guards, who welcomed the news as much as the Americans did. And as the bombing raids over Romania became more frequent, it added to the prisoners' belief that the war was drawing to a close.

General Gerstenberg's defenses took their toll, however. German antiaircraft guns shot down 286 U.S. planes, leaving almost 2,900 crewmen killed or captured. The final mission over Ploesti was carried out by 78 RAF bombers on the night of August 17, 1944. One of them crashed on the grounds of Princess Caradja's estate, as Britt's *Chattanooga Choo Choo* had done a year earlier.

The princess saw the burning plane go down and then two parachutes float to earth. One of the flyers was on fire. She rushed to save him but his burns were too severe. "She drove him to a physician. On the way the airman held his peeling arms away from his body and blinded eyes and conversed calmly. He had three children and was trying to win the war." He lived another 15 hours. She brought the body home and buried him in the family cemetery, next to Frank Kees, the flight engineer from *Chattanooga Choo Choo*.

Eight days later, on August 26, 1944, King Michael of Romania informed General Gerstenberg that he was severing his country's alliance with Germany. Gerstenberg would be allowed to withdraw his troops from Romanian territory using certain designated mountain passes, one of which was close to Timisul. The king also agreed to an armistice with the Russians, which would allow the Red Army to pass through Romania unchallenged.

The flyers held at Timisul shouted with joy at the news. And so did the guards, who ran throughout the camp hugging the prisoners. At four o'clock in the morning, several high-ranking Romanian officers from Bucharest arrived to advise the men to stay in the compound for the time being, for their own safety. The officers explained that although most Germans were leaving Romania, some were holding out in Bucharest, fighting in the streets.

However, it was not safe for the POWs to remain at Timisul for long; the Germans might try to take them to Germany. The Romanian officers said they would try to find a place to hide the Americans until it was safe for them to go on to Bucharest.

For her part, Princess Caradja continued to deliver supplies to her orphans, trying to avoid contact with the advancing Russians. She also headed for Timisul to see what she could do to find a haven for her boys.

Russian soldiers intercepted her car. A colonel ordered her out and told her that they would trade cars at once, her gleaming well-kept 1937 Plymouth for his rusty 1926 Chrysler that had no starter. It had to be pushed to get the engine running. She finally reached Timisul and urged the Americans to leave before the Russians arrived, but said they should avoid Bucharest where the fighting was still fierce. The camp guards rounded up four trucks for the Americans to board, urging them to stay hidden beneath tarpaulins in case the convoy ran into Germans. They set off over treacherous mountain roads in search of a place to stay until the Germans were out of the country. The flyers knew they were in greater danger now than at any time since their capture nearly a year ago.

Col. James A. Gunn, III, was shot down August 17, 1944, on the last raid over Ploesti, one week before the Romanians changed sides. Gunn was taken to the officer's camp in Bucharest, which was near the enlisted men's compound and the hospital for wounded prisoners. German forces surrounded the city and some troops wandered the streets in search of food and medical supplies. They were likely to open fire on anyone they thought was behaving suspiciously. German planes had begun to bomb the city, further endangering the American prisoners.

Colonel Gunn was the senior officer present, responsible for the care and safety of the men. He wanted to get them out of the country before the Germans decided to execute them all or take them back across the border. Another danger was that they might be caught in the crossfire between German and Russians troops. Somehow, Gunn decided, he had to get word to an American airbase in Italy to warn his superiors about the dangers facing the downed flyers from all the Ploesti missions. First, Gunn expressed his concerns to Rico Georgescu, the Romanian secretary of state. Goergescu arranged for a plane to take Gunn to the American airbase at Bari, where plans could be made to evacuate the flyers.

Time was critical. The Russians were moving closer by the hour and the Germans had stepped up their bombing raids. On the morning of August 26, only nine days after Gunn had been shot down, he was transported to an airfield 15 miles outside of Ploesti and got a glimpse of the airplane that would take him to Italy, if it could fly that far without falling apart. The plane was an Italian Savoia-Marchetti twin-engine bomber. It was in terrible shape and neither the Romanian pilot nor the two soldiers with him understood English. They even seemed a little frightened of Gunn. The old bomber managed to get airborne but after 20 minutes the pilot turned back, landing at the same field where they had started.

After deplaning, an interpreter told Gunn that the pilot reported engine trouble, an explanation Gunn did not believe.

The engines had sounded fine to him. He thought the pilot was too scared to make the flight. While Gunn waited beside the plane, wondering what to do next, a dashing, handsome Romanian pilot appeared, offering an intriguing suggestion. In fluent English he said, "Colonel, if you will crawl into the belly of a Messerschmitt 109 I will fly you to Italy."

The pilot was Capt. Constantine Cantacuzino, Romania's leading ace, having shot down more planes—including B-24s and B-17s—than anyone else in the Romanian Air Force. He was also credited with downing 12 German planes in the short time since Romania had switched allegiance. Before the war Cantacuzino had been a pilot with Romanian National Air Lines, as well as a stunt pilot with his own biplane adapted for daredevil flying. He was wealthy, well educated, a member of the aristocracy, and a cousin of Princess Caradja.

Perhaps because he sensed doubts about Gunn's estimate of his flying ability, or maybe he merely enjoyed demonstrating his skill as a pilot, he hopped into his biplane and took off. Staying close to the field so Gunn could watch, Cantacuzino put on a dazzling display of aerial acrobatics, "the likes of which I'd never seen," Gunn remarked.

The flight to Italy was a bold and risky undertaking that seemed to have little chance of succeeding, but neither man hesitated about trying it. The ME-109 was a one-seater plane; Colonel Gunn would have to make the two-hour flight hunched in the tiny radio compartment behind the cockpit, with his head between his knees. He would not be able to look out and of course there was no room for a parachute. Their route would take them over German-held territory for 300 miles and then 100 miles over American-held ground. They would attempt to land their German plane at an American base and had no way to make radio contact with the air traffic controller. They did not even have a map of Italy. Gunn found a piece of cardboard and drew a sketch from memory. He gave it to Cantacuzino, and told him how to reach the airfield. Their only other safeguard was to paint American flags on the fuselage.

They took off at 5:20 on the afternoon of August 27, heading west. Gunn described it to a historian as follows.

> It was very cold in the cramped space strung with control cables, and the lack of oxygen and space limited Gunn's physical movements. The lesser air density of their high altitude [19,000 feet] added to his breathing problem and the dizzying effect (hypoxia) of being without oxygen.

As the ship neared the American air base at San Giovanni, Cantacuzino followed Gunn's instructions to keep from being shot at. Still some distance from the field he lowered the flaps and landing gear and approached slowly, wagging his wings from side to side. It worked. No one opened fire on them. But as soon as the plane rolled to a stop, armed MPs surrounded it. They grabbed Cantacuzino the instant he climbed down from the cockpit.

"Gentlemen," the pilot announced in his clear diction and perfect English, "I have a wonderful gift for you. Will someone quickly get me a screw driver?" A mechanic handed one over and the growing crowd watched in amazement as Catacuzino removed the access door to the radio compartment, revealing a pair of regulation Army Air Corps boots. Colonel Gunn carefully made his way out of the compartment and stood up slowly, stretching his cramped limbs. Someone shouted his name. Then more people recognized him and they broke into applause.

"It wasn't a pleasant trip," Gunn remarked.

The Operation Tidal Wave airmen in Romania had been taken to a safe haven in the Transylvanian Alps in the village of Piertrosita, a two-hour drive from Timisul. They were quartered in private homes along with a number of young women refugees who had fled the fighting in Bucharest and who were delighted to meet Americans. The village offered little more than a café and bar, grocery store, pharmacy, barber shop, and manicurist, who also was the town's prostitute. One of the flyers described their time there.

> Maidens with whirling skirts danced the *hora* to strumming balalaikas and guitars. A fallen Sky Scorpion [389th Bombardment Group], Sergeant James Sedlak, took to the band pavilion with his trumpet and lined out a screaming chorus of "Flat-Foot Floogey." Princess Caradja said, "Those boys had all the fun there is in this world."

But soon the novelty wore off. The village was small and there was little for the men to do. Life at Timisul began to seem a lot better than it had been.

One day hope arrived in an expensive roadster driven by a chauffeur clad in an immaculate, black, gold-trimmed uniform. The passenger in the sleek automobile, which had been confiscated from General Antonescu, was one of the American flyers shot down over Ploesti in a later, high-altitude raid. He brought news: U.S. planes were being dispatched from air bases in Italy to take the men out, but first they would have to join up with other flyers at a field near Bucharest.

Trucks took them past Bucharest's marshalling yards. Richard Britt recalled,

Bomb craters in the road made the going slow. Rails were twisted into every conceivable shape. Buildings surrounding the yards were demolished. Boxcars had been blown apart, scattering boards everywhere. Tank cars were squashed flat, overturned, standing on end, or upside down. As far as the eye could see was devastation.

They drove past the city and came to a sight that made them feel that finally, truly, they were going home. It was the American flag high atop a pole at the entrance to what once had been a military base. The airmen already there—the ones who had been shot down during the raids over the previous six months—rushed over to greet them. They had much to tell the flyers from Timisul, but the best news was that American planes were coming in the morning to take them out.

All the men were told to stay in that night and not, under any circumstances, to venture into Bucharest. It was still considered too dangerous. Several men held in POW compounds in the city limits had already been wounded and nine had been killed in the continuing German air raids.

Although the prisoners held in Bucharest had been officially freed by the Romanians on the night of August 23, they found themselves in a difficult situation. As one historian described it, "They were hundreds of miles from any allied troops. They were still in enemy territory with at least one German air base a scant 20 miles to the north, some German troops near Bucharest, and a Russian Army bearing down from the east."

Many of the Americans were suffering from dysentery. With the guards and the compound staff now gone, they did not know where to obtain food or medical assistance. "The civilian population had its own disastrous situation with lack of food and good water, little medical attention, and fear of the military, be they armies flying overhead, or Germans retreating, or Soviets advancing."

Harry Fritz, a B-24 gunner from one of the high-altitude groups, sought shelter during a German air raid in a 14-story city building. He huddled in a corner, the only American in the crowd, doubled over in pain from the dysentery and terrified he was going to die there alone. "I was ready to break physically and emotionally," he recalled. As the bombs fell all around him, he cried. He survived that bombing, but there were more to come.

At the American air base at Bari, Italy, Operation Gunn, designed to rescue the approximately 1,100 downed flyers in Romania, was about to get under way. Planning had begun shortly after Colonel Gunn climbed out of the radio compartment of the ME-109. By later that night, August 27, the ambitious plan had been developed and by the next day it was fully approved. The Americans would be flown out of Romania on August 31.

On the 29th, phase one of the operation began. Captain Cantacuzino was given a P-51 fighter plane to fly back to the airfield at Popesti with three other Mustangs flown by American pilots. When they reached the airbase, Cantacuzino was to land and send up a flare if it seemed safe to proceed with the next phase of the operation. No one told Captain Cantacuzino that the American pilots had been ordered to shoot him down if he deviated in any way from the flight plan or did anything else that looked the least bit suspicious.

After word had been received from the P-51 escorts that the Popesti field looked safe, two B-17s and 32 Mustangs took off from Italy and headed for Romania. The bombers carried a dozen OSS men in addition to the regular crew to serve as an advance party making final arrangements for the rescue.

Col. George Kreiger was in charge of the advance contingent. Their job was to establish radio communications for Operation Gunn and to locate all the POWs and get them to the airport on time. Kreiger carried food rations as well as medical personnel and equipment to treat the wounded. His party was met at the airport by Romanian Secretary of State Georgescu, who took him to the home of Demeter Bragadiru, Princess Caradja's son-in-law.

Colonel Kreiger and his men faced two major problems, finding enough trucks and buses to transport the POWs to the airport, and rounding up the men. There were several prison camps in and around Bucharest and at least one hospital in which some were being housed.

The men in those facilities would be fairly easy to find. But there were several hundred more staying in private homes or wandering the streets on their own. They had to be contacted and informed of the time and place of departure, but the information had to be kept from the German forces.

No general announcement could be made. Instead, the news was spread from man to man, alone or in groups, throughout the city streets, in bombed-out buildings, at the hospital, at and around the camps, wherever they could be found. And it was done in whispers: "Tomorrow morning. Be at Popesti Airdrome. We're leaving."

At the Bari airfield, 38 B-17s were being stripped of all nonessential equipment so they could carry as many men as possible. The bomb bays were covered with plywood flooring. There would be no seats for passengers. Each plane carried a crew of 6 instead of the usual 10, and the planes were scheduled to land in relays, to stay on the ground no longer than necessary to load their human cargo and take off as quickly as possible.

The bombers left Italy in groups of 12, beginning at 8:00 on the morning of August 31. Every hour another group of 12 took off to make the 1,000-mile round trip. More than 250 P-51s and P-38s were constantly in the air as escorts during the operation, including the famed Tuskegee Airmen, the only squadron of black fighter pilots in World War II.

Operation Gunn went off as smoothly as a peacetime maneuver. Nearly 1,000 prisoners of war were waiting at the airfield for the first ships to arrive. Colonel Krieger had obtained bread and cheese to stave off their hunger, and he had lined the men up along the edge of the runway in groups of 20, each group precisely 150 feet from the next so that the planes could roll up to them as they landed.

The men from Timisul were all present, waiting patiently, laughing and joking nervously. Richard Britt remembered,

> A new group of B-17s landed and it was our turn. At first, Riffle, my radio operator, held back. I didn't blame him, we were all nervous. It was the first time we had been close to a plane since the raid. We all remembered our last flight ended in a crash. For most of us, it was a "white knuckle" flight. Any unusual sounds from the engines, or turbulence in the air, caused anxiety. It was a relief to touch down safely.

Their mission to Ploesti was finally over.

PART VI

AFTERMATH

The Columbia Aquila refinery left in ruins by aircraft of the 44th Bombardment Group. (National Archives)

14

GOOD SHOW—BUT YOU
LOST TOO MANY

H ER REAL NAME WAS Mildred Gillars, but millions of
Americans knew her as Axis Sally. The 43-year-old
Maine native with the sultry voice broadcast her nightly propaganda program, *Home Sweet Home*, from Berlin between 8:00
and 2:00 in the morning. She played popular American music
and teased the GIs with taunts about how their wives and
sweethearts at home were cheating on them.

A few days after the mission to Ploesti, Axis Sally had a message for the leader of Operation Tidal Wave. "Good show,
Brereton, but you lost too many!" She was right. The cost had
been far too high: one of every three men and aircraft had been
lost. And the results had been too ineffective. Within weeks, oil
production at Ploesti was higher than before the raid.

What had gone wrong? The planning and the rehearsals had
been meticulous, unprecedented in depth and detail, and it had
appeared as though every eventuality had been anticipated. The
men knew what they were supposed to do and how to do it.
They had studied the models and executed low flights over the
simulated targets on the desert floor. Yet it had all gone wrong

even before they reached the target; some say even before they took off.

Faulty intelligence about the strength of the defenses around Ploesti was one factor. The bomber crews had been told that the defenses were weak, with the majority of the antiaircraft guns manned by poorly trained Romanian soldiers who were likely to run for shelter at the first sight of planes overhead. That was not the case. Ploesti was one of the most heavily defended sites in all of Europe at that time, and the guns were manned by highly trained German crews.

A Romanian pilot who had defected a few days before the raid had brought this information to the Americans, but his story was discounted, perhaps in part because he had changed it from an earlier version. But more likely it was ignored because the orders for the raid had come from the highest level. By then, the project had assumed a momentum of its own and could not be stopped.

A second problem that may have doomed the raid was the decision to bomb from a low altitude. The assumption was that the defenders would be taken by surprise and would therefore have no time to respond. That idea was faulty also; the Germans knew well in advance that the planes were coming. Another reason for making a low-level approach was the belief that gun crews would be unable to track accurately any aircraft zooming past directly overhead. That idea should have been quashed when British gunners aboard ship in Benghazi harbor reported in a test run that they had no problem whatsoever swinging their guns fast enough to track the Liberators flying over them. Had they been firing, the British gunners told the Operation Tidal Wave planners, they would have shot down most of the planes.

That information was not shared generally and would probably not have changed the situation even if it had been. It was too late to make such a basic change in the preparations for the mission. Too much was at stake, too many people had signed off on it. Powerful voices from Washington and London had spoken, voices of opposition among the military had been silenced, and so much training had already taken place that nothing could derail the project.

By then, no facts contradicting what everyone thought they knew about the target, how it was defended, and the best way (indeed, the only way) to catch its defenders by surprise—would be believed or even discussed. It was too late to change the mind-set of the commanders, even though many of those who were about to embark were convinced it was a suicide mission from which few would return.

A former Marine Corps pilot, Jay Stout, who has made an intensive study of Operation Tidal Wave, concluded that,

> What made this mission so horrible was its low-level execution. The bombers were within the lethal range of everything from sticks and stones to heavy antiaircraft artillery. Once an airplane was mortally hit, there was little that the crew could do to survive. A few men managed to bail out and survive at the extremely low altitudes that were flown, but really there was little choice but to ride the aircraft into the ground.

Had the planes reached their targets on time and in the designated order, the destruction of the refineries might well have been more severe. At least then, the staggering casualty rate might have been justified. The loss of men and planes might indeed have affected Germany's ability to continue the war.

Then the mission could truthfully have been said to be a success, as General Ent erroneously described it on his return to Benghazi.

Unfortunately, due to human error, intransigence, and personal animosities, the bombers did not arrive over their targets as planned. They did not reach the target area as a group because of the failure of Col. John R. Kane and Col. Keith Compton to agree on the proper engine settings, leading to the fatal difference in airspeed.

The mutual antipathy of the two men prevented them from cooperating. Kane refused to follow the speed set by Compton, or by anyone else. Robert Sternfels, a pilot in Colonel Kane's 98th Bombardment Group, wrote that Kane was "blunt about his feelings towards the 'Washington Experts' who came into his area telling him how to run the 98th Bomb Group and how to fly the B-24 on missions he had already been flying for months." Kane was older and had more combat experience than Compton.

General Brereton later criticized Kane for failing to keep up with Compton's forward group. However, as far as is known, General Ent was never admonished for his failure to demand agreement between Kane and Compton, who were both his subordinates, or to order Kane to fly with the same engine settings used by Compton.

But in the final analysis the separation of the two groups turned out to be advantageous, in that Kane's group and the two behind him arrived on course over their specified targets. If not on time, at least they were in the right place, which is more than can be said for the two forward groups led by Colonel Compton and General Ent.

In a 1999 examination of the mission, Lt. Col. Robert Modrovsky prepared a report for the Air War College and concluded: "If it had not been for the wrong turn made at Targovista, there is every indication that the Ploesti mission would have succeeded in accomplishing all of its objectives; destroying 90 percent of the refinery complex."

General Brereton admonished General Ent as mission commander for the wrong turn, and also for the way in which the attack was then carried out. Brereton wrote: "The decision of the commander to execute an attack from the south after his formation had been lost and missed its IP was unsound. It resulted in wrong targets being bombed, destroyed coordination, and sacrificed the benefits of thorough briefing and training of the crews." Curiously, Brereton added that "no blame is attached to any commander or leader participating in the mission for decisions which were made on the spot under the stress of combat."

Three men took responsibility for the faulty turn. Two did so publicly nearly 60 years later and the third, whose life was cut short a few years after the mission, did so privately to his family. Harold Wicklund, the navigator on *Teggie Ann*, wrote that he gave Colonel Compton the wrong estimated time of arrival to the target: "The error was mine. I did not correct him during the turn. I simply made a mistake."

When Colonel Compton learned that Wicklund had assumed responsibility, he protested. "That is just not totally correct," Compton responded. "It was also my decision, my mistake, and was my responsibility." General Ent's nephew reported that although the general had left behind no writings about the Ploesti mission, he had told his family that he "assumed full responsibility for the error of the wrong turn on this mission."

Regardless of hindsight and later judgments, recriminations, or charges, no one can deny the bravery of the air crews and their leaders. Nothing can diminish their courage and dedication. Most of the men are now gone but their memories remained with them throughout their lives.

Jack Warner survived the war. The navigator aboard *Euroclydon*, whose life was saved by Red Franks, stayed in the Air Force until his retirement in 1966 to suburban Dayton, Ohio. Every August 1st he revisited the past at the sprawling United States Air Force museum, now only a short drive from his home.

A B-24 is there, painted desert pink, fully restored to look like it did in North Africa in 1943. It is named *Strawberry Bitch*, and although it did not fly on the Ploesti mission, seeing it conjures up images of all those men and all those planes never seen again.

Inside the museum, Jack Warner stopped to see a special exhibit, the shirt he wore during the raid that was ripped and torn by German shells. "Clearly visible is the stitching around the shoulders and down the back where Romanian nurse Elana Andreise sewed up the 35 tears and holes from shrapnel." Warner kept it for years and donated it to the museum.

Jim Sedlack, a radioman aboard *Boomerang* in the 93rd, relived his fragment in time in a different way. On Veteran's Day of 2004, 61 years after Operation Tidal Wave, he took a ride in a B-24. He flew in a fully restored ship called *All-American* from a field in Kennesaw, Georgia, "grinning like a kid all the way." During the hour-long flight, he hunched over the radio, as he had done all those years ago. A newspaper reporter for the *Atlanta Constitution*, whose name, coincidentally, was Jack Warner, went along and later wrote about it.

There are headphones over his ears and a telegraph key by his hand. Except for the gray in his military mustache and a few wisps of white hair sticking out of his cap, he must have looked like this [in 1943]. Sedlack clambered around the drafty, deafening B-24 with greater agility than men 20 years and more his junior, looking for all the world like a man returning to the house where he grew up.

Sedlack talked to the reporter about the mission over Ploesti. "I was standing up behind the pilot and copilot when we went in. I'll never forget the sight of that brick smokestack. We lifted up over it, let go our bombs and dropped back down. I heard the burst that got us. It severed some of the hydraulics and knocked out number four engine."

Boomerang went down in a cornfield near Ploesti and Sedlack and his crew, all of whom survived the crash-landing, were taken to Timisul. Sedlack was a trumpet player and started a band in the camp. After the war he played with the Atlanta Symphony Orchestra and, as of 2004, was leading a 17-piece band, The Nostalgics, playing the forties' music that makes them sought after by World War II veterans' reunion groups.

Many of the men on the mission attended the annual reunions. In 2004, all five bombardment groups held a grand gathering in Salt Lake City, Utah. Norman Whalen, navigator on board Kane's Hail Columbia, was there. It was thanks to him that they made it to Cyprus.

After the mission Whalen completed his first combat tour and volunteered for a second. He eventually made 75 missions, but Ploesti was the one that stood out. "It was the most horrific raid I went on," he said. When asked why he volunteered for a second tour, knowing that his chances of survival would be slim, he answered, "I felt an obligation to the men over there. In all the raids, I never even got a scratch. I always attributed it to Divine Providence."

Henry Lasco also attended the reunion. He was the pilot of *Sad Sack II* who had been wounded so badly in the jaw that one of his own crewmen did not recognize him. He spent a year undergoing reconstructive surgeries. He stayed in touch with Joe Kill, his copilot, who died a few years before the 2004 reunion. "But his daughter and granddaughter still come to these reunions," Lasco said. "They think of me as their surrogate Dad, and to me, they're my family too." For many of the men, the mission was a deep and lasting bond. Now their families are maintaining those ties, keeping alive the legacy.

There was another reunion in 2004 in Vancouver, Washington, where 23 of the Ploesti crewmen and their families gathered. They were among the 48 remaining of the more than 100 flyers who had been shot down and who spent 13 months imprisoned at Timisul. "We have a camaraderie most people don't have," said Al Mash. He had been a waist gunner on *G.I. Gal* of the 44th Bombardment Group. "It was a great group of men," he added. His son Joe had helped organize the weekend. He said, "We've been fighting the war over and over again all weekend. The best thing is that we win each time." "You get a little teary during these ceremonies," said Norman Adams, a navigator on *Jersey Bounce*, at the Timisul reunion. "But it's great to see these people again."

Even Princess Caradja held reunions with her boys from Timisul, but not until after she escaped from the Communists who took control of the Romanian government in 1949. All of her property was confiscated, including the estate near Ploesti and the orphanage. She later told an American reporter, "My crime was being a landholder [which] was worse than being a murderer."

She was labeled a woman of "unhealthy social origin," as a member of the aristocracy, and was not permitted to have a food ration card or to take any kind of gainful employment. People of her class were supposed to "wither away and die. Many jumped off tall buildings, others committed suicide in different ways." She managed to survive until her daughter, then living in Paris, helped her escape from Romania 1952, by hiding in a tiny compartment on a barge. The trip down the Danube took 62 days; the weather was freezing and there was no heat in her cramped cubbyhole.

She spent the next three years giving talks on "Life Behind the Iron Curtain." Her lecture tours took her throughout France and were broadcast on the BBC and Radio Free Europe. After three years of bureaucratic delays trying to get a visa to the United States, to visit her "boys," she finally succeeded in 1955. When she arrived in New York, she was promptly invited to appear on *Today*, a popular television talk show hosted by Dave Garroway. From there, she went to Comfort, Texas, to visit Richard Britt, whose life she had saved when his plane crashed on her estate.

For the next 35 years, Princess Caradja divided her time between Comfort, Baltimore, and Kansas City. She attended reunions of Ploesti survivors and traveled widely, as Britt described it, "speaking at Rotary, Lions, Women's clubs, at high schools, colleges, and churches, and to anyone who would listen to her" about the threat of Communism. "Her mode of travel was by bus, sleeping in YMCAs where she could find one. She always refused any monetary offering other than her needs for transport, sustenance, and lodgings."

On August 28, 1972, 28 years to the day after her Ploesti fly-ers were freed from Timisul, she arranged a reunion in Dallas, Texas, for as many of them as she could locate. This became an annual tradition that continued for more than 10 years. In 1991, when she was 98 years old and confined to a wheelchair, her boys honored her with a farewell banquet in San Antonio. She was returning to Romania, where a more liberal govern-ment had restored part of her estate and planned to welcome her back. She died in 1993, two days after her 100th birthday.

The Russian domination of Romania in 1944 also affected the lives of those who had defended Ploesti against the bombers of Operation Tidal Wave. Gen. Alfred Gerstenberg was ordered to take over the city of Bucharest when the Romanians signed an armistice with the Allies. On the morning of August 24, 1944, he led 2,000 troops into the city, where they were met with such fierce resistance from the Romanian populace that Gerstenberg was forced to retreat to the Otopen Airport on the outskirts of town, where he and his remaining men were soon surrounded.

They held out for two days and on August 27 were rein-forced by a battalion of commandoes who parachuted into the airfield to rescue Gerstenberg. But even with the fresh troops, the Germans were unable to break out of the encirclement and the following day were forced to surrender. Gerstenberg was taken prisoner and held by the Russians for 11 years before being released in 1955.

The Romanian and Bulgarian fighter pilots who flew for the Germans also had a difficult time under Communist rule. Lt. Stoyan Stoyanov, Bulgaria's leading ace who tangled with the *American Witch*, was celebrated as a hero, having shot down more American planes than any other pilot in the Bulgarian Air

Romanian Air Force pilot, Capt. Constantine Cantacuzino, right, shakes hands with Col. James A. Gunn after flying him to safety in Italy. (*Paul A. Sihvonen-Binder*)

Force, but that was of no help when the Communists took over. He was dismissed and stripped of all rights. He was not allowed to have a career or a steady job. He wrote, "At first I worked as a construction worker, and then for five years I performed as a mute actor and lighting specialist in different theaters. After that, the State Committee for Culture sent me to the Rila Monastery where I spent almost 30 years in seclusion."

When Stoyanov wrote his memoirs, the government suppressed the book until Communist rule ended. Finally published in 1992, it became a national best-seller. Once again he was declared a hero and restored to the rank of major general. By then he was in poor health; redemption had come too late. For five more years he lived in Sofia, "in an attic that could only be reached by climbing 85 steps. Forgotten by almost everybody, he was cared for only by his wife, Mina, until he died on March 13, 1997."

The Romanian fighter pilot who had flown Colonel Gunn to Italy, Capt. Constantine Cantacuzino, was allowed to keep the P-51 he had been given to lead the advance units back to Romania. He used it to fight the Germans until the Russians arrived and confiscated the aircraft. He escaped from Romania in 1955 and went to France. His repeated requests for a visa to visit the United States were rejected. He died in 1969, in Spain, while undergoing emergency medical treatment for an intestinal ailment.

Most of the U.S. commanders from the Ploesti raid went on to prominent careers in the air force, as did the raid's planner, Jacob Smart. He flew 29 combat missions until he was shot down and spent a year as a POW in Germany. Smart rose to four-star rank and had several high-level postwar assignments including commander of all American forces in Europe. After he retired from the air force, he joined NASA to work on the Hubbell Space Telescope. He died in 2006 at the age of 97, in the house in which he had been born.

Maj. Gen. Lewis Brereton won a promotion and a larger command. In August 1944, he took over the newly created 1st Allied Airborne Army, consisting of British and American parachute troops, for Operation Market Garden, which involved landing 35,000 men in Holland, behind the German lines. (The failed operation was the subject of a popular book and movie, A Bridge Too Far.) Brereton then served in various administrative posts. He died on August 1, 1967, 24 years to the day after the mission to Ploesti.

Uzal G. Ent was sent back to the States a month after the Ploesti mission. He was later promoted to major general and given command of the 2nd Air Force in Colorado, a major training outfit. Part of Ent's responsibility was to oversee the

· training of the B-29 crews who would drop the atomic bombs on Japan. He personally selected the commander, Col. Paul Tibbets.

On October 10, 1944, Ent was taking off in a B-25 from an airfield in Texas when a propeller blade sliced into the cockpit, leaving him permanently paralyzed from the waist down. Confined to a hospital bed from the age of 44, he devoted his time to designing braces and other devices to assist paraplegics. Gen. Omar Bradley, head of the Veterans Administration after the war, was so impressed with Ent's designs that he had them put into production. Ent began to study law, intending that to be his future career, but he died in 1948. The cause was an infection from a hot water bottle burn he got in the hospital.

Of the four bombardment group commanders who survived the raid, all but one was promoted to the rank of general. Keith Compton of the 376th, who had made the wrong turn, retired as a lieutenant general after a succession of high-level appointments: vice commander of the Strategic Air Command, inspector general, deputy chief of staff for plans and operations, and a deputy for the Joint Chiefs of Staff. He died in 2004.

Jack Wood, commander of the 389th, retired as a major general after serving as air attaché in London, director of the budget for the air force, and deputy inspector general. He died in 1994. Leon Johnson, who led the 44th, retired in 1961 as a four-star general and died in 1997.

Killer Kane never received another promotion after Ploesti, despite having been awarded the Medal of Honor. Kane was sent back to the States six months after Ploesti to serve as base commander of an airfield in Idaho. He was never given another combat command. After the war he held a series of administrative posts in Colorado, Alaska, Idaho, Libya, and Morocco.

He retired in 1954 and set out on a two-year odyssey in a trailer, along with his British wife whom he had met in North Africa after the Ploesti mission. He said he was "dropping out of the rat race," looking for a quiet place to live, which he found on top of a mountain in the Ozarks. They camped in a tent for two years while they built their rustic home by hand. Kane attended reunions of the 98th for awhile but stopped going when he was in his early seventies. "They met too far away," he said, "and I got tired of getting together with all those old guys." He died in 1996, at age 89, in a VA nursing home in Pennsylvania. A few months earlier, he recorded his memories of the Ploesti mission. "I still recall the smoke, fire, and B-24s going down, like it was yesterday. Even now I get a lump in my throat when I think about what we went through."

NOTES

Prologue: Frozen in Time

"He looked like Clark Gable" (Hadley obituary, *Wichita Eagle*)

"He chewed us out for saluting him" (Hadley obituary, *Wichita Eagle*)

"The seven of us" (Hadley obituary, *Wichita Eagle*)

"I feel this was a good payback" (Hadley obituary, *Ponca City News*)

"I tell you" (Shubert, p. 8)

"Worst catastrophe" (Turner, p. 43)

"One of the bloodiest" (Modrovsky, p. 38)

"A watershed event" (Stout, foreword)

"Ploesti was producing" (Modrovsky, p. 29)

"It was strange to me" (Butler, p. 7)

"Look, there's another one" (Martin, pp. 142-143)

"One bomber" (Stout, p. 53)

"Two pieces of metal" (Britt, p. 49)

"When we got there" (Hill, p. 89)

"Near the refinery" (Hill, p. 91)

"It was a horrible sight" (Hill, p. 141)

"I don't know how I made it" (Dugan and Stewart, p. 122)

"I was not getting much pressure" (Dugan and Stewart, p. 134)

"My stomach turned over" (Dugan and Stewart, pp. 186-187)

"In one case" (Colley, p. 146)

"Tumbled out of their ships" (Stout, p. 74)

"I made it back" (Dugan and Stewart, p. 218)

"Our squadron is no more" (Adlen, pp. 132-133)

Chapter 1. Operation Soapsuds

"I was woken up"; "From every point of view" (Churchill, vol. 4, pp. 604-605)

"The P.M. is at a disadvantage" (Moran, p. 86)

"Taproot of German might" (Stout, p. 7)

"So reduced were inventories" (Wolff, p. 77)

"Now all we need" (Larrabee, p. 184)

"A cross between" (Larrabee, p. 184)

"Short and square-set" (Copp, p. 211)

"You are not" (Sterner, p. 7)

"To us, the briefing" (Sterner, p. 7)

"Can we help it" (Sterner, p. 7)

"The general impression" (Unitt, part 1, p. 18)

"This is the beginning" (Dugan and Stewart, p. 15)

"No mission before or after" (Copp, p. 414)

"A bad idea" (Way and Sternfels, 2002, p. 42)

"Of all aircraft" (Dugan and Stewart, p. 38)

"Nobody with any sense" (Colley, p. 9)

"Had photographs been taken" (Copp, pp. 416-417)

"Ridiculous and suicidal" (Way and Sternfels, 2002, p. 42)

"Very comfortable" (Gilbert, p. 420)

"The imaginative Churchill" (Dugan and Stewart, p. 40)

"General Eaker has given me" (Copp, p. 415)

About code names for U.S. operations, see Hoffman

"On reflection" (Gilbert, p. 424)

Chapter 2. Some Idiotic Armchair Warrior in Washington

About "Hot-Foot Louie" Brereton, see Hastings, p. 57; Miller, 2000, 2001; "Brereton Is Named to Andrews's Post"

"Distinguished by the amount of time" (Luce, quoted in Miller, 2000)

"Postwar problems" and "who does not apply himself" (Miller, 2000)

"Boys, bombing Japs" and "About the only fun" (Miller, 2001)

"I knew that the Liberator" (*Brereton Diaries*, p. 192)

"We estimate that 75 aircraft" (Ent, 2000)

"What about the balloons" (Wolff, p. 98)

"I wish I could believe" (Adlen, p. 30)

"It's strange" (Adlen, pp. 32-33)

About "Killer" Kane, see Buller, p. 1; Calhoun, pp. 126, 129; Turner, p. 41

"Get the hell off the air" (Sterner, p. 10)

"Since Kane took the outfit over" (Adlen, pp. 87, 88, 91-92)

"He was a controversial figure" (Sterner, pp. 10-11)

"A courageous, able bomber pilot" (Way and Sternfels, p. 142)

"I found out I couldn't stand" (Turner, p. 40)

"I sponged off my dad" (Calhoun, p. 131)

"Some idiotic armchair warrior" and "We're going to knock out Ploesti" (Turner, p. 41)

"Ted's Traveling Circus" (U.S. 93rd Bomb Group)

"A good commander" (Rooney, pp. 135-136)

"Walk around the B-24 bases" (Dugan and Stewart, p. 45)

"Colonel Johnson told us" (Dugan and Stewart, p. 44)

"We did practice" (Wolff, p. 99)

Chapter 3. A Bird's-Eye View of Impending Death

About the B-24 Liberator, see McCrary and Scherman, p. 186; Colley, p. 13; Childers, pp. 20, 24; Stout, p. 69; Fay, p. 11; Longo, p. 6

"When the book was started" (O'Leary, p. 6)

Comparing the B-24 and the B-17, see O'Leary, pp. 6-7; Longo, p. 3; Johnsen, pp. 6-7

"Battle damage" (Kinsey, p. 6)

"The B-24 handled" (Rooney, p.75)

"Men who are picked to fly" (Johnsen, p. 7)

"It was so tight" and "The only way to do this" (Longo, p. 6)

"Sat for hours on end" (Perkins, Crean, and Patterson, p. 19)

"Bird's eye view" (Colley, p. 28)

"Death of the Ball Turret Gunner" (quoted by Longo, p. 5)

"Once inside it seemed" (Longo, p. 5)

"Complicated beyond reason" (Stout, p. 23)

"Oxygen masks" (Bowman, p. 46)

"The noise was more than deafening" (Longo, p. 5)

"Here a bit of cloak and dagger" (Hill, p. 18)

"The idea was taken one step further" (Hill, p. 19)

"Silly pants" (McCrary and Scherman, p. 201)

"Virgin target" (Rooney, p. 136)

"I would say" and "And so at the end of the film" (McCrary and Scherman, p. 202)

"The defenses" and "No one headed for Ploesti" (Rooney, pp. 136-137)

Chapter 4. When Are You Going to Bomb Ploesti?

"Gerstenberg was a dedicated man" (Dugan and Stewart, p. 25)

"DS Secret" (Hill, p. 23)

"The days were hot as blazes" (Cotter, p. 755)

"The dust moved every day" (Hill, p. 25)

"Daily, for hours and hours" (Way and Sternfels, 2002, p. 46)

"The sun beat down" (Hill, p. 25)

"Chow in camp" (Fay, pp. 3-4)

"Take a shower?" (Hartley, p. 25)

"There were grasshoppers" (Hill, p. 27)

"To make things more exciting" and "You can tell a rookie" (Hartley, p. 24)

"We took 8mm. shells" (Ardery, 1978, p. 95)

"Parts of collapsed buildings" (Cotter, p. 758)

"Our recreation room" (Cotter, p. 761)

"There were never any dull moments" (Cotter, p. 764)

"Everybody eats tangerines" and "The standard horror story" (Notes from North Africa, p. 5)

"Had served for Italians" (Wolff, p. 104)

"By far the finest city" (Adlen, p. 90)

"Bill and I spent the day" and "Bill took off" (Adlen, p. 57)

"Security around this headquarters" (Dugan and Stewart, p. 59)

"I was visited by" (Dewez, p. 5)

"With great secrecy" (Kane, Spring 1983, p. 40)

"It was suicide" (Turner, p. 41)

"Tedder indicated" and "I opposed Tedder's view" (*Brereton Diaries*, p. 197)

"The general feeling" and "The brass felt" (Hill, p. 34)

Chapter 5. We Dreaded This Mission

"For days" (Ellis, p. 77)

"Flying a B-24" (Colley, p. 14)

"Many of our high-level pilots" (Wolff, p. 14)

"When you go 200 miles per hour" (Ardery, 1978, p. 97)

"After passing a village" (Britt, p. 34)

"I guess I hold" (Wolff, p. 107)

"The bird hit the center section" (Hill, p. 32)

"I guess we received" (Ellis, p. 7)

"Each vital pinpoint target" (Dugan and Stewart, p. 62)

"We practiced coming in" (Ardery, 1978, pp. 97-98)

"The charm of the plan" (Colley, p. 16)

"There were major differences" (Way and Sternfels, 2002, p. 47)

"Probably the most discussed question" and "It's something beyond belief" (Dugan and Stewart, p. 64)

"Lobbing basketballs" (Colley, p. 15)

"You will be on a southeast heading" (Hill, p. 33)

"We could hit a target" (Wolff, p. 108)

"To the observer" (Hill, p. 35)

"Each man was given" (Colley, pp. 16-17)

"Timberlake's face" (Sterner, p. 20)

"There was a growing pessimism" (Dugan and Stewart, p. 65)

"We dreaded this mission" (Wolff, p. 15)

"This is where the Ninth Air Force" and "Tomorrow, when you advance" (Sterner, p. 18)

"If you do your job right" (Sulzberger, p. 3)

"We sat stunned" (*Wichita Eagle*, January 8, 1997)

"A strange silence" (Way and Sternfels, p. 93)

"There was universal high morale" (*Brereton Diaries*, p. 199)

"Our Saturday evening supper" (Way and Sternfels, p. 93)

"There was a quietness" (Colley, p. 21)

"We talked about death" (Colley, p. 17)

"This is the biggest mission" (Hill, p. 38)

"Dearest Dad" (Colley, pp. 105-106)

Chapter 6. Not Here! Not Here!

"That dream was embedded" and "Outside the plane" and "Lieutenant Scrivner" (44th Bomb Group: Walter Patrick, pp. 1-3)

"You'll never get back" (Britt, p. 42)

"I hope the son-of-a-bitch" (Barbee, p. 5)

"I had no objection" (Hill, p. 44)

"Young waist gunner" (Dewez, p. 10)

"It was an odd punishment" (Colley, p. 25)

"At 0655, Johnny turned over number one engine" (Kane, Summer 1983, p. 129)

"Flying blind" (Britt, p. 42)

"With a sickening jolt" (Wolff, p. 130)

"That was a bad omen" (Kane, Summer 1983, p. 129)

About the order of assembly, see Fay, pp. 103-104

"Got into formation" (Shubert, p. 2)

"Every once in a while" and "Those guys look too happy" (Dugan and Stewart, p. 92)

"This percentage" (Wolff, p. 131)

"Looks like we're getting" (Adler, p. 131)

"Look at that" (Colley, p. 33)

"As we approached Corfu" (Britt, p. 43)

"Then, out of a blue sky" (Shubert, p. 2)

"We were in serious trouble" (Britt, p. 44)

"A cold chill" (Baker, p. 1)

"Knowing Kane" (Way and Sternfels, p. 85)

"Who insisted on flying slower" (Stout, p. 46)

"It is unclear" (Sterner, p. 24)

"Like that Kentucky bluegrass" (Sulzberger, p. 4)

"I wondered when I saw the Danube," "After several minutes," and "The houses were brightly colored" (Kane, Summer 1983, p. 130)

"A girl beside him" (Colley, p. 70)

"When my gunners began to shoot" (Kane, Summer 1983, p. 130)

"Not here!" (Sterner, p. 25)

"We're going to Bucharest" (Hill, p. 57)

Chapter 7. My God! We're Sitting Ducks!

"If this is the correct turn" (Dugan and Stewart, p. 133)

"Tramping the pedals" (Dugan and Stewart, p. 134)

"Something I couldn't do" (Dugan and Stewart, p. 136)

"We're going wrong" (Colley, p. 73)

"Look at nine o'clock" (Colley, p. 72)

"There was no doubt" (Sterner, p. 27)

"Damned cleverly done" (Sterner, p. 28)

"All hell was breaking loose" (Baker, pp. 1-2)

"Fire at anything you see" (Colley, p. 75)

"Look at that" (Colley, p. 77)

"We pulled up" (Hill, p. 59)

"Baker had been burning" (Dugan and Stewart, p. 117)

"I tried to use the intercom" (Hill, p. 68)

"Two men out" and "Like a blazing star" (Colley, p. 79)

"I immediately reached" and "Too seriously wounded" (Unitt, part 2, p. 33)

"Red pushed me out" (Colley, p. 283)

"Always spoke of Red" (Colley, p. 284)

"Bartlett with his big top guns" (Hill, pp. 60-61)

"We rolled the left wing" (Dugan and Stewart, p. 118)

"Don't look now" (Hill, p. 61)

"Hey, there's a little girl" (Dugan and Stewart, p. 128)

"I never saw him" and "Our number 3 engine . . . we zigzagged" (Baker, p. 2)

"Sliding down a street . . . a plane hit a barrage balloon" (Dugan and Stewart, p. 118)

"Wires snapped" (Hill, p. 65)

"Flaming petrol" (Dugan and Stewart, p. 127)

"They were practically flying," "It was like hell," and "He expected to simply blow up" (Nitu, pp. 2-3)

"Gasoline squirted" (Dugan and Stewart, p. 122)

"A guy hit a barrage balloon" and "We got away from the target" (Ferrell, p. 2)

"We weren't going to make it," "I knew I was hit" and "I lifted my leg to try again" (Hill, p. 66)

Chapter 8. The Furnace of Hell

"I turned to General Ent" (Way and Sternfels, p. 177)

"Ent would not allow" (Hill, p. 77)

"Grand tour of Romania" (Hill, p. 78)

"With the bombs gone" and "I was not called upon" (Way and Sternfels, p. 182)

"It was a mess" (Hill, p. 74)

"Let's tuck in now" (Sterner, p. 31)

"At 200 miles per hour" (Hill, p. 78)

"Roofed with three layers" (Dugan and Stewart, p. 142)

"In the distance toward Ploesti" (Kane, Summer 1983, p. 130)

"To this day" (Fay, p. 110)

"I did not think it was possible," "I thought I was low" and "We had to shoot our way in" (Kane, Summer 1983, pp. 130-131)

"The gunners aboard the train" (Stout, p. 56)

"I did not think I was going to live" (Sterner, p. 35)

"Suddenly we were enveloped" and "We must save the engines" (Kane, Summer 1983, p. 131)

"Quit trimming the hedges" (Hill, p. 84)

"It was just like a movie" (Sulzberger, p. 42)

"They got me too" (Sterner, p. 42)

"I never want to see" (Sulzberger, p. 42)

"For a split second" and "By this time" (Sulzberger, p. 43)

"That I had the control yoke" (Way and Sternfels, p. 60)

"Full throttles" (Way and Sternfels, p. 62)

"When we were in the smoke" (Way and Sternfels, p. 64)

"Suddenly and without warning" (Hill, p. 84)

"Looked like the furnace of hell" (Hill, p. 86)

"When we got there" (Hill, p. 89)

"The next thing I knew" (Hill, pp. 86-87)

Chapter 9. We Were All Dead Anyway

"We flew through sheets of flame" (Wolff, p. 156)

"William, you are on target" (Dugan and Stewart, p. 146)

"Ahead the target" (Hill, p. 103)

"The ground was littered" (Sterner, p. 33)

"We found that we could weave" (Wolff, p. 157)

"Balloon cables," "At least a hundred fighters" and "Calaban got away" (Dobson, p. 20)

"This would be a day" (Worley, p. 2)

"A German fighter plane" (Worley, p. 4)

"Saw Lieutenant Winger" (44th Bomb Group Roll, p. 91)

"We then went down" and "With the two waist gunners" (44th Bomb Group Roll, p. 93)

"For whom crew members" (House, p. 2)

"This proved to me" (Hill, p. 102)

"Began to have grave doubts," "I received shrapnel wounds," "We were very low," "The navigator was kneeling," "I tumbled" and "Was blindly thrashing about" (44th Bomb Group Roll, pp. 88-89)

"People ask me" (Dugan and Stewart, p. 161)

"Glanced sideways" (Hill, p. 121)

"A German sergeant" and "An old lady" (Hill, p. 122)

"Those poor oxen" (Hill, p. 123)

"I saw dogs" (Hill, pp. 126-127)

"Too soon" (Ardery, 1978, pp. 102-103)

"We found ourselves" (Ardery, 1978, p. 104)

"We were on target" (Britt, p. 47)

"Roof tops and trees" (Britt, p. 48)

"Looking down at the housetops" and "The next few seconds" (Britt, p. 49)

"Poor Pete" (Ardery, 1978, p. 104)

"A moment later" (Ardery, 2001, p. 85)

"It was a horrible sight" (Hill, p. 141)

"Tracers, red, white" and "The boys told me" (389th Bomb Group, 2002, p. 5)

"The sky was a bedlam" (Ardery, 1978, pp. 106-107)

Chapter 10. A Wing and A Prayer

"Quickly we looked around," "Amazed at the capacity," "Corn, wheat, and sunflowers" and "We buzzed over small villages" (Ellis, p. 80)

"It was so terrible" (Semerdjiev, 1999)

"I felt my heart" and "I press triggers" (Stoyanov, pp. 2-4)

"We either had to shoot," "Let's move back" and "The trip home" (Ellis, p. 81)

"Every time Utah Man's speed" (Hill, p. 148)

"I've never been so out of gas" and "You call this an ocean" (Hill, p. 163)

"The greatest game of chance" and "Hell, I don't know" (Hill, p. 151)

"Sorry for the bedraggled thing" (Fay, p. 130)

"As they lay on the beach" (Fay, pp. 131-132)

"Mission successful" and "A feeble attempt" (Wolff, p. 167)

Chapter 11. The Last Plane Back

"Hadley called me" (Way and Sternfels, 2002, p. 99)

"Do you want to bail out" and "Am I going to die" (Sulzberger, p. 43)

"We hear it was a big raid" (Sulzberger, p. 44)

"I told 'Wilkie,'" "Coming in too steep" and "As the dust settled" (Baker, p. 3)

"Berserk with curiosity" (Dugan and Stewart, p. 197)

"Our time in the Yeni Hotel" (Zimmerman, p. 22)

"Leaves blowing off the trees" (Hill, p. 154)

"I damn near died" and "With a roar" (Shubert, p. 7)

"Our nerves" and "We listened to our radio" (Shubert, p. 8)

"The silence was deafening" (Shubert, p. 2)

"We have about as much chance" (Dugan and Stewart, p. 198)

"What are you doing" and "I did not dare" (Kane, Summer 1983, p. 132)

"A prop from the dead engine" and "I sat down in a daze" (Kane, Summer 1983, p. 133)

"What a helluva situation" (Way and Sternfels, 2002, p. 113)

"I haven't had time" (Way and Sternfels, 2002, p. 112)

"As if by magic" (Way and Sternfels, 2002, p. 113)

"There are no gas trucks" (Way and Sternfels, 2002, pp. 113-114)

"Had been riddled" (Kane, Summer 1983, p. 133)

"Tempted to fall flat" (Cotter, pp. 767, 768)

"Downcast" (*Brereton Diaries*, p. 200)

"I originally blamed" (Way and Sternfels, 2002, p. 187)

"It's the ugliest piece" (Hill, p. 163)

"The trip home" (Ellis, p. 81)

"We saw some red flares" and "We could never go around" (Ellis, p. 82)

"The ground crew lit up" (Ferrell, p. 3)

"The ground crews waited" (Hill, p. 165)

"Madge and I listened" (Cotter, p. 768)

"Horrified at the blank spaces" (Kane, Summer 1983, p. 134)

"The next day" (Martin, p. 146)

Chapter 12. Nights Were Not Happy Times

"Those skimming bombers" (Colley, pp. 259-260)

"Send to Dr. Jesse D. Franks" (Colley, p. 259)

"The Romanian women" (Modrovsky, p. 32)

"Initial inclination" and "I figured" (Unitt, part 2, pp. 33, 34)

"They jumped me" (44th Bomb Group Roll of Honor, p. 89)

"I must have scared them" and "Looked at the note" (Hill, pp. 171, 172)

"There was a nurse,""I just wanted something" and "The doctors and nurses" (Britt, p. 211)

"A big ox of a man" (Britt, p. 78)

"I was still in the plane,""People peering" and "An agitated reaction" (Britt, pp. 2-3)

"I felt no pain" (Britt, p. 6)

"In the most impolite German" and "I thought the Germans had won" (Britt, p. 7)

"The houses were picturesque" (Britt, p. 71)

"The graceful spiral staircase" (Britt, p. 94)

"Nights in the hospital" and "Was in constant pain" (Britt, pp. 82, 83)

"Seemed to be missing" (Britt, p. 88)

"Not a pretty sight" (Britt, p. 89)

"Fool things" and "You can't catch me" (Britt, p. 93)

"The sloppy patients" (Britt, p. 104)

"We realized that our treatment" (Britt, p. 105)

Chapter 13. The Gilded Cage

"Probably the best prison camp" (Britt, p. 114)

"Imprisoned us" (Fili, 1991, p. 199)

"Fresh butter" and "With white tablecloths" (Unitt, part 2, p. 35)

"For some strange reason" (Britt, p. 119)

"Exhausted, grouchy" and "In a calm" (Britt, p. 122)

"Exploded with a tirade" and "I am taking your Ping-Pong table" (Britt, p. 124)

"I'm worried about you" (Britt, pp. 132-133)

"One day began to merge" (Britt, p. 127)

"I looked at her" (Britt, p. 145)

"A feeling of gloom" (Britt, p. 151)

"We were being paid" (Dugan and Stewart, p. 259)

"The party was over" (Britt, p. 177)

"She drove him to a physician" (Dugan and Stewart, p. 277)

"Colonel, if you will crawl" (Fili, 1991, p. 263)

"The likes of which" (Cubbins, p. 248)

"It was very cold" (Cubbins, p. 250)

"Gentlemen, I have a wonderful gift" (Fili, 1991, p. 271)

"It wasn't a pleasant trip" (Williams, p. 85)

"Maidens with whirling skirts" (Dugan and Stewart, p. 281)

"Bomb craters in the road" (Britt, p. 230)

"They were hundreds of miles" and "The civilian population" (Williams, pp. 75, 76)

"No general announcement" (Williams, p. 93)

"A new group of B-17s" (Britt, p. 234)

Chapter 14. Good Show—But You Lost Too Many

"Good show, Brereton" (Sterner, p. 41)

"What made this mission" (Stout, p. 77)

"Blunt about his feelings" (Way and Sternfels, 2002, p. 174)

"If it had not been" (Modrovsky, p. 29)

"The decision of the commander" and "No blame is attached" (Stout, p. 78)

"The error was mine" (Way and Sternfels, 2002, p. 176)

"That is just not totally correct" (Way and Sternfels, 2002, p. 175)

"Assumed full responsibility" (Way and Sternfels, 2002, p. 176)

"Clearly visible" (Colley, p. 282)

"Grinning like a kid," "There are headphones" and "I was standing up" (Warner, pp. 1, 2)

"It was the most horrific raid," "I felt an obligation" and "But his daughter" (House, pp. 1, 2)

"We have a camaraderie" and "You get a little teary" (Priniotakis, pp. 1, 2)

"My crime" (Reis, p. 4)

"Unhealthy social origin" (Britt, p. 264)

"Speaking at Rotary" (Fili, Princess Caradja, pp. 3-4)

"At first I worked" and "In an attic" (Semerdjiev, 1999, pp. 6, 7)

"Dropping out of the rat race" (Turner, p. 43)

"I still recall the smoke" (Sterner, p. 43)

BIBLIOGRAPHY

Adlen, Robert N. (1985). *In the Lion's Mouth: The Story of a WWII Aviator.* Canoga Park, CA: Emis Publishing.

Ardery, Philip (1978). *Bomber Pilot: A Memoir of World War II.* Lexington: University Press of Kentucky.

Ardery, Philip (2001). A veteran of the August 1943 Ploesti raid reveals long-hidden details of the costly operation. *World War II* (July), pp. 85-90.

Axis Sally (Mildred Gillars). Biography. *http://users.rlc.net/catfish/liberator-crew/11_Axis%20Sally.htm;*

http://womenshistory.about.com/library/prm/blaxissally1.htm.

B-24 Liberator Flight Manual (1942). Appendix: How to start, taxi, warm up, take-off and land the B-24D airplane. September 15.

Baker, Edwin C. (1984). Ploesti. *Second Air Division Association Journal* (March), pp. 1-3.

Ball of Fire Quarterly Express (93rd Bombardment Group) (2005). Newsletter, Fall.

Barbee, Darren (2000). WWII aviator Ernest Fogel shares his diary, bitter-sweet memories for Memorial Day. *Corpus Christi (TX) Caller-Times,* May 28.

Bowman, Martin W. (1998). *Consolidated B-24 Liberator.* Wiltshire, England: Crowood Press.

Brereton, Lewis H. (1946). *The Brereton Diaries: The War in the Air in the Pacific, Middle East, and Europe: 3 October 1941–8 May 1945.* New York: William Morrow.

Brereton, Lewis Hyde. Biography. *www.arlingtoncemetery.net/brereton.htm.*

Brereton is named to Andrews's post. *New York Times,* February 7, 1943.

Britt, Richard W. (1988). *The Princess and the POW: The True Story of Princess*

Catherine Caradja and Richard W. Britt. Comfort, TX: Gabriel Publishing.

Buller, H. L. (2002). *Killer Kane's Raid!* Chatsworth, CA: Challenge Publications.

Butler, R. D. "Dick." (2002). The recovery of Hadley's Harem, 98th Bomb Group. *Briefing* [Journal of the International B-24 Liberator Club], (Summer), pp. 6-8.

Calhoun, Fillmore (1944). Killer Kane. *Coronet* (July), pp. 126-134.

Cantacuzino, Constantin. Biography. *www.worldwar2.ro/arr/*.

Caradja, Catherine Olympia. Biography. *www.tsha.utexas.edu/handbook/online/articles/CC/fcaca_print.html*.

Childers, Thomas (1995). *Wings of Morning: The Story of the Last American Bomber Shot Down over Germany in World War II*. Reading, MA: Addison-Wesley.

Churchill, Winston S. (1950). *The Second World War. Volume 4: The Hinge of Fate*. Boston: Houghton Mifflin.

Colley, David P. (2004). *Safely Rest*. New York: Berkley Publishing Group.

Compton, Keith Karl. Biography. Air Force Link, *www.af.mil/bios/*.

Copp, DeWitt S. (1982). *Forged in Fire: Strategy and Decisions in the Air War over Europe, 1940-45*. Garden City, NY: Doubleday.

Cotter, Margaret (1944). Red Cross girl overseas. *National Geographic* (December), pp. 745-768.

Cubbins, William R. (1989). *The War of the Cottontails: Memoirs of a WWII Bomber Pilot*. Chapel Hill, NC: Algonquin Books.

Davidson, Thomas E. (1976). Ploesti leader questioned. *Briefing* [Journal of the International B-24 Liberator Club] (Spring), pp. 1 ff.

Dewez, Luc (2005). To North Africa and hell. *www.bcwarbirds.com/PLOESTI/to_north_africa_and_hell.htm*.

Dobson, Edward M., Jr. (1994). Ploesti, Ed Dobson remembered. *Second Air Division Association Journal* (Summer), pp. 20-21.

Dugan, James, and Carroll Stewart (2002). *Ploesti: The Great Ground-air Battle of 1 August 1943*. Dulles, VA: Brassey's. (Originally published by Random House, New York, 1962.)

Ellis, Lewis N. (1983). Ploesti: A pilot's diary. *American Heritage* (October-November), pp. 76-82.

Ent, Uzal G. Obituary. *New York Times*, March 7, 1948.

Ent, Uzal W. (2000). BG Uzal G. Ent commanded the American bombers that raided Ploesti in August 1943. *World War II* (March), pp. 70 ff.

Ent, Uzal W. (2005). Leading the Ploesti raid. *Military History* (January-February). *www.thehistorynet.com/mh/letters_02_05/index.html*.

Fay, William J. (1998). *Maternity Ward: Final Flight of a WWII Liberator, and the Diary of Her Waist-gunner, S/Sgt. William J. Fay.* Edited by M. M. Aronowitz. Prescott, AZ: Pine Castle Books.

Ferrell, Paul (2004). The last plane back: The Memorial Day story of a local World War II hero. May 27. *www.newsreview.com/issues/sacto/2004-05-27/news.asp*.

Fili, William J. (1991). *Passage to Valhalla: The Human Side of Aerial Combat over Nazi Occupied Europe.* Media, PA: Filcon Publishers.

Fili, William J. Biography of Princess Catherine Caradja, Romania, 1893-1993. *www.ploiesti.net/Gallerys/Princess/*.

Frisbee, John L. (1994). The ordeal of Sad Sack II. *Air Force Magazine Online: Journal of the Air Force Association* (December). *www.afa.org/magazine/valor/0195valor.asp*.

Frisbee, John L. (1995). Operation Gunn. *Air Force Magazine Online: Journal of the Air Force Association* (January). *www.afa.org/magazine/valor/0195valor.asp*.

Gates, Verna (2004). Churchill was his copilot. *MOAA* [Military Officers Association of America]: *Today's Officer* (October). *www.moaa.org/todaysofficer/*.

Gerstenberg, Alfred. Biography. *www.geocities.com/~orion47/WEHRMACHT/LUFTWAFFE/Generalleutnant/GER*; *www.olokaustos.org/bionazi/leaders/gerstenberg.htm* (translation by Nick Scrima from the Italian of Top Secret memorandum, USDIC, UK).

Gilbert, Martin (1986). *Winston S. Churchill, Vol. VII: Road to Victory, 1941-1945.* Boston: Houghton Mifflin.

Goodwin, Doris Kearns (1995). *No Ordinary Time: Franklin and Eleanor*

Roosevelt: The Home Front in World War II. New York: Simon & Schuster.

Hadley, Gilbert. Obituary. *Ponca City (OK) News,* January 7, 1997; see also *Tulsa World,* December 26, 1996; *Wichita (KS) Eagle* (Knight-Ridder/Tribune News Service), January 8, 1997.

Hartley, Gene (1993). 389th Green Dragon Flares: Benghazi revisited. *Second Air Division Association Journal* (Summer), pp. 24-25.

Hastings, Max (2004). *Armageddon: The Battle for Germany, 1944-1945.* New York: Alfred A. Knopf.

Hill, Michael (1993). *Black Sunday: Ploesti.* Atglen, PA: Schiffer Publishing.

Hoffman, Lisa (2003). Naming conflicts—a fine art. Scripps Howard News Service, March 20. *www.knoxstudio.com/shns/story.cfm.*

House, Dawn (2003). WWII bomber crews recall horror of Ploesti. *Salt Lake Tribune,* August 2.

Johnsen, Frederick A. (1999). *B-24 Liberator: Rugged but Right.* New York: McGraw-Hill.

Johnson, Leon William. Obituary. *New York Times,* November 15, 1997.

Kane, John Riley ("Killer"). (1983). The war diary of John R. "Killer" Kane: Out in the blue [part 3]. *American Aviation Historical Society Journal* (Spring), pp. 32-40.

Kane, John Riley ("Killer"). (1983). The war diary of John R. "Killer" Kane: Out in the blue [part 4]. *American Aviation Historical Society Journal* (Summer), pp. 126-139.

Kane, John Riley ("Killer"). Biography. Air Force Link, *www.af.mil/bios/;* see also *www.af.mil/history/person.asp?dec=&pid=123006489*

Kane, John Riley ("Killer"). Congressional Medal of Honor citation, *www.medalofhonor.com/recipients/JohnKane.htm*

Kinsey, Bert (1993). *B-24 Liberator in Detail.* Carrollton, TX: Squadron/Signal Publications.

Larrabee, Eric (1987). *Commander in Chief: Franklin Delano Roosevelt, His Lieutenants, and Their War.* New York: Harper & Row.

Lindsey, Rex (1997). Eulogy. *VFW* [Veterans of Foreign Wars], September, p. 44; see also Flight of the Phoenix Aviation Museum, Gilmer, TX. *www.flightofthephoenix.org/storyboard.htm.*

Longo, Robert "Smiley," as told to Max Pottinger. Above the clouds at thirty below: A true story of a B-24 Liberator crew member. *www.b24.net/stories/longo2.htm.*

Martin, Ralph G. (1946). *Boy from Nebraska: The Story of Ben Kuroki.* New York: Harper & Brothers.

McCrary, John R. (Tex), and Scherman, David E. (1981). *First of the Many: A Journal of Action with the Men of the Eighth Air Force.* London: Robson Books. (Originally published 1944).

Miller, Donald L. (2006). *Masters of the Air: America's Bomber Boys Who Fought the Air War Against Nazi Germany.* New York: Simon & Schuster.

Miller, Roger G. (2000). A "pretty damn able commander": Lewis Hyde Brereton: Part I. *Air Power History* [Air Force Historical Foundation] (Winter), pp. 4 ff.

Miller, Roger G. (2001). A "pretty damn able commander": Lewis Hyde Brereton: Part II. *Air Power History* [Air Force Historical Foundation] (Spring), pp. 22 ff.

Modrovsky, Robert J. (1999). 1 August 1943—Today's target is Ploesti: A departure from doctrine. Research report, Air War College, Air University, Maxwell Air Force Base, Alabama. AU/AWC/170/1999-04. April.

Moran, Lord (Charles Wilson) (1966). *Churchill: Taken from the Diaries of Lord Moran: The Struggle for Survival, 1940-1965.* Boston: Houghton Mifflin.

Nitu, V. (2001). Operation "Tidal Wave"—from Romania view. *www.elknet.pl/acestory/tidalwave/tidalwave.htm.*

Notes from North Africa. (1943). *Air Force* (February), pp. 4-5.

O'Grady, John E. (1990). Ploesti—August 1, 1943. *Second Air Division Association Journal* (Fall), pp. 30-32.

O'Leary, Michael (2002). *Consolidated B-24 Liberator: Production Line to Front Line.* Oxford, England: Osprey Publishing.

Perkins, Paul, Michelle Crean, and Dan Patterson (1994). *The Soldier: Consolidated B-24 Liberator.* Charlottesville, VA: Howell Press.

Priniotakis, Manolis (1995). B-24 mission. *Vancouver (WA) Columbian,* August 10.

Rahmi M. Koc Museum, Ministry of Culture, Istanbul, Republic of

Turkey. Salvaged cockpit and artifacts from the B-24 Liberator Hadley's Harem. *www.kulturturizm.gov.tr/portal/arkeoloji_en.asp?belgeno=3862*

Ravitts, Gail (1999). Amos Nicholson and the Seven Dwarfs. *Friends Journal* (Spring), pp. 38-41.

Reis, Jim (1997). Romanian princess embraced family here. *Cincinnati Post,* September 15.

Romanian Military History Forum. Personal communication regarding Nikolae Teodoru. *www.worldwar2.ro/forum/.*

Rooney, Andy (1995). *My War.* New York: Times Books, Random House.

Semerdjiev, Stefan (1999). Ace in defense of Bulgaria [interview with Smerdjiev]. *Military History* (August), pp. 50 ff.

Semerdjiev, Stefan (2003). Bulgarian Eagles: The Bulgarian Messerschmitt Me 109 fighters in the Second World War. *Airpower* (September), pp. 14 ff.

Shubert, Lyndon (2004). Eyewitness to the raid on Ploesti. *www.thehistorynet.com/ahi/blvagabondraid/index.html.*

Smart, Jacob E. Biography. *www.af.mil/bios/.*

Smart, Jacob E. Obituary. *New York Times,* November 16, 2006; *Washington Post,* November 17, 2006.

Smart, Jacob E. (1943). The Ploesti mission of August 1, 1943. Unpublished transcript of briefing before Gen. H. H. Arnold, August 26. AAFRH-3 (official)

Sterner, C. Douglas (2004). The Ploesti raid: When heroes filled the sky [Wings of Valor, Part II, World War 2]. *www.homeofheroes.com/wings/part2/09_ploesti.html*

Stout, Jay A. (2003). *Fortress Ploesti: The Campaign to Destroy Hitler's Oil.* Havertown, PA: Casemate.

Stoyanov, S. (2000). Stoyan Stoyanov—the Bulgarian top ace. *www.elknet.pl/acestory/stojanov/stojanov.htm.*

Sulzberger, C. L. (1944). Life and death of an American bomber. *New York Times,* July 16.

Taddonio, Joseph (2004). 376th Heavy Bomb Group Veterans Association: Birth of a combat crew. *www.376hbgva.com/memoirs/taddonio.htm.*

Turner, Thomas E. (1983). "Killer" Kane: A hero from our heritage. *Airman* (August), pp. 38-43.

Tutt, Bob (1993). WWII remembered: Survivors recall "hell of Ploesti" during WWII. *Houston Chronicle*, August 1.

U.S. AAF Headquarters, Directorate of Weather (1943). The other North African battle. *Air Force* (February) [no page].

U. S. 44th Bomb Group Roll of Honor and Casualties (revised, winter 2004). *www.greenharbor.com/ROHPDF/ROHAU43.pdf*.

U.S. 44th Bomb Group Veterans Association. M/Sgt. Walter M. Patrick and the Fighting Lady. *www.44thbombgroup.com/fighting lady.html*.

U.S. 93rd Bomb Group: The Traveling Circus. *World War II* magazine. *www.thehistorynet.com/wwii/blthetravelingcircus/index.html*.

U.S. 389th Bomb Group (1973). *Newsletter* (June). Ploesti aftermath.

U.S. 389th Bomb Group (2002). *Newsletter:* Ploesti revisited: An original letter by Lt. John McCormick.

Unitt, Pete (1998-99). Ploesti at low level: Prelude to the raid. *Friends Journal* (Winter), pp. 17-24. [part 1].

Unitt, Pete (1998-99). Ploesti: At low level. *Friends Journal* (Winter), pp. 29-37. [part 2].

Ward, Ray (1989). *Those Brave Crews: The Epic Raid to Destroy Hitler's Ploesti Oil Fields.* Waverly, NY: Weldon Publications.

Warner, Jack. Flight into the past. *Atlanta Journal and Constitution*, November 12, 1993.

Way, Frank, and Robert W. Sternfels (2002). *Burning Hitler's Black Gold.* (Published by authors.)

Way, Frank, and Robert W. Sternfels (2003). An epilogue to *Burning Hitler's Black Gold: The Sandman—then and now. Briefing*, pp. 8-11.

Williams, William G. (2003). *Rescue from Ploesti: The Harry Fritz Story—A World War II Triumph.* Shippensburg, PA: White Mane Books.

Wolff, Leon (1957). *Low Level Mission.* Garden City, NY: Doubleday.

Wood, Jack Weston. Biography. Air Force Link, *www.af.mil/bios/*.

Worley, Bob (1994). Ploesti: Fortunes of war prevented a daring raid from crippling German oil supplies. *Commemorative [Confederate] Air Force Dispatch* (Winter). *www.rwebs.net/dispatch/output.asp?ArticleID=47.*

Zimmerman, Earl (1991). Hethel highlights. *Second Air Division Association Journal* (Summer), p. 22.

Index

ACKNOWLEDGMENTS

Anyone attempting to tell the story of an event long past (in this instance, well over 60 years) owes a debt of gratitude to many individuals and organizations. For me, this list includes those who lived through the raid on Ploesti and left behind the records and accounts of their experiences, the dedicated archivists and librarians who so faithfully preserved and catalogued those records, and the past authors who presented their views of Operation Tidal Wave in books and articles.

It is a pleasure to acknowledge the help of Jenny Christian at the Memorial Library of the 2nd Air Division the USAAF in Norwich, England, who not only sent copies of all the articles I requested, but also found other relevant ones I had not known about.

In addition, I would like to express my thanks to Pearlie Draughn, Research Librarian at the Air Force Association in Arlington, Virginia; Maia Armaleo, Editorial Assistant, American Heritage Group; 1st Lt. Megan A. Schafer, Associate Editor, *Airman Magazine*; Jamie Blankenship, *VFW Magazine*; George Welsh, *Bomber Legends Magazine*; and Lisa Veysay, *The Atlanta Constitution*. All responded promptly and graciously to my many requests. I am also grateful to Candace McDaniel of the Clearwater (FL) Public Library for so cheerfully and competently dealing with my interlibrary loan requests over the years, often requiring detective skills to locate obscure and esoteric materials.

Little research on the Ploesti raid would be possible without the dedication of the many editors of the journals and newsletters of the bombardment groups' survivors' associations. They diligently recorded the stories, making them a part of history.

My gratitude also to General Dénes, who answered my query about the Romanian pilot who defected in 1943, which had been posted on the Romanian Military History Forum only seven minutes earlier.

I thank my literary agent, Robin Rue, of Writers House, for her patience, persistence, and sage counsel, Bruce H. Franklin of Westholme Publishing for his enthusiasm and dedication to the book, Trudi Gershenov for her striking book jacket, and Noreen O'Connor-Abel for her careful and caring editing. And, as always, I thank my wife, Sydney Ellen, who continues to make everything better, including this book.